TWO SONS OF CHINA

Also by Andrew Lam

Saving Sight: An eye surgeon's look at life behind the mask and the heroes who changed the way we see

TWO SONS OF CHINA

A Novel of the Second World War

ANDREW LAM

BONDFIRE
B O O K S

TWO SONS OF CHINA

Bondfire Books, LLC.
7680 Goddard St, Suite 220
Colorado Springs, CO 80920

See full line of Bondfire Books titles at www.bondfirebooks.com
Electronic edition published 2014 by Bondfire Books LLC.

Cover art copyright © 2014 by Bondfire Books, LLC.

ISBN 978-1-62921-373-6

Published in the United States of America.

For my parents,

Wilfred and Esther Lam

AUTHOR'S NOTE

A father of five named Chung Tam was a civil servant of the Nationalist government in Chungking during World War II. When the Communists took control of China in 1949, he escaped and fled to Hong Kong, leaving all of his land and possessions behind. There his family lived in poverty for many years.

A student named Wing Ching Lam, the scion of a wealthy family, left China in 1937, just ahead of the Japanese invasion. He didn't know he would never see his homeland again.

These two sons of China built new lives for their families in America. They were my grandfathers.

In my youth, Grandfather Lam painted a picture of pre-Communist China, a country rich in ancient traditions but crippled by overwhelming poverty and abuse by Western nations. Later, I discovered the incredible true story of the courageous American Foreign Service Officers who conceived and participated in the Dixie Mission during World War II, America's best chance to evaluate and understand the Chinese Communists who would later form the People's Republic of China.

Thus were the seeds of this narrative planted.

———

In general, the novel employs the pinyin system of romanization. Exceptions occur for names of people and places that are more familiar to a Western audience or would have been used by the characters in their time. In these instances the older Wade-Giles romanization is used, such as with "Yenan" or "Chiang Kai-shek" instead of "Yan'an" or "Jiang Jieshi."

CONTENTS

Japanese forces invade China in July 1937, swiftly conquering the eastern seaboard and driving Chiang Kai-shek's beleaguered Nationalist government far inland, to the city of Chungking.

The United States enters World War II in December 1941 and sends a handful of Foreign Service Officers to Chungking. Finding the Nationalists reluctant to engage the enemy, they consider reaching out to another group rumored to be battling the Japanese from their northern base of Yenan. These fighters are Chiang's enduring adversaries, the Chinese Communists.

———

The story that follows was inspired by true events.

MONGOLIA

KOREA

Peking

Tianjin

Baoding

HEBEI

Taiyuan

SHANDONG

Yenan

SHANXI

Xian

Yellow River

SHAANXI

Nanking

SICHUAN

Shanghai

Yangtze River

Chengdu

Wuhan

Chungking

Changsha

Hengyang

JIANGXI

Kunming

Guilin

Xiamen

FORMOSA
(TAIWAN)

Hong Kong

EASTERN CHINA

Areas of Japanese Occupation
Spring 1944

PART ONE

Chungking—Yenan

May 1944 – July 1944

ONE

Near Wuhan, May 1944

It definitely wasn't an animal.

Lieutenant David Parker froze, mid-step, at the faint scuffling between the trees. His hand dropped to the Colt .45 at his belt, the checkered grip slippery against his sweaty palm. He squinted at the forest of hemlocks and birch, into the setting sun, which cast a swath of sparkling light across the ripple of the river.

No one. Nothing.

He lifted his foot, a step toward the men, but his boot sole made a mud-sucking sound that froze him again.

He shot a look at the three Nationalist soldiers, the ones he'd handpicked for this mission. Gong, a wiry eighteen-year-old with unruly hair, was chortling over some joke his friend Lee had made. Lee was shorter, more stocky—a former warlord's bodyguard. Lee had heard the noise too; he shoved Gong, quieting him. The last man, Cheng, clutched his box-like radio close to his chest, as if he might succeed in hiding behind it.

Now all three were alert, sitting on the trunk of a fallen oak whose upper branches touched the river.

Again, the scuffling sound. A rustle of leaves, twenty yards away, off to the left, then...silence.

David exhaled slowly. *Spread out*, he motioned with his hands. Lee, quick to obey, crept deeper into the woods. Cheng set the radio down. He crouched low and slid downriver. Gong didn't seem to know where to go. He jumped at the rapid flutter of a crow alighting on a branch overhead.

Behind them: the snap of a twig and a low curse.

David spun, drawing his pistol.

Ten feet away, a balding, middle-aged Chinese man stumbled onto the riverbank. He wore spectacles with round lenses that in China suggested accountant or banker. The sleeves of his white, pinstriped shirt were rolled up and dirt-smudged.

The newcomer shook his head and a few pine needles fell out of his hair. David pointed his gun at the man, who looked up in surprise.

"They sent a white man to do such a dangerous job?" he said, addressing Gong in brisk, staccato Mandarin.

David frowned and took a step forward. "Ni wei shenme zheyang shuo?" *Why should you say that?* he replied evenly.

The man's brows rose. The American's fluency was unexpected. Now he studied David more carefully.

"Are you not too valuable to risk getting killed?" he said.

Ignoring the question, David lowered his pistol, but his face did not hide his annoyance. He'd expected the spy to look more…capable. "We've come a long way," he replied. "Just tell us what we need to know."

The spectacled spy stumbled a few steps closer and whispered, "Very well, but not in front of *them*."

David looked toward his men.

"Why not?" he asked.

But the spy was already moving clumsily into the trees.

David followed. The ground was covered with damp pine needles and decaying leaves.

The spy stopped in a small clearing and knelt down to take off his right black leather shoe. He removed a small piece of folded paper from inside the shoe and stood up.

"I'll tell you first about the bridge. It's around the bend ahead, only three hundred meters upriver." He pointed toward a tall granite escarpment that was visible through the trees. "Leave the raft here. Hide it. Haul charges along the bank. Then go into the water after dark."

"Okay, good." David looked back at the men. Lee punched Gong on the shoulder, both of them laughing at another inane joke. *Do those two ever get serious?* He stretched his neck to see that the crates of explosives were still bundled on the raft.

"You might like to know there will be a train at six minutes after six in the morning," the spy added.

"What?"

"A train. I checked the schedule myself. The Japanese always run on time. If it is scheduled to leave the local station at six, it will take six minutes to reach the bridge."

"Why would they run a train so early in the morning?"

The man's dry expression transformed into something resembling both pride and resignation. "It may have to do with the other thing I've found out. They are moving many men and supplies because of something new—a new offensive."

5

"You mean an attack?"

The spy nodded.

"But the lines here haven't changed for years. Are you sure? How do you know?"

The Chinese man's eyes flickered with irritation as he glanced at his watch. "I have no time to explain. The Japanese want your American airfields, especially the one at Hengyang. American planes are sinking ships around Formosa. Many ships."

David let the surprising news register and felt a grudging respect for the spy. He thought of the war being waged in the Pacific and the long Japanese lines of supply. He searched for a reason to doubt the man, but in his gut, he knew it was the truth. *It's exactly what the Japs would do.*

"You must warn them," the spy said. Beads of sweat glistened on his brow. "I do not know when the attack will begin, but it will come."

David didn't reply. He was still thinking of the implications.

Suddenly, the spy clenched the front of David's army jacket. "You must understand the importance of this! Warning Changsha is far more important than blowing up a bridge."

David forced an awkward smile. Then he took a step back and the man let go of his jacket.

"Don't worry. We'll get this job done and make it back, too. I'll deliver the message."

He waited for the spy to say more, but now the man just stared at him, as if weighing David's trustworthiness all over again.

We're some pair. David thought. *He's worried about me; I'm worried about him.*

"All right then. Thanks for your help," David said as he turned away from the spy. There was still a lot of work to do before sundown.

"Wait," the spy hissed, glancing over his shoulder to check the soldiers by the raft. Now he brought forth the small piece of folded paper that David had forgotten about.

"I risked my life many times to compile this list," he whispered. "The names of double agents in Wuhan and Shanghai."

"You mean—"

"All the Nationalist spies who have been turned by the Japanese. They were captured. Most were tortured. Now they send back bad information while still pretending to work for Chiang Kai-shek's network. This is one reason Chiang does not know about the attack."

David reached out for the paper, but the man held it back.

"You must understand. The enemy has eyes and ears everywhere: in the Chinese army, among the people. Their spies are more likely to be paid-off Chinese than Japanese. You cannot show this to *anyone* until you return to Chungking. When you arrive there, show your American general…"

"Stilwell," David said.

"Yes, Stih-weh," the spy repeated. "No one can see it before Stih-weh."

He held out the small square of paper. David wiped his palms on his pants, took the paper, and unfolded it. In neat, formal characters there were more than a dozen names.

"Put it away," the spy said. "Do not let your men see."

David slipped the paper into his inside jacket pocket. *This could be big.* He pictured himself handing the paper over to Stilwell, basking in the Old Man's approval. Then, glancing at his unit, he saw they were still goofing off. *God, they're just a bunch of kids…How the hell am I supposed to pull this off by myself?*

He exhaled, then drew a deep breath. They'd been tramping through the backcountry with heavy explosives for almost a week. Tonight, they would accomplish their mission. But this odd spy had complicated things. David wanted to ask him about his cover and how he'd managed to sneak away to this riverside rendezvous, but when he turned around, the spy was gone.

Two

The river's long ripples drifted out of focus. David blinked and wiped away the sweat, trying to clear his vision, but a fog of exhaustion clouded his brain. He rubbed his forehead and slumped against a large granite rock, pressing its coolness against the side of his face. *I should close my eyes. The others will tell me when to get up.* He shut his lids, surprised at the effort to keep them down despite their heaviness. They opened. *No use.*

He resolved to stay awake. Still, he couldn't keep his mind from drifting. And there was Rita Hayworth, reclining on a chaise lounge in a gossamer négligée, lips puckered up to the end of a cigarette. David enjoyed the image for a moment, but the pin-up soon evaporated, becoming one with the last wisp of low-lying fog.

Turning on his right side, he peered over the rock at the bridge. The red-orange dawn now lit its top, the railing and span in bright contrast to the strong timbers below, which remained cast in shadow. Crisp, cool air filled David's lungs and he shivered, his clothes still damp from the night swim. He moved his arms and legs, working the stiff joints.

Gong was up ahead, thirty yards closer to the bridge and more easily seen with the light of dawn. *Too close*, David thought again, until he remembered the cord wouldn't let out any farther. He smiled as he remembered Gong's eager face glowing in the moonlight just hours before, when he'd suggested Gong blow the charges. Nationalist soldiers were rarely rewarded for their initiative, and these men had risked much for this moment.

Close by, to his left, David saw Lee lying flat on his stomach behind a rotting log. *Sleeping?* Grains of sand mixed with Lee's stringy, black hair. Cheng, the radioman, crouched behind a boulder five yards back. In the shadows, his grease-darkened face made him almost bat-like, the whites of his eyes faintly blue in the dim light, eyes that were glued to the bridge.

"Ni ting jian shenme ma?" *Hear anything?* Cheng whispered to David.

David shook his head.

Suddenly, the thuddish sound of steps on the bridge made David sink low, hand going for the trigger guard of his M-3 submachine gun. Tilting his head back and right, he saw the sentry again, lazily walking the span for the second time that night. *He's about to get the surprise of his life*, David thought. Then he remembered what the spy had said and felt inside his jacket to make sure of the list. *Still there.* He raised his watch close to his face. *Almost six o'clock already. He said six after six.* Again, David questioned himself.

It's not too late to just blow the bridge and leave.

He rubbed the tiny grains of wet sand between his fingers.

No, too late to play it safe...Could've pulled it off two hours ago...We aren't leaving now.

A flock of sleeping pigeons erupted into flight from the top of the bridge, their wings thrumming the air. David risked another look, careful to spot the sentry, who was almost out of sight on the far side. He scanned the bridge, the river. Quiet. Yet the wing beats of the birds echoed in his mind.

Then, a low mechanical hum gradually rose out of the dark silence. It grew in volume and turned into a sluggish, but persistent, chugging sound. *The train!* Gong glanced back from his position by the bridge. He'd heard it too. David nodded. He flicked some sand at Lee, who sat up with a start, his hair matted from lying close to the ground. David pointed to his ear.

The chugging sound came on stronger, more uniform.

The earth rumbled and pebbles near the water trembled like loose marbles. David gripped the stock of his M-3, checking to make sure the action was clear of sand.

The sound of the train amplified.

Still crouched behind the boulder, David stared at the empty space, to the right, waiting for the engine to appear. The sentry was jogging back to the near side of the bridge. Clenching his hands, as if he could feel the cold metal himself, David saw Gong raise the detonator handle.

The black locomotive steamed into view, huffing slow and loud, puffing smoke and steam, one above, one below. The sentry stood to the side, staying clear of the huge cowcatcher. The coal car followed, then a rusty brown freight car.

Blow it! Blow it now! David hollered in his head.

Upwind, he saw Gong staring, frozen.

What the hell's wrong?

The locomotive seemed to slow at the midpoint of the bridge.

Now! David's inner voice screamed.

Gong plunged the handle down.

Nothing happened.

The locomotive was almost across with four cars in view.

Then—two bright flashes at the waterline.

Twin explosions thumped the air.

David ducked behind the boulder, eyes closed, and saw the after-image—the sudden incandescent flashes—followed by the dullish thuds of explosion. Then he was up and looking again. Huge timbers were bent, split apart. The span quivered, then buckled. Pieces of wood hit the river, followed by a storm of splinters that knifed the black water in an ever-widening circle.

The bridge began to list. Freight cars derailed and disconnected.

The locomotive, leaning sideways, gave an iron cry and cranked to one side, as if begging to stay. Then it tumbled over, rolling mid-air, wheels revolving, smoke billowing. It struck the river with a volume of spray that seemed like white horizontal rain.

The center of the bridge had collapsed. Water boiled brown with wood and steel detritus. David scarcely believed the plan had worked. He glanced up and to the right. Intact freight cars stood atop the remains of the broken bridge.

Lee shook his shoulder. Eyes wide, he jabbed the air with his thumb. *Get back?* David thought. *Yes, we should.* He took one last look at the bridge, a smoking ruin. A sense of accomplishment suffused his tired body.

"Zou ba," *Let's go*, he said in Mandarin, signaling for Lee and Cheng to get up. Cheng turned around and bent low to put his arms through the straps attached to the bulky radio; its long antennae was bent in a loop and hooked to the bottom of the box.

Then David heard the rolling rumble of many footsteps on the bridge.

"Sokoni irukara ute!" The Japanese words were clear in the crisp air.

A rifle shot cracked. David ducked and froze, his back to the bridge. The bullet splattered sand three feet to his right. Cheng looked back, surprised. His hands came up, hurrying to cinch his straps. Another shot rang out. The bullet struck the radio on Cheng's back, throwing him forward onto the sand.

David spun around. Japanese troops were crowding the bridge railing. More streamed out of the freight cars. Fingers pointing, rifles raised, soldiers taking aim. He was close enough to see their angry faces. His eye caught the movement of one soldier bending down to adjust a metal tube. Another dropped a ball into the tube, followed by an immediate, silent puff of smoke.

A wave of panic coursed through David's body. *We're too close, too exposed. We've got to move back.*

Whump!

The close explosion deafened him, but his eyes saw the shattering of Cheng's leg. This image he took into darkness as he squeezed his eyes shut against the sand that stung his face.

A second mortar shell exploded on his right.

This blast carried David off his feet; he landed hard on his back, three yards away. Pain burned deep within his right thigh.

I can't hear.

He touched his right ear. Nothing.

He rolled onto his stomach and opened his eyes. Cheng was asprawl at several different angles. Dead.

In his left ear, oddly echoing, David heard bullets whine and stab the cratered sand. The riverbank was narrow. A fifty-foot-high granite wall rose abruptly near the water's edge to a flat plateau above. The rock face that had concealed their advance to the bridge now limited their movement. He had to move. He looked for Lee and saw him crouched behind the rotten log. Lee wasn't firing; he stared at David, frozen, eyes full of fear. David clambered to his side.

"What now?" Lee shouted. David looked ahead and saw Gong, closer to the bridge, firing toward the Japanese.

"We must go!" Lee screamed, unconvinced he was being understood. He grabbed David's arm and pointed at the forty enemy soldiers scrambling down the ridge near the bridge.

David shouted at Gong but could not be heard above the gunfire and explosions. Gong's attention remained forward. David made a decision. The sense of purpose dampened his fear.

"We can't leave him."

Lee protested, but in an instant, David was moving forward.

Something was wrong with his first step. His right leg bowed. He looked down. Blood drenched his pant leg and soaked the laces of his boot. Against his skin the blood felt cold, like ice. He lurched forward. He was fifteen yards behind Gong. Ten. Five. Gong looked back. Their eyes locked and David gestured empathically with his free hand. "Get back!" he yelled, desperate to be heard above the piercing explosions. He clenched Gong's khaki shirt, jerking him backward. The two scrambled back toward Lee, who was emptying a clip at the soldiers on the ridge above.

Their only chance was the raft. It was tied up two hundred yards downriver. The previous day had been an exhausting upriver effort, but now the current could be their ally.

The Japanese were gaining on them. Bullets ripped the water on their right and ricocheted off the steep rock face on their left.

A narrowing of the riverbank lay ahead, where only ten feet separated the water's edge from the sharp rise in the granite escarpment. Boulders dotted the bottleneck, and the three men scrambled over them. David felt a tug at his shoulder. It was Lee, grabbing at his weapon and ammo.

No, it should be me. I'm wounded already.

But Lee had already stripped Gong of his rifle and three grenades. Precious seconds passed. The fear had left Lee's face; he was grim, firm.

There was no time. David ducked his head under the strap of his submachine gun and handed it to Lee. Shouldering it, Lee turned and, with a burst of fire, killed the two closest Japanese only twenty yards away. Close behind, a dozen others scrambled for cover as Lee peppered the beach and rocks.

David and Gong stumbled toward the raft. They reached it and climbed aboard. The current was strong, and the duo pushed frantically with poles to hasten their retreat. David kept his head down. Rivulets of sweat ran down his brow, dripping off his eyelashes, stinging his eyes. Repeatedly, he plunged the long bamboo pole into the water, found the soft river bottom, and pushed off.

He slowed after several minutes of hard exertion. Across the muddy water he could barely see Lee. He saw him throw a grenade. He heard the small explosion and recognized the sound of his own weapon. A few minutes passed. Gong was poling steadily, calmer now. Soon a bend in the river would prevent them from seeing Lee. David strained his ears as they turned the corner; he realized the firing had stopped.

They pushed for another half hour until they were convinced they were safe. Then there was silence, save for the current lapping and their rasping breaths.

THREE

Yenan, May 1944

Outside a door cut into a steep hillside, Lin Yuen sat on a small wooden stool cleaning his gun. His thirty-nine-year-old face was darkly tanned with rugged, weather-beaten creases on either side of his mouth. Although he stood just five feet, five inches tall, he was very muscular. Friends said he resembled bamboo and cypress: strong and venerable.

The narrow doorway to his cave-home was arched above. Rectangular windows, covered with paper, adorned the walls on either side. A wide ledge cut out of the hillside led from the valley floor like a ramp past his door and continued sloping upward to additional dwellings beyond his.

Yuen's weapon was a Russian PPS-43 submachine gun. It was disassembled, and he had the barrel in his lap. Using a metal cleaning rod with a patch of oiled cloth at the eyelet-end, he swabbed the piece several times. Then he removed and carefully folded the cloth patch. He placed it in a small box which also contained two unlabeled bottles, one with oil and one with grease. The rifle was thin and black, with a folding stock. It weighed seven pounds unloaded. There were few such weapons left among the Communist guerillas, and these were only entrusted to platoon leaders—men who could be trusted to use them effectively.

Yuen looked up from his work and took in the view from his hillside perch. Yenan was a desolate place. The brown loess landscape was hard-packed, moisture-starved ground covered by a superficial dusting of fine-grained clay and silt. Low, adobe-style buildings populated the valley floor. Yuen squinted at the sun, high and bright. Most comrades were taking the midday meal now, and only a few pedestrians and one ox-drawn cart occupied the lanes between the buildings. The surrounding cliffsides contained dwellings like his. Loess hills sliced easily along vertical planes, making them conducive to excavation of rooms. It took time for Yuen to get used to the claustrophobic, underground feeling, so different from the years of outdoor living he'd grown accustomed to during the years the Communists had spent in Jiangxi Province and on the Long March. He'd also learned to suppress his fear of earthquakes, which could bury cave dwellers alive.

To the men he commanded, Yuen was a stoic and reserved veteran. Any passerby watching him clean his weapon would not dare to interrupt his concentration. He was a leader, a scout, a tracker, and above all, a killer. He never counted how many enemies he'd killed over the years, and he wasn't about to start now. He was numb to the fear of battle and indifferent to any close encounter with death. He killed without hesitation, even in close combat with his hands, and thus, he was a legend among other men. Still, he was not a talkative leader, and the men who served under him knew better than to ask him about his past. Unlike other Party members his age, Yuen wasn't an outspoken communist. New soldiers heard gossip that he'd once been zealous, that he'd even participated in some of the Party's earliest meetings, but all this was shrouded in myth. Yuen himself said nothing about it.

A young girl began to climb the path toward Yuen's home. Her rich, black hair was drawn into two long ponytails that reached halfway down her back. Yuen looked to his right and caught sight of her. His face broadened into a wide smile. His men would be surprised he was capable of such warmth. They didn't know how much Yuen loved his eight-year-old daughter, Mei Fong.

Even among enlightened communists like Yuen, it wasn't unusual for fathers to care nothing for their daughters. But, during the long months away on guerilla missions, Yuen lived for the moment when he could embrace Mei Fong again. She was friendly and outgoing, and she drew great confidence from knowing that few sacrificed more for the Cause than her father. Her self-assurance had led some teachers to complain she was bossy at school, but Yuen was blinded to her faults.

Nearing the front door now, Mei Fong carried two buckets of water on either end of a long pole balanced across her shoulder. Seeing him, she smiled and quickened her pace. Yuen got up to help her set the buckets down.

"Ba Ba! Where will you take me today?" she asked eagerly.

"Your chores are done?"

Mei Fong pouted. "Ma Ma said to bring the water *and* clean the floor. To her I am a water buffalo."

Yuen tried to frown but found it difficult to suppress a smile. His daughter's attitude was improper, disrespectful, and he had to be careful not to encourage this. Already, his wife was worried about finding a good match for her—no man would tolerate a disobedient wife. Even so, it was next to impossible for Yuen to be upset with her.

"Tell me your school lessons. What are they?"

Mei Fong rolled her eyes and said quickly: "Build China. Loyalty to the Chairman. Serve the Revolution. Serve the People."

Recitation done, she flashed her prettiest smile and hopped up and down. "Ba Ba, let's go! Can we?"

Yuen sighed, then smiled. "All right, perhaps we shall climb the high mountain. We can sit atop the Phoenix's Perch," he said with an upward gesture.

"That would be a fine adventure!"

The front door opened.

A young-looking thirty-year-old woman stepped out over the threshold.

"What do you say?" Yuen's wife, Jiang Hong, said. "This daughter is no good. No work. No worth. What man would marry such a lazy dog?" Jiang Hong eyed her chastened daughter. "Well?"

"Yes, Ma Ma," Mei Fong uttered. She went inside to mop the floor with the water she'd brought.

Jiang Hong turned to Yuen. "With you she gets away with everything. With you she thinks whatever she wants, so she whines and complains. This is *not* good to teach her."

"She is not so bad," Yuen replied. "Jade must be chiseled before it can be considered a gem, yes? We just want to have some fun today. I hardly ever see her."

"That's right, you're hardly ever here. You're gone for months and come back for a few days. You spoil her, and she becomes disrespectful. It takes me weeks to correct what you do to her."

Yuen remained silent. It was no use arguing with Jiang Hong.

"Instead of wasting time wandering around," Jiang Hong continued, "you could be talking to the men of the Central Committee. How else will they know of your sacrifices? Do you *like* going out to get shot at when you could stay here with us and become one of the great men of the Party? Everyone respects you and would listen to you. You must think of the future. We will not be living in this place forever."

Yuen sighed. "I won't discuss this again. I am not a politician; I am a soldier." Quietly, he added, "I only...I just want to be with my daughter."

His wife's expression did not soften.

"If it brings you happiness," Yuen offered, "this afternoon I go to Comrade Peng Dehuai to report."

Yuen thought he saw his wife's eyebrows lift at the mention of the Red Army's deputy commander-in-chief, but the sternness remained. She turned to reenter their home and said, "Well, you should tell him you want to do more than be a common soldier."

Yuen fingered the metal pieces of his gun. Jiang Hong was a beautiful woman, certainly among the most beautiful women in Yenan. Years ago, when they'd first met in Shanghai, he was surprised by the much younger girl's crush on him. He assumed his status in the Party impressed her. They were happy for a few years, but now the intimacy they'd once shared had been lost for as long as Yuen could remember.

Mei Fong hurried to finish washing the stone floor of their two-room home. The front door opened into the main space, which contained a small stove, wooden table, and three stools. Pieces of the room's yellow, earthen walls would crumble off if rubbed hard. In a tiny back room there were two separate floor mats for husband and wife. At night, Mei Fong unrolled a mat and slept near the stove.

Yuen finished re-assembling his gun. Down the street he saw a neighbor chasing a chicken and a Party official posting signs for the lectures to be held that week.

Mei Fong jumped on his back, "Ba Ba! All done—let's go!"

They walked down the narrow ramp to where it joined the main street at the bottom of the hill. Mei Fong picked up a long, straight stick, shouldered it like a rifle, and play-acted marching like a soldier.

"Ba Ba, when can *I* go with you to fight the invaders?"

Yuen chuckled. "Ah, xiao peng-you—*little friend*—I've been fighting so you needn't do that. Even girls will have important work to do. 'Women hold up half the sky,' Chairman says. Learn as much as you can; China will need people like you."

"But I want to fight now, Ba Ba! I run fast. I can carry messages. I can help with sick people."

"Mei Fong, don't think about these things."

"I want to go."

"It is better for you to stay and learn. Help your mother. That is also what a good daughter should do."

"Yes, Ba Ba," Mei Fong responded mournfully, kicking at the dust under her feet as she walked.

Yuen felt obliged to add, "You should respect your mother more. She carried you in her belly and still survived the Long March. There are not many women who could say they did that, eh?"

"Yes, Ba Ba. I know." Yuen could not place the moment when Mei Fong had stopped listening to him with adoring attentiveness. *Was it months ago or years ago? Is this normal for an eight-year-old?* He had to admit, she *was* a little rebellious. Each time he returned home, he was surprised by how much she'd grown, by how much she'd learned in school. But this time was different. Though she still looked like a child, he felt like he was talking to an adult. *When did this happen?* he wondered.

FOUR

Yangtze River, north of Changsha

Verdant hillsides rose up on both sides of the wide river. Solitary fisherman, few and far between, tended lines and stared with detached interest at the two men and their raggle-taggle raft. Cormorants, drying their wings on the banks, saw them coming and flew to higher ground. The river rolled on silently in its long journey to the sea.

First Lieutenant David Parker was twenty-five years old. He stood five feet, eleven inches; his hair was wavy and chestnut brown. He was not muscular, but he was agile. At the army's new Ranger school his nickname had been "The Rabbit" for his wild way of sprinting the obstacle course full out, and he rated top ten at the distance run. His test scores in tactics and general knowledge elevated him to near the top of the class, and he expected to have his pick of duty once America finally got into the war. He leaned toward the Airborne, not because he liked the idea of jumping out of an airplane but because it seemed to be the most exciting duty he could opt for. He'd also noted that women seemed to swoon over parachutists.

It was his damn *rare gift* that thwarted his plans. He didn't like to talk about being born and raised in China; it was embarrassing to tell anyone his parents had been *missionaries*— the word itself was enough to make him cringe. But he hadn't seen the harm in listing "Mandarin Chinese" on the Officer Candidate application under "Foreign language abilities." Soon after the Japanese attack on Pearl Harbor in December 1941, he learned that this *rare gift* dictated his assignment to General Joseph Stilwell's staff in Chungking. Others considered working for the commander of the China-Burma-India Theater to be a plum posting, the perfect way to wait out the war, but David detested it. He couldn't imagine a place farther from the action.

The Chinese had been battling the Japanese since 1937, but when David arrived in Chungking in the summer of 1942, it took him only a few weeks to realize the Nationalists were hardly fighting. In fact, their leader, Generalissimo Chiang Kai-shek, seemed content to let Japan occupy China's eastern seaboard without opposition. Scuttlebutt was that he was more concerned with halting the expansion of the Chinese Communists—his archenemies—a group he had been trying to eradicate for almost twenty years.

David spent a year and a half training Chinese soldiers to use U.S. Army weapons and tactics, but he'd yet to see any of the units he'd taught engage in battle. The time spent translating documents for Stilwell's staff was drudgery, so when his long-awaited request to observe a Nationalist battalion in the field came through, he was pleased. And when the adjunct orders followed, permitting him to assemble a small force and operate independently behind Japanese lines, he was overjoyed.

But Chungking was a distant memory now.

David looked back at Gong, who wielded a thin plank of wood as a paddle and rudder at the stern. David had never seen him so...forlorn. *He's shell-shocked and he doesn't know it.*

David turned to watch the river. The sun-sparkled water winked at him. He closed his eyelids. *Cheng and Lee—dead. Was it worth it?* He pressed the heels of his palms against his eyes. *They were good men.*

His mind kept returning to the simple words which just hours ago he'd thought would make him happy: *mission accomplished.* Yet he couldn't feel the satisfaction, and he couldn't shake the feeling of failure. *Why didn't I sacrifice myself so the others could escape? Am I a coward?*

He shuddered, blinked, opened his eyes into the river's glare. *Better to not think about what happened. Better to think about what's happening.*

"Your leg..." Gong said, but he didn't finish.

David saw fresh pinkish blood filtering through the cloth tourniquet. He tightened it and ripped his pant leg below to inspect the wound more closely. A piece of shrapnel from the mortar shell was lodged inside his flesh. He gritted his teeth and dug at the metal with his fingers. The twisted steel was blood-slick, slippery. A flash of pain throbbed through his entire leg, but the jagged piece of steel came out. Then he took off his shirt and tied it down hard over the wound.

David was trying to calculate how far they'd traveled when the feeling hit him: a wall of fatigue that seemed to sap every cell in his body. It felt as if someone had opened his veins and was letting the blood drain out.

After joining the main body of the Yangtze they'd turned southwest and passed two exhausting days paddling upriver against a slow but unceasing current. David's malaise mounted by the minute and a fever came on. The ache in his thigh prompted him to untie the grimy cloth bandages. Viscous yellow mucus filled in the void of his wound. It was blood-tinged. The skin at the edge was everted and deep blue.

It's infected.

A wave of dread coursed through him. The image of a Civil War battlefield hospital materialized in his mind—screaming soldiers, saw-wielding surgeons, and piles of amputated limbs outside a lantern-lit tent. He re-tied the bandages and tried to calm himself as Gong stared ahead at the bow, attentive to the river.

Within an hour, David could no longer stand, could no longer kneel. He lay down on his side. Gong slid to the back of the raft wearing an expression that told David he looked as bad as he felt.

"You're pale," Gong said as he felt David's forehead. "And very hot, too."

Gong's voice sounded far off. David's thoughts ran together. The weight of sleep closed over him—like a black shroud. He fought it, fearful of giving in to death.

"What do I do?" Gong pleaded, despair in his voice. David's eyes were closed. He didn't answer. Gong put two fingers over his mouth to see if he was still breathing.

At the same time, David's eyes opened. Glazed and unfocused, they sought Gong's face though it was right there in front of him. Then, with effort, he murmured, "Changsha..."

Gong nodded, relieved to get any response. He crouched down at the stern behind David and started to paddle.

The sun was high and white.

The raft was rising and falling.

David awoke. He tested his arms and legs. It was as if they had no bones in them.

Where am I?

With concentrated effort, he was able to turn onto his side, and he saw that Gong was waving his arms like a bird and dancing on the raft.

What is he doing?

"Chinese! We are Chinese!" Gong shouted toward the riverbank.

A distant voice came over the murky water. "Chinese?"

"Yes, Chinese!" Gong shouted again. And then, pointing at David, he hollered, "American!"

David raised a hand, shielding his eyes from the sun. The riverbank was bright with thin birch trees whose white bark and green leaves punctuated the otherwise grayish woodland. Squinting, he made out a scrawny Chinese soldier leaning against a slender tree. The man had a rifle resting in the crook of his arm.

David wished Gong would stop yelling, but he was too weak to summon more than a faint groan, and the rocking of the raft gave him the urgent need to vomit. His mind filtered the thoughts his mouth couldn't say. *That soldier could be a Jap spy.* But Gong continued calling out to the man, flapping his arms in a ridiculous way.

David struggled up to a sitting position as Gong paddled them to the riverbank. They saw the man for what he was—a stick. *Too starved to be a Jap,* David thought. A wine-colored mole covered the crest of the soldier's right cheek, and a long, solitary hair grew out of it.

Gong tossed the soldier a rope, and the bone-faced, skeletal man dragged the raft close in. Gong gave him a quick report of their mission. The soldier, who said he was a picket for the Nationalist army, seemed awestruck by the tale.

The raft secured, Gong reached down to lift David up by the armpits. David's right leg was dead weight. Stumbling off the edge of the raft, he leaned on Gong and splashed into the muddy water. Once ashore, Gong set him down against a tree.

"How far is Changsha?" Gong asked the soldier.

"Changsha? Two days by river. On land perhaps four." The picket looked at David. "But I don't think the American can walk."

Gong nodded. "River is best."

"Please, share my food," the picket said, holding out a small tin pot. Gong accepted it and scooped a small lump of brown rice into David's open right hand. David lifted his palm. The rice smelled like spoiled milk, and one of the grains was moving—a maggot. David nudged it away with his forefinger and forced himself to eat.

Being still brought David relief from his nausea, but now the sharp thigh pain filled his consciousness. The more he tried not to think about it, the more overwhelming it became. He curled up in a ball, grimacing, trembling. He half-wished for a guillotine to chop off the leg—anything to stop the pain.

The emaciated soldier stared at him. His sunken eyes looked huge, and David stared back at the strange orbs for a while before realizing there was feeling behind them. *Was it sympathy?*

The picket then knelt beside David's outstretched leg. He reached into his shirt pocket and withdrew a small ball of brown paste stuck between two thin squares of wax paper.

David's eyes widened. *No.* He wanted to push the man's hand away, but he was too weak to lift his arm.

Not noticing, the man unwrapped the blood-saturated bandages wound around David's leg. He took a pinch of the sticky paste and began to rub it into the open wound, an act that made David writhe in pain. The picket beckoned Gong to hold the leg still, which he did. And then, even before the soldier had finished re-bandaging the leg, the pain began to lessen.

The soldier handed the rest of the paste to Gong. David's head drifted sideways and slumped against the tree.

Minutes later he was fast asleep.

FIVE

Yenan

M ei Fong sprinted halfway up Fenghuangshan—*Phoenix Mountain*—the tallest hill north of the city. It was their custom to race, with Yuen trotting backward as a handicap. The initial sprint winded Mei Fong, and she fell behind. Passing her, Yuen watched the way her twin ponytails danced behind her head.

At the summit, they settled down beside each other on the flat top of a dusty boulder. Yenan spread before them. The settlement itself was three thousand years old, formerly an important point of trade between Chinese, Mongols, and other travelers from the north and west. Japanese bombing had flattened many of the freestanding buildings, driving Yenan's denizens to resettle in caves. Though the city had a university, hospital, theater, and other modern institutions, Yuen thought it would never lose its primitive, rustic feel.

His eyes followed the shallow, rock-tumbled Yan River as it meandered past the city on the valley floor. Cave dwellings dotted the surrounding tan-colored hillsides. Beyond Yenan, the rugged mountain land rose up as far as the eye could see, a beautiful yet forbidding panorama.

"Ba Ba, what is the rest of China like?" Mei Fong asked. The question surprised Yuen, until he remembered that Mei Fong had never been outside Yenan. He wrapped his arm around her and pulled her in close.

"It is very beautiful."

"Do you think it is beautiful here?"

"It is beautiful in some ways, but there are more beautiful places in China."

"Where?"

Dozens of images flurried through Yuen's mind: wild backcountry, latticed rice paddies, icy peaks. One image lingered: a rain-soaked campsite with comrades huddled in groups, sleeping. Yuen was cold and fighting to stay awake. Of all the nights spent keeping watch, he didn't know why this one stuck out, but it did. Sadly, he couldn't remember where the place was.

"Ba Ba?" Mei Fong persisted.

Yuen glanced at her and smiled. "Yes, China is very beautiful. On the coast there is the vast blue ocean. We have rounded mountains, often covered by mist and clouds. There's also waterfalls, farmland..."

Mei Fong nodded. "Yes, yes, go on."

"Someday I will take you. I promise."

"Ba Ba?" "Yes?"

"I heard Ma Ma say this is a bad place. She told her friend it was barren here, and she wanted to leave."

"You mean she wanted to leave—now?"

Mei Fong shook her head. "Not now. Someday."

Yuen didn't say anything.

"Do *you* want to leave?" Mei Fong asked.

A gust of wind kicked up some loose silted loess and made a spinning dust devil. Yuen squeezed his daughter, shielding her face with his open hand. At that moment, he felt a sudden sense of regret. *This wilderness is no place to raise a child. Shouldn't a father do everything for his children? Whatever is necessary to keep them from eating bitterness, as we have?*

"Mei Fong, this is our home. Our home is wherever we are together, and so this is our home."

Yuen had no idea when they would ever be able to leave.

He recalled the overwhelming feeling of relief when they'd settled here in 1936, after the end of the Long March. This landscape wasn't barren to him then; it was a sanctuary. Their year-long, six-thousand-mile trek had winnowed the Communists until only the most hardy and resourceful men and women remained. Only one in ten of the eighty thousand who began the journey survived. Yuen would never forget the weariness in his bones, the days without food and water, the feeling that becoming a Communist might have been the biggest mistake of his life. Sometimes he still had nightmares of being hunted, but he always woke just after the *feeling* recurred. The *feeling* was like the nadir of hell, that there was no place on earth he would be safe from his enemies. In the usual dream, Yuen was the last soldier; all others were gone, dead. The Nationalists had taken everyone and everything dear to him, and now they wanted *him*; they would never stop.

Slowly, they descended the hill and headed home. They walked down the center of Yenan's dusty streets, avoiding flies and piles of manure along the way. Yuen heard his name called out.

"Comrade Lin!"

He turned and recognized an old acquaintance, Chen Zhen Guo. Like him, Zhen Guo was a longtime Party member, a veteran of the Long March. If there was a picture of the quintessential Communist soldier, Zhen Guo was it. He was tall for a Chinese, almost five foot ten. His sharp, angular facial features, also unusual for a Chinaman, were both handsome and gave an impression of fortitude. He was affable and always greeted Yuen with warmth, yet there was something about Zhen Guo that made Yuen feel that he should keep up his guard. Perhaps this was because Zhen Guo worked so hard to please other people, to be liked by all.

Zhen Guo shook Yuen's hand vigorously and slapped him on the shoulder.

"Hello, Comrade," Yuen answered in a friendly, though less enthusiastic tone. "Busy today?"

Technically, Zhen Guo was Yuen's superior, in overall command of Communist guerilla units, but between veterans such as these, rank mattered little.

"Yes. Gathering reports from the various groups," Zhen Guo said. "What a busy spring! It's good to see you, safe and healthy…and here is Mei Fong!"

Zhen Guo knelt before her. "Growing more beautiful every day," he said playfully. "You take after your beautiful mother, not this ugly dad of yours."

Mei Fong didn't find this very funny, and she pulled away when Zhen Guo tried to tousle her hair. Zhen Guo shrugged and chuckled. Standing up, he put a hand on Yuen's shoulder.

"Yuen, I long to be out there with you, fighting the enemy, not stuck in boring Yenan pushing papers all day long."

Why don't you then? Yuen thought, but he said, "This is true?" He focused his gaze on Zhen Guo's smiling face.

"Certainly. Killing the invaders—that's what I'd like to be doing."

"Perhaps you should request a transfer."

"If only I could." Zhen Guo's grin faltered a little as he returned Yuen's stare. "Yuen, I would not wish my responsibility on anyone," he said. "Sending men off to fight and die robs my sleep each night."

Yuen nodded. "I understand. Will you have a new assignment for us soon?"

"Perhaps." Zhen Guo smiled once again. "But try to relax and enjoy yourself. You deserve a good rest. Enjoy your family!"

With a sweeping wave of his arm, Zhen Guo said farewell and sauntered off.

There's a soldier who transitioned well to politics, thought Yuen. He felt the tug of Mei Fong's hand.

"What? Oh, yes. Let's go home."

Yuen ate a quick meal of rice and steamed cabbage. Then he left his home, walking through the city and across the river to Red Army Headquarters. Every time he approached the small, one-room adobe building, he found it remarkable there was no sign, nameplate, nor guard post to indicate that anyone significant worked there, much less the deputy commander-in-chief of the Communist army.

Yuen knocked.

"Come in," came a gruff voice from behind the thin door. Yuen could see inside through the gaps between the door's wood planks.

Peng Dehuai looked up from his desk as Yuen entered the austere space. The only decoration was a gossamer paper map of China pasted to the wall. A shaft of sunlight through a glass-paned window illuminated the myriad dust particles that hung in the air and cast light across Peng's simple desk. Yuen always found it surprising that this modest structure had been fitted with a glass window, a rare luxury in Yenan.

Comrade Peng resembled a bulldog. He was a revered soldier, known for pugnacity and stoicism, but Yuen found him quite warm when it came to his personal relations. Like many Chinese, Peng looked younger than his age, but the lines of his face and his hardened skin left no doubt that he'd already lived a long, difficult life.

Peng pushed aside a stack of papers. He removed his wire reading glasses and set them on the desk.

"Comrade Lin, welcome back. I have been expecting you." With an open hand, he gestured for Yuen to sit in the wooden chair opposite him.

"Thank you, Comrade Peng. It is good to see Yenan bustling again. I would like to report on our last campaign."

"Excellent. Go ahead."

"At the start of our excursion three months ago, our force numbered one hundred and fifteen men. We returned with seventy-five. We spent all three months behind Japanese lines in southern Shanxi. We engaged and harassed the enemy as much as possible."

Unfolding a piece of paper with figures, Yuen continued. "Railroad sections blown up: seven; engagements: five; estimated enemy killed: one hundred; our casualties: forty. These figures are all in my formal report."

Yuen handed the paper over. Peng put his reading glasses back on and glanced over it.

"Tell me, Yuen, was it a rough one?"

"It was about usual."

"You mean you expected to lose this many men?"

Yuen's eyes drifted to the floor. "I never expect to…we would have done better, but a dozen men I sent into a village for food ran into a Japanese regiment there. They killed all our men."

Peng put the papers down. "It wasn't a criticism, Comrade. Your job is tough, but you are tough. You are doing fine."

"Thank you, Comrade."

A knock at the door interrupted them.

"Come in!" Peng said.

The door creaked. Heavy footsteps fell on the wood floor, and a man entered the small room. Immediately, Yuen was on his feet.

"Hello, Comrade Lin."

"Hello, Chairman. It's good to see you." Yuen felt his face grow flush as he stood before Chairman Mao Zedong.

Mao wore his typical blue cotton tunic, brown pants, and black slippers. From the waist down he was a peasant, but his tunic gave the impression of a scholar. His hair was slicked back, revealing a generous forehead. He was thin, and his dark, piercing eyes took in everything at a glance.

"Comrade Lin has just been telling me of his latest successful excursion behind enemy lines. Would you like him to repeat some of his figures?" Peng asked.

"No, that isn't necessary. Please sit down." Mao leaned against a wall and crossed his arms over his chest. He was tall, and his head almost touched one of the narrow rafters. "Just tell me how we can help you do your job better."

Yuen paused. *Isn't it obvious?* He decided to say it out loud. "We could have done more damage if we weren't so short of ammunition." *And rifles. And supplies.*

Mao surprised Yuen by laughing heartily.

"I've said that power comes from the barrel of a gun...but I suppose the ammunition is just as important as the gun itself!" He chuckled at his own cleverness for several seconds while Yuen remained silent. Finally, Mao said, "Of course, we'll keep trying to get as much as we can for you."

Yuen nodded.

"Now I do have another question for you," Mao said. "If there was an urgent need, do you believe we could mount a sizable force as far east as Shandong? As far as the coast?"

"Shandong? So far?"

Yuen saw that the question was a serious one.

"With respect, Chairman, we embark on each mission on foot. There are no vehicles to transport even small forces such as the groups I lead, and not enough horses to spare. It takes us weeks to reach the Japanese lines. I do not know much about the disposition of our comrades in Shandong, but it seems very far to me."

Peng asked, "How large a force do you think you could take there if you needed to?"

Yuen furrowed his brow. *Walking to Shandong took months. It would be impossible to get a lot of men that far behind Japanese lines without running into complications and disaster. Why are they suggesting something so outlandish?*

"Comrades, it would be quite difficult. I don't think I could expect to take more than"—he sought a low but realistic number—"thirty men that far." Mao and Peng stared at Yuen, and he quickly added, "Undetected, I mean."

Mao and Peng remained expressionless.

"May I ask why you are interested in Shandong?"

The two men exchanged glances, but Yuen could not read either of their faces.

Finally, Mao nodded at Peng. The old soldier returned the nod and then looked at Yuen. "I suppose it is no secret," Peng said, "that there is a chance the Americans will land in China. They are battling up the Pacific island by island. They need a land base that is within bombing range of Japan. If they come, Shandong will be the place, and we need to know how much support we could offer them."

Yuen did not try to hide his surprise. "Support them? How? The Japanese control that territory. We may have a few thousand comrades ready to organize some underground resistance there, but we would never be able to meet them on the beach for a handshake—if that is what you are hoping."

Mao chuckled lightly. With a toss of his right hand, he said, "Of course, of course. It is a far-fetched idea. But there may be a time when America needs us, and it would be in our interest to help them. It would be good for us politically, and they could give us weapons and supplies. Wouldn't that be helpful to you?"

"America? Since when have they been interested in us?" Yuen failed to keep the sarcasm out of his voice.

Mao did not take offense. "You're right, Yuen. They have not been—at least not yet. But Comrade Zhou Enlai is in Chungking now with instructions to invite the Americans to visit us here—"

Yuen coughed, and raised a fist to his mouth.

This time Mao paused, raising an eyebrow.

"Forgive me, Chairman, I did not mean to interrupt," Yuen said.

"What is wrong, Comrade?" Peng asked.

Yuen chose his words carefully. Although he had known Mao and Peng for many years, they were still the Party leaders and speaking with excessive familiarity would be disrespectful.

"Comrades, I only harbor reservations that the Americans would ever be interested in helping us."

Mao frowned. Then he rubbed his chin and stared out the window. "I admit I am doubtful they will come," he said. "We cannot put much hope in it."

Six

Chungking, June 1944

David was hooked again.
And he hated himself for it.

He was fifteen the first time he'd smoked opium, after a Chinese schoolmate had introduced him to it. The sense of euphoria, of well-being, had astonished him. His mind was blank and clear at the same time. He loved the way it made him forget about life: the schoolwork he hated, his father's disapproval, and the memories of his mother.

He managed to kick the habit two years later, not through an exercise of willpower but simply because he'd run away from home by hopping a slow freighter to San Francisco, and his opium stash ran out halfway across the Pacific. He spent the next week suffering the shivering, restless agony of withdrawal alone in the bowels of the ship.

It wasn't until the Nationalist soldier smeared the thick, tarry ball into his leg—an act of mercy—that David had been pulled back. Gong understood and had used it to ease David's pain more than once. But now the usual amount was no longer enough to sate his need. He'd need a fix soon.

Still, it was good to be back in Chungking. The city was beautifully situated on a rocky delta that rose like a small mountain between the convergence of two rivers: the Jialing and Yangtze. The surrounding countryside held an ancient, fairy-tale charm, with fertile plains glimmering seductively between jade-blue mountains and small villages geometrically divided from the green and watery paddy fields.

David owed his survival to Gong, who had paddled two days straight to reach Changsha, and to penicillin, which was administered to him by a Chinese doctor at a Red Cross hospital. At the present time, his wound was a cratered depression in the side of his thigh, covered by a sinuous scar. The skin still wept a little, and he kept a dressing on it. But physically, he was growing stronger and walking almost without pain.

While recovering, he'd managed to tell a Nationalist colonel about the impending Japanese attack, and the man promised to pass the intelligence up the chain of command. News of the massive Japanese offensive came a few days after David left the city, an operation the enemy code-named *Ichigo*. Changsha's defenses collapsed in a matter of days. Now the American airfields were sure to fall, a half dozen of them strung like a string of pearls across southern China, and David wondered if his warning had made any difference at all.

And now he was back in an office—not just any office, either—this was part of General Stilwell's headquarters located in a palatial residential complex. Manicured lawns and meandering pathways traversed the property. Being back among Americans, all scurrying about, hearing English spoken rapidly—all of it felt odd to David, like a childhood memory relived. His workspace, tucked away in a corner of the building, was small and cluttered. Documents and books in English and Chinese lay scattered on his desk next to a massive Underwood typewriter.

A brief knock at the door was followed by a sudden, brash voice. David jumped at the intrusion.

"You're back, Lieutenant?"

David climbed awkwardly out of his chair and saluted the officer in the doorway.

"Yes, sir, Major Enfield. It's good to be back."

The major bestowed a rather routine smile and said, "Don't trouble yourself to rise on my account, Lieutenant. Word's out you're the *big* hero."

David sighed uncomfortably. He lowered his arm and half-tried to assume a more casual stance.

Enfield grinned. He seemed to enjoy David's indecision. "You deserve a rest, Lieutenant. Of course you do."

The major glanced around the room, missing none of the disarray. "Same old paperwork, eh? Same creepy, inept Chinamen running around the place doing as little as possible in the most amount of time."

David drew his feet together. "Yes, sir."

"Tell me, what took you so long getting back?"

"I spent some time at the hospital in Changsha...and now, well, I'm ready to get back to work."

"Are you?" There was a hint of mockery in the major's voice. "Yes, well, when you find the time, I expect to see your full report on my desk."

"Yes, sir," David answered. "That'll be no problem."

Major Enfield nodded, turned crisply, and left the room. David sunk back into his chair.

Enfield had originally been stationed in China as an attaché in 1939. No one understood how that posting had come about, because the major knew no Mandarin and seemed to hate being in China. Nevertheless, he was an ambitious officer, and right after Pearl Harbor, he'd convinced General Stilwell that he had a keen understanding of the Chinese. During Stilwell's long absences to command troops in Burma, Enfield reveled in his augmented power. The major used his phony charm to get most things he wanted. Grudgingly, David admitted the man did have a certain handsomeness about him, a kind of B-grade movie star appeal. This, coupled with his storied reputation with women, made some men look up to him.

Pleasant way to start the day, David thought, starting to file the papers scattered about his desk.

The sheet in his right hand was trembling.

No, it's my hand that's shaking.

David gripped his right wrist with his left hand to stop it.

Already, he thought. *Damn.*

He resumed what he was doing, but even so, there was now a bizarre, restless energy in his chest. It was slight enough that he could ignore it...for now.

A moment later, a friendly face appeared in the doorway. David looked up and smiled. It was his buddy, Jack Service.

"Welcome back," Jack said.

"Hey! Great to see you, Jack."

"Same here, youngster." At thirty-five, Jack Service was the "old man" of the Foreign Service in Chungking. Tall and lanky, he dressed like all the State Department boys: khaki shirt, khaki trousers, thin khaki tie just a shade darker than the shirt. Jack's

Chinese was impeccable, for he, like David, had been born and raised in China.

"Heard you were back. Also heard you had a rough time out there. How's the leg?"

David shrugged. "Good, I guess."

"Good enough for a Purple Heart, right?" Jack sat on the corner of David's desk.

"Yeah, right. How's everything here?" David asked, moving away from the topic of his glorious injury.

Jack sighed, raised his hands. "Busy. Memos and meetings with Chiang's people. All's calm and polite on the surface, but underneath—who knows? All boils down to Stilwell and Chiang…"

"What?"

"…hating each other."

"So nothing's changed," David said.

"No. Nothing except for the *big arrival,* of course."

"What big arrival?"

"You don't know? The vice president is coming tomorrow."

"The vice president of what?"

Jack guffawed. "The United States, you idiot!"

"Henry Wallace? Coming here?"

Jack beamed, enjoying David's disbelief. "Yup, big honor for our Chinese allies." Lowering his voice, he added, "And do you remember what we talked about before you left?"

"Of course."

Jack shut the door. He pulled up a chair and sat close to David. "Davies and I have been nudging it along. Been lots of Nationalist roadblocks, of course, but also from State."

"State? What's their issue?"

"They hate Communists."

"Even if they're helping to defeat Japan?"

"Even so. They don't understand how dysfunctional things are out here. From their perspective, the Chinese Communists are a sideshow to a sideshow. It's off their radar screen. The day-to-day action's in trying to get back into Europe right now."

"Yeah, maybe. But I'll tell you something, this war seemed pretty damn real when the Japs were shooting at me."

Jack grinned. "True enough, buddy." He patted David on the shoulder. "Still, I think we're close. We're hoping Wallace can put us over the top and convince Chiang to look the other way."

There was a knock at the door. Jack rose and opened it.

"Having a nice reunion, gentlemen?"

David stood, and he and Jack saluted Colonel David Barrett. The Colonel was short and balding, the image of the benevolent uncle—round-faced and merry-eyed. Barrett had spent almost his entire army career in China, and he loved everything about the country—the food, scenery, and people—a surprising level of affection for a man who hailed from Colorado and was well-nurtured in everything American.

"Just catching up with our hero, sir. But I was on my way to deliver some memos, actually." Jack slid past Barrett and went through the open doorway. "See you soon, David. Good to have you back."

"Thanks for stopping by, Jack."

"Good to have you back, indeed," Colonel Barrett affirmed as he shook David's hand. "You look well, Parker. Fine work."

"Thank you, sir. But do you mean the bridge or the intel on the Jap attack? Because you might have noticed I lost most of my men, and the Japs still had a field day."

Barrett couldn't help grinning at David's honesty. He sat down in the chair Jack had vacated. "Yes, I heard about all that. Don't beat yourself up. You did good, far as I'm concerned. In battle, a man's got to make quick decisions. Please sit down, and by all means—at ease."

David lowered himself into his chair, keeping his injured leg as straight as possible.

Barrett said, "Still, I wanted to get the story directly from you. I know you caught some lead, son. Take your time."

David told the colonel his tale as succinctly as possible.

When he finished, Barrett shook his head a number of times.

"Lieutenant, you are one lucky son of a bitch to be alive."

"There's one more thing, sir."

"What?"

David took the folded list out of his pocket. "Giving you this will be a big relief. I've carried it for almost a month because I only trust you with the info. I know you'll give it to General Stilwell and do what's best with it."

The colonel took the yellowed paper. "What is this?"

"A list of names—names of Nationalist spies who've been turned by the Japs and are now sending back misinformation. At least, that's what the spy told me when he handed it over. I can't say whether it's true for sure, but I believed him, and he was right about the Jap attack."

Barrett hummed softly as his eyes ran down the list. "If you're right, this could be huge. You say you haven't showed this to anyone till now? Not anyone?"

David shook his head. "The spy warned me against it, worried something would leak or some Jap spy would find out."

"He was probably right. We'll have to share this with Chiang, of course, but we should vet it first and check on a few things ourselves. Then we've got to make sure we show it to the right people. Wouldn't surprise me at all if some of Chiang's inner circle are working for the Japs."

David sat back and exhaled. "Like I said, I'm glad to be passing it off to you."

Tucking the list into his shirt pocket, Barrett gave David an approving nod. "You did well with this too, son. Nice work, you deserve a rest."

David looked out the window at a passing bird. "The war didn't end while I was in the hospital."

"No, it did not," Colonel Barrett agreed. "And I'm anxious to make our mark here. But unfortunately, we're allied to a piece of crap!"

David chuckled.

The colonel continued, "They're trying to run this broken-down country while fighting with one eye on the Communists. They won't fight the enemy. They hoard our supplies. Our war here, if you could call it that, is a *farce*. And I mean to change that. From what I hear, the Communists are the ones actually *fighting* the Japanese, and we have yet to make any official contact whatsoever."

"Jack mentioned the VP might be able to help us out."

Barrett nodded. "That's the plan. Along those lines, you'll be most interested in whom I've invited to the press conference tomorrow, to meet with us afterwards."

"Who?"

Colonel Barrett stood up and moved toward the door. "Just have a good time, Lieutenant," he said, waving off David's curiosity, his eyes smiling as usual. He added wisely, "Watch for new faces, and make sure you stay sober so you can catch the dimes that are dropping." Barrett gave David a wary look but only for a split-second.

"Is someone coming that Chiang won't approve of?"

"I wouldn't worry about it just yet. Actually, I still have to make sure this man can make it. Anyway, it's our party, we'll meet with whomever we want." Barrett clapped David on the shoulder. "I'll see you at the press conference. You should bring that girl of yours—British reporter, right? A woman always helps to loosen things up."

David reddened. *She's not my girl*, he wanted to say, but Barrett, in his typical manner, was already walking off, humming to himself.

SEVEN

"*A bit too hot in there for you?*"

Katherine Payne's first words to David, six months ago at the British legation's stuffy Christmas party. She was a pretty, brown-haired British journalist, and even as he'd made preparations for his mission at the bridge, even as he lay half-dead in the hospital, he'd thought often of her voice, her precise words, and the night they met.

The room *was* hot. Steaming. General officers and ambassadors milled about, dressed in layers of full regalia, sweating like pigs in the windowless room and subtropical humidity.

David circled the large ballroom alone, nursing a drink and searching for someone else of mediocre rank to talk to. He desperately wanted to leave, or at least loosen his tie.

Then he heard her voice, British and alluring, and all other sounds of the ballroom became distant.

"You don't really mean that, do you, Ambassador?" Her tone was assertive, almost challenging,

David took a step back, closer to the voice.

"My dear," the British ambassador had said with a professorial air, "I served in Washington in 1919. I saw what happened to the League of Nations. They rejected Wilson's own idea! You will never get Americans to care about anything beyond their shores, even after this war. It falls to us to police the world, for civilization's sake, and that is one thing that will never change."

"But surely you can't deny all that they're doing now. Without them I daresay we might have floundered."

The old man emitted a patronizing chuckle. "Yes, yes. All credit to Roosevelt for getting them behind us. But don't forget it wasn't until they were *attacked* that they came in. And don't expect them to care after it's over, mark my words..."

David's back was to the ambassador. He turned and glanced at Katherine over the gray-haired man's shoulder. She was slender, pale...lovely. Her lips pursed when she listened, as if formulating her next response. There was a hint of mirth in her light green eyes.

"Forgive me for saying so, but it's my opinion that we owe a lot to our old cousins," she said to the ambassador.

The old man grunted. "In my day, we weren't used to women sharing their opinions," he said, though there was no judgment in his voice. He sounded reflective, as if reminiscing. He leaned closer and spoke in a suggestive way, "But Miss Payne, rumor has it that *you* cannot be objective on the matter, as I believe you were *involved* with an American, were you not?"

A rush of color came into Katherine's cheeks. The full front of her tight-fitting gray business suit swelled as she took a deep breath, and David hardly realized how far forward he was leaning over the ambassador's shoulder.

Suddenly, Katherine looked right at him.

David immediately turned his head, mortified. A heat wave passed through his body. He tried to walk away casually, in no particular direction, just away from the embarrassing stare of the woman who'd intrigued him, and he paid no attention to where he was going.

"Hey, look out!" exclaimed a tall American holding a cocktail in one hand. David collided with him, and the tall man made an exaggerated show of sweeping his arm to keep his glass from spilling.

"Oh! Sorry, Ray."

"Parker, you klutz. How'd they ever let you become a Ranger?" Ray Ludden grinned. He was a friend, a Foreign Service Officer like Jack.

"Very funny. Nice job saving your drink."

"I know, maybe I should've joined some commando group instead of this gig I got. Could've put my agility to better use."

David chuckled politely, but he was already looking back in Katherine's direction. "Wouldn't have been too sad if you'd made me spill this." Ray made a face at the drink. "It's terrible. Can you believe they're also serving hot tea over there? In this weather?"

"Awful..." David said absently. He couldn't see her near the ambassador anymore.

"Chinese think hot tea cools you down because it makes you sweat. Crazy, right? 'Course, the Brits love their tea. I guess that just leaves more liquor for the rest of us..."

David wasn't listening. He circled the ballroom again, but there was no trace of her, and now he was just hot.

He walked outside on to a patio overlooking a small English garden. Two wrought iron benches with weathered wooden slats straddled the path leading down to the garden. He sat down on one, opened his collar, and loosened his tie.

"A bit too hot in there for you?"

David turned and rose, taking in the tall, graceful beauty who'd appeared out of nowhere.

"You might say that. I was trying to get some air," he replied, but the moment the words tumbled out of his mouth he wished he'd said something more witty and memorable.

"I imagined I'd get used to the humidity, but actually, I don't believe I ever shall. I'm Katherine Payne, by the way."

She extended her hand. David took it gently, noticing the cluster of light freckles on the ridge of her nose, which gave her an innocent, girlish look. Her skin was soft and cool.

"I'm David Parker...um, *Lieutenant* David Parker."

"American, I presume?"

"Yes, I work for General Stilwell."

Katherine smiled. "Pleasure to make your acquaintance. And happy to have you Yanks on our side. Where do you come from stateside?"

"Born and raised in Tianjin, actually." David watched the mild surprise spread over Katherine's face.

"Lovely! How did you manage to hail from there?"

"My father worked there. He was a missionary."

"You must speak Mandarin then?"

David nodded. "Pretty well, actually."

"Is that right?" Katherine returned, teasing him.

David, hastening to be done with his awkwardness, said, "And you're from England?"

"To be more accurate, Wales. I grew up on a farm near Cardiff, a half-day's tramp from the Bristol Channel. Do you know Britain at all?"

"Not that well."

"It's not ideal farming weather, I assure you. I had three brothers, and I pitched in to do all the same work they did."

"So, what are you doing way out here?"

"I'm a journalist, with London's *Daily Mirror*."

"Really?" David had guessed she might be a secretary—or bad luck indeed—some distant officer's wife.

"Yes, I've been here three years already. I daren't ask what you were doing three years ago—were you out of school yet?"

David blushed, more annoyed than embarrassed. Katherine appeared so youthful, but her manner was quite sophisticated. It was hard to tell her age, and he wondered if she could be thirty to his twenty-five. He decided not to answer her question. Instead, he fumbled for something else.

"Do you still like it here?"

Katherine's amused eyes dropped slightly when he phrased the question, with perhaps a little less enthusiasm but with the same polished, self-contained manner. "Why, of course I do. Yes, it's bloody boring much of the time, but truth is, the people back home don't know a lot about what's happening here, and they *do* want to know. At least that's what I tell myself."

They conversed for a few minutes more, David feeling like he was holding his breath, his heart out of rhythm, while Katherine was so confident and cool, watching him stumble along and sort of enjoying it—or so he thought. He wondered if she might be cultivating him as a source, hoping to garner some inside information on future government dealings, but it didn't bother him.

A lithe Chinese girl came out on to the patio with a zippered dispatch pouch. She walked briskly and tossed her hair to one side as she walked up to Katherine.

"Excuse me, Miss Payne?"

"What is it, An Li?"

"This just arrived from London. I'm sure you'll want to look at it."

Katherine accepted the dispatch. "Forgive me, Lieutenant. I hope you'll excuse me. Perhaps we'll talk again sometime," she said, smiling.

"I'd like that," David said. There was a lump in his throat, and his voice sounded foggy, old. Katherine and the pretty Chinese girl turned and walked back into the ballroom.

A week later, David's spirit soared when Katherine accepted his invitation to dinner. They wandered the streets and alleys for almost an hour, until Katherine chose a little, out-of-the-way spot that smelled of steamed pork and slightly burned dough. A small sign hung on the door, three characters.

Chi Jiao Zi. *Eat Dumplings.*

An hour later, they had each consumed thirty delicious dumplings. They were small, oval-shaped morsels. The first bite of each dumpling released a scalding flow of meat juice that burned their tongues, until they learned to eat with the large spoon designed to collect the fluid, which could then be sipped.

When they exited the restaurant, David felt the sweat at the back of his neck dry in the unexpectedly cool air. Then, they were suddenly swarmed by a half-dozen Chinese children.

"Cigarette, G.I.? Cigarette?" the boys and girls called out to David. He stared at them for a moment, mesmerized by their energetic, sooty faces.

Hands up, he said, "Sorry, no cigarette. No cigarette."

The children followed them for half a block, pestering them.

"If please, cigarette?"

David was becoming annoyed. "I told you, no—"

Two of the boys, taller than the rest, gave David and Katherine a hard shove into an alleyway. Then they disappeared into the crowd.

David brushed the front of his jacket with his hands. "What was that about?"

There was a scuffing sound behind them. David smelled something foul.

A crackly voice demanded, "Qian na lai!" *Give me your money!*

David spun. He stared at the mugger, a thin wisp of a man, with pocked skin and a big cauliflower lump on the side of his neck. His eyes were fierce, and he had a crudely sharpened dinner knife in his right hand. He pointed it at David's throat as if it were a gun.

Katherine slapped the mugger hard across the face. "Get out of here!" she shouted at the top of her voice.

The mugger shook his head, his face showing a mixture of shock and fear.

A riverboat's siren wailed in the distance.

The thief, hearing it, spun around and ran in the other direction.

David let out a deep breath.

"It's so sad, these poor people," Katherine said, rubbing her hand.

David looked at her in wonderment, and nodded.

That night David felt sure he loved her. No other girl in China could come close to her. The women he'd met on base in training were chatty and nice, but so little informed, so drab in appearance, so American in manner—he'd had no interest in them. Katherine, however, was in a league of her own. She was honest and decisive, and she spoke with the easy authority of a man who didn't fear what he was saying or to whom he was saying it. Surely, other men in Chungking desired her, but David thought his odds of successfully wooing her were far better here than on an army base in England, and for the first time, he considered himself lucky to be stationed in China.

—

David was still mulling over whom Colonel Barrett had invited to meet the vice president when he ran into Jack Service at the American officer apartments. Jack knew, and when the name crossed his lips, the shock and surprise left David speechless. *I don't believe it. This is going to be phenomenal!* He couldn't wait to find Katherine. This would be a story she would not want to miss.

He went looking for her at her usual haunts, weaving through the crowded streets, relishing the exercise and lack of pain in his thigh. He found her seated under an awning at a makeshift café by the British consulate, chatting with a couple of secretaries. After he was sure that Katherine caught sight of him, he ducked out of the crowded street and went down an alley and across the bridge leading toward the Nationalist Army compound. The compound had been targeted on a Japanese bombing raid, and the wall of one of the buildings had crumbled to a heap of bricks. Once, Katherine had insisted on climbing up the rubble for the fun of it.

She jogged across the bridge five minutes later. She wore a dark green cloth over her long hair and loose-fitting brown pants typical for a laborer. As she approached, David couldn't help but smile. The drab clothing was too short for her long limbs, and her pants were hiked almost halfway up her shins, exposing her slim ankles and fair skin.

"Hello, young man," she said, setting herself down beside him on the rubble pile.

"Good afternoon."

"You look happy. What's the news?" she asked, lighting a cigarette.

"Trying to decide how to tell you," he said mysteriously.

"Oh, a secret? I *like* secrets. Fag?"

"No thanks."

She sucked on hers, then queried, "So?"

"There's a press conference tonight at the mansion."

"I know, your vice president. I'm a reporter, remember?" She smiled. "Is that all?"

"I imagine you might be interested in a couple of the guests."

"Matchmaking, are you?"

"Love at first sight, I should think."

"So who am I to fall for—other than you, of course?"

At this, David felt his face grow warmer. He looked away and stammered, "Um...the generalissimo will be attending."

Katherine smirked. "Dashing character, but not very exciting."

"Colonel Barrett, too."

"That jolly American officer? Charming."

"Not to mention Major Robert Enfield, of course." David hesitated, watching for Katherine's reaction. Word had it that she and Enfield had been together near the very beginning of the war, before David had come to Chungking.

Katherine laughed softly. "Oh dear, why dig up an old grave?"

This time she looked away, downriver. A group of ducks alighted and coasted on the water, leaving expansive, converging wakes. Then she looked David full in the face again. "Come now, David. This is hardly whetting my appetite. In fact, it's a trifle annoying—if you really want to know."

He didn't wish that, so he hastened on. "There's another guest—and I almost forgot to mention him."

"Hm," she murmured, gazing at her feet.

"Zhou Enlai."

Katherine's half-grin evaporated. "Bugger off! Really?"

David grinned. "Oh yes. Zhou is here. Can you imagine what it'll be like to have him *and* the generalissimo in the same room?"

"Chiang would never allow it!" Katherine exclaimed. With her right hand she tapped one slender finger to her lower lip, as if to underscore what she'd said.

"It's not his choice," David said.

"And why in the world would you risk an incident?"

"Tell me that you're not as fascinated with this man as I am."

"Well, who wouldn't be? Shanghai? The Long March? The man is a perfect legend."

"Like I said, love at first sight." David sat back, satisfied.

"And how can you be so sure that Zhou will come?" Katherine challenged.

"Because he wants to meet Wallace. In fact, he wants to meet any American who will give him an audience. That's precisely why he's here."

"Marvelous, just marvelous," Katherine said, shaking her head and studying her hands as if they were holding the story she had yet to write.

"So if you've got a dress in the closet…"

"Don't worry," she said, rising to her feet. "Just tell me where to be and at what time."

David turned his hand in the air with a flourish. "My dear, come to the mansion at half past four. I'll make sure you get a front row seat."

"Crikey!" she said. And then, swift as a bird, she flew in close to his face and kissed him quickly on the lips. Before he could react, she was turning and heading back the way she'd come through the late golden afternoon. David watched, chuckling to himself, as her smooth, gliding motion disappeared like a white flower petal lost in the throng of dark heads and shoulders moving up and down the main thoroughfare of Chungking.

Eight

Yenan, May 1944

Yuen stood at the open doorway, backlit by the morning sun. His home stay had been one week, and now he was ready to leave. But not really ready, for Mei Fong clung to him like a vine, her arms around his thigh.

"I must go," Yuen said to his daughter. Letting go and standing up, Mei Fong said, "You have to?"

He nodded. "I don't *want* to, I *have* to."

Jiang Hong stopped washing dishes, lifting plates from the wooden bucket of soapy water to the bucket of clean water. Sighing, she said to herself as much as to her daughter, "Your father must leave now."

Yuen looked into his wife's eyes. *She's not as sad as she is resigned. No different from me.*

Jiang Hong rose from her stool and stepped close enough to Yuen to hug him, but then, eyes downcast, she held back. He embraced her. She accepted his embrace but left no opening for a kiss.

Comrades were not encouraged to display affection openly, but there had been a time when Jiang Hong had ardently savored Yuen's kisses. She was a giddy girl from the backcountry then. That young spark in her eyes had since dulled, replaced by a darker, more calculating look that hard times had driven deeply into her face. *The trials,* Yuen thought. *No woman should have to go through them the way she has.*

He remembered their flight from the Nationalists, and the miscarriage of their first child that would have been a boy. *That hardened her heart more than anything,* he remembered. He did not blame her for any of these feelings, rather, he felt her sorrow as if it were his. In truth, it *was* his.

"I will come home soon."

"You have to," Jiang Hong said in a voice that was both numb and hopeful at the same time.

Yuen said nothing.

Jiang Hong pressed his hand. "I know you will," she added, but even as she said it, her voice dropped and became almost inaudible, as if he wasn't there anymore.

Yuen released her from his embrace and turned to his daughter. Saying goodbye to Mei Fong was far more difficult. Tears slid down her round cheeks as she hugged his leg in mute silence.

"Zai jian, Ba Ba." *Goodbye.*

"Zai jian, Mei Mei." *Goodbye, little sister.* Even though Mei Fong was an only child, Yuen called her Mei Mei in memory of the brother who had never drawn breath.

"Come home soon," she whispered, her eyes glistening.

"I will," he replied, and felt, just then, his own tears begin to well up.

Yuen had ordered the men to form up at Yenan's eastern edge. This mission was different, more dangerous. Penetrating to the area east of Taiyuan would be a deep incursion into Japanese territory. The two hundred fifty mile trek, some of it over mountainous terrain, would be slow going, and this time he preferred a smaller force, only thirty men.

His men were veterans, ranging in age from seventeen to forty-three. There was easy camaraderie as they marched, but also an understanding that it was bad form to laugh or talk loudly at the start of a mission. Flanked by rocky, yellow hillsides devoid of vegetation, the road was familiar, the men subdued. *It always starts this way,* Yuen thought. *They're thinking of family and the hard living to come.* He knew this feeling, and there was comfort in the routine. He felt his spirit calm, away from the city, away from Jiang Hong. *There is only one goal now: to accomplish this mission.*

No. There is another: to keep these men alive, if I can.

Things loosened up by nightfall. The campsite felt almost like a celebration, a reunion of old friends. The men told dirty jokes and complained about their wives. Jou, a former actor, sang songs from his repertoire of Chinese opera. He had a rich voice with a wide range, impressing his comrades with his ability to sing the parts of multiple characters, even that of the shrill female lead. Jou was lithe and not particularly strong, but his talent and affability made him well-liked.

After the singing, Han, a recent university graduate, delivered a lecture aimed at the illiterate soldiers. With his glasses, wide forehead, and close-shaven head, he looked the part of a monkish scholar. Although he could be supercilious, Yuen liked Han because he was quick-thinking and reliable. He was the Party's perfect political mouthpiece, used to educate and inculcate the ones who'd never been to school.

"It has been a long struggle, and it may go on for many more years, but we are succeeding! We loosen the landlords' grip on the people. We throw out the Japanese. China will not be the concubine of Western nations. Together, comrades, we can ensure that every person in China is safe and has food to eat. In 1911, our fathers revolted to overthrow the Qing Emperor. Now we must finish the work they started!"

The men cheered Han. They liked his pep talks, but Yuen was tired of the theatrics. He knew what would happen next: a series of hard luck stories from men who liked to hear themselves talk—who maybe *needed* to hear themselves talk. Yuen wondered if anyone else could see how shallow the whole thing was. He scanned the circle of men and, judging from the smiling eyes around the fire, he was the only one who was bored with it.

The first to speak was a soldier named Bao. He was exceptionally tall and heavyset for a Chinese man. The brawny soldier was sometimes self-conscious about his lack of education, but by nature he was a gregarious man, and he liked to surprise the others by doing crazy things, like biting the head off a live cockroach, or walking around naked. This time, however, he spoke gravely of his past.

"For twenty years, my family worked for the same landlord. Then famine came, and the landlord drove us off. He said we did not produce enough to be worth feeding. We broke up after that. My younger sisters were sold to a brothel. I went to the city and became a stonecutter. I never saw my parents again."

His fellow soldiers nodded in sympathy; some mumbled, "Shame, shame." The firelight flickered in the shadowy darkness. Stray sparks flew up and away, carried by the wind.

There are thousands of stories just like Bao's, Yuen thought. *Everyone's lost someone, every family's been touched, hit, devastated in some way. Now the Party's become their family. This platoon's become their family.*

Yuen marveled at the way the group hung together as one. Farmers and rickshaw pullers, side by side with scholars and merchants. In a country where most people never ventured farther than a day's walk from the village of their birth, this was extraordinary.

—

The platoon crossed into areas of nominal Japanese control after two weeks of marching. Despite the ever-present risk of Japanese reprisals against them, civilians along the way fed and sheltered them. Yuen relied on this, and to his men he stressed the importance of treating civilians with respect. *We always pay for goods. We never steal. It is better to sleep outside in the open than to intrude on civilian homes.* The support of the people was crucial to the Communists' ability to operate behind enemy lines.

He remembered this area well; they'd passed by here just two months ago on their return trip to Yenan. The soil was shallow and poor; hard clay lay underneath. Thin, wasted poplar trees dotted the drab, hilly landscape. One of his men had been severely wounded. They'd stopped at a small village, only a dozen huts. Though the villagers were poor, Yuen had been humbled by their generosity. They fed his men and let them stay the night. When they offered to care for the wounded one, Yuen hesitated, but agreed. He knew the man probably would not survive the rest of the journey to Yenan.

Now what's that? Smoke?

Yuen's pulse quickened.

Twin trails of smoke rose in the distance, to the northeast.

"Jou! Han! Run ahead," he ordered. The rest double-timed it, jogging after the sprinting scouts.

Yuen's stomach tightened. He sensed what had happened.

As they closed in on the smoke, the sky blackened. *The same small road, the same trees. I'm coming from another direction, but I recognize it.*

It was the same village.

They came in sight of it. Jou and Han were already searching for survivors. Nearly every building was burned to the ground and smoking. Yuen guessed the attack had come the day before.

Jou hollered from one of the still-standing huts. Yuen dashed to it, pushed aside the gray blanket covering the doorway. His eyes were blinded by the sudden darkness.

A couple moments later, he saw something stretched out on the floor. *What's that? A body? There's a humming in here, unless it's in my head.*

He knelt beside a girl, perhaps twelve or thirteen, naked. There were stab wounds all over her chest.

Jou vomited, spat, wiped his mouth with his sleeve. Yuen waved him outside.

The humming in the hut continued, growing in volume.

Yuen took a series of abbreviated breaths. The smell of death, burnt huts, and vomit penetrated his nostrils. As his mind reeled, he fought to maintain his focus.

He turned around and saw two people, possibly the girl's parents, dead in a corner. Turning over their bodies, he noticed their hands and feet were bound. They, too, were peppered with stab wounds—now black with coagulated blood and flies. Yuen brushed some of the flies away, but they returned in an instant, humming more loudly. He gazed at the bodies for a moment longer, mesmerized by the unnatural scene, then he felt the bile rise in his throat, and he rose to his feet and staggered out of the hut.

Outside, the smoke hung low, but the death smell was less. Yuen joined some of his men who'd discovered more charred bodies inside another standing hut. These were barely recognizable as human forms—limbs truncated and scorched, heads burnt, with the teeth being the only white thing in the midst of all that black. The hut itself was not much damaged. *Burned alive,* Yuen concluded.

Walking then to the center of the village, he heard a moan from underneath a pile of machine-gunned bodies. Bao heard it too. They rushed toward the pile. Bao moved the bodies aside, one after another until he uncovered a teenage boy.

Barely conscious, the boy was coated in dried blood. Bao lifted him gently and laid him down apart from the others. The youth looked dead, but his mouth was open and his lips moved. Yuen carefully opened his shirt, revealing three gaping gunshot holes. Overhead, the specks of vultures wheeled. Dark-winged, circling, lowering their angle of flight. Drawing down so that Yuen could see their naked heads.

Bao held the boy's head with one hand while he offered him his canteen with the other. The boy sipped like a bird, coughed. His eyes opened wide and he cried, "Ma Ma! Ba Ba!"

"You are safe now," Bao said soothingly.

"Mei Mei!"

The boy's eyes rested on Yuen.

"Where are they?" Yuen asked. He remembered this boy. *He was the one who wanted to hold my gun.* "The Japanese," Yuen said. "What happened?"

The boy blinked. His breath came in sobs. Laboring to speak, he said, "They came...Tong told them...about the man you left."

"When?"

"Yesterday. Your man came out...they shot him." He paused. Bao tried the water again, but the boy twisted his face away. "They killed everyone."

Yuen showed no emotion. The band of men, Yuen's soldiers, were all there, no one saying anything, just staring. The vultures dropped nearer in concentric circles, some landing in nearby trees.

Minutes later, the boy in Bao's arms closed his eyes for the last time. Yuen sent pairs of men to scout the woods and fields, and to follow the truck tracks that wound to the east.

For the rest of the day, the clank of shovels and the harsh cries of carrion birds punctuated the stillness of the dead village.

NINE

"There are only ten of them," Han whispered into Yuen's ear as the two of them surveyed the long, green valley. The sun was setting. Its fiery glow lit the sky behind them, and long shadows cast by the grassy hills extended across the valley floor. Yuen nodded. *Their truck must be broken down. Why else would they stop here—in the middle of nowhere and out in the open?*

From their hidden position on a hill above the Japanese soldiers, Yuen could see the tan clay valley road for a quarter mile in each direction. *Would we have enough warning if any more arrive?* The scouts had followed the road leading from the village for two miles and found it joined a larger road. They split up:

one going north, one south. The northern scout discovered the enemy soldiers one mile from the junction.

"Do you think these are the ones who attacked the village?" Han whispered.

Yuen shrugged. *Does it matter? They are the enemy. Every one of them would gladly kill us. They rape girls, don't they?* He felt his anger rise, but he checked himself. *Keep your head. No room for revenge. He who seeks revenge should remember to dig two graves.*

The Japanese were mostly teenage boys and middle-aged men. Their dark green uniforms looked black in the dim light. A pair of them lit cigarettes—glowing points of light that tracked their hand movements. By their lack of any effort to set up a camp, Yuen figured they did not plan on waiting more than one night.

Calmer now, he wondered if it would be wiser to pass them by. *An ambush would increase enemy patrols.*

The light was fading. Yuen had to make a decision. *The smart move is to go around. The men are tired and hungry.* Their last meal had been breakfast: rice porridge and three-day-old sticks of you tiao—*fried dough twists.* But then he looked at the men, surprised to find many staring at him, waiting for orders. *They want revenge. They need it. How can I deny them this?*

And though he tried to stem it, though he rarely let emotions cloud his judgment, Yuen couldn't shake the image of the blood-smeared girl in the hut. He tightened his grip on his rifle.

"What's your plan?" came a deep voice. Yuen looked over his shoulder at Yang Lu Gao, his second-in-command who had crawled up behind him. Yuen made the decision.

"We surround them and attack just after dark."

Lu Gao considered this. His face gave no indication of what he thought or felt. At last, he nodded, slunk back, and disappeared into the tall grass.

It helped knowing that Lu Gao would spread the word and ready the men; he was very good at details and doing things properly. The oldest man in the group, Lu Gao was accorded respect as well as allegiance to rank. This was reinforced by his refusal to become too friendly with any of the men.

Yuen could hear murmurs of assent as Lu Gao delivered the plan of action.

Darkness came slowly.

In the valley, the Japanese soldiers built a fire near the truck and broke out ration tins. *They will not leave the truck*, Yuen thought. Army vehicles were valuable and almost impossible to replace in inland China. *We have plenty of time…wait long, strike fast.*

Silently, the Communists snuck down the hillside and surrounded their enemy, crouching in the waist-high wild grass that densely covered the valley floor.

The Japanese soldiers' fire crackled and smoked. The air carried the fragrance of burnt pine. In the wind-blown smoke, the dark forms of men were clearly visible. Yuen studied the serpentine hills he and his men had come down from and wondered if they had enough cover. The night was not fully settled yet, and the sky was clear enough that the twinkling stars gave off even more light. Cricket song began pulsating in the gathering darkness, and the air grew colder and crisper.

Yang Lu Gao tapped Yuen on the shoulder, indicating the men were ready.

Yuen squinted to see in the shadow-light and confirmed the men were in position.

He drew a deep breath and bellowed, "Attack!"

Men on the western flank popped up out of the grasses and opened fire. In mere seconds, five of the ten Japanese were hit. Ducking back into the grass, the Chinese heard their comrades on the eastern flank fire a volley that killed three others who had fled to that side. The two remaining soldiers jumped into the truck bed, which had a canvas cover stretched over it.

"Cease fire!" Yuen ordered. Lu Gao loudly echoed the order.

Moments passed. Smoke from the Communist guns twisted and twined with the pine smoke from the campfire, floating away in the breeze. The groans of wounded Japanese soldiers mixed with the loud sparking of the fire; and then, first from one and then another, cricket song started up in the grass—and made it seem as if nothing had happened.

A shout in Japanese came from the truck.

"Utanaide kure!" *Don't shoot!*

Yuen scoffed. Early in the war he had rarely seen the enemy surrender. Doing so was shameful to the Japanese. *Now they send the worst soldiers to China.* Though these were likely to have been bookkeepers, shop workers, or ex-convicts, he still found it ironic how little they cared to die for their emperor.

Two boys emerged from the truck with hands held high. They looked fifteen or sixteen years old. Their eyes grew wide with surprise as they watched Yuen's thirty-man platoon emerge from the shadows into the firelight. One of them began to sniffle, failing to hold back tears. The other remained stone-faced.

There was a thud at the front of the truck, near the fender, followed by a groan. *What is that?* Yuen wondered. There was another thud, then another. Yuen came around and saw Han kicking a body, a soldier who had been shot in the abdomen. Dark blood dribbled from the soldier's lips as he murmured something in Japanese.

Han stopped, leaned over the wounded man, and spoke to him.

For a moment, the soldier was stunned that Han, the university graduate, could speak Japanese. His face seemed to soften, but then Han un-holstered his pistol, cocked it, and aimed at his head.

The man's eyes widened and he began to sputter. Yang Lu Gao walked up to Han's side and whispered in his ear. Yuen couldn't hear what was said, but he saw Han lower his pistol.

The men searched the truck. Besides ration boxes and the soldiers' Arisaka rifles, they did not find any useful supplies or intelligence. The hungry Communists divided and ate the Japanese canned fish and cooked rice. They also found miso powder to be mixed with water and stuffed Kanpan hardtack crackers in their pockets for later.

As Lu Gao forced the two boys to load their dead and wounded comrades into the truck, Yuen asked Han, "What did he say?"

Distracted, Han said, "Who?"

"The one you had words with."

"He said, 'I didn't hurt anyone. I want to go home.'"

"Then what did you say?"

"I told him, 'You should have thought about it before you invaded my country.'"

After this, Han stalked off into the darkness and stood at the umbra of the fire's glow, pausing as if deep in thought. In a short time, the two boys completed their task of loading the bodies into the truck. Cowering at the tailgate, one of them began to beg for his life.

Lu Gao looked to Yuen, who nodded.

Lu Gao strolled up to the other one, the stone-faced boy, and struck him with the butt of his rifle. The boy crumpled, and his comrade wailed more loudly. All at once, several of Yuen's men descended on the pair and began beating them. Yuen looked away. He derived no pleasure from this, none at all. Yet, a short while ago he'd wanted it, wanted to kill each and every one of them.

This is war. They began it. We will finish it.

Finally, Yang Lu Gao ordered the men to stop. The Chinese forced the beaten boys into the truck and tied them to the metal ribbing that supported the canvas stretched over the truck bed. Lu Gao methodically walked around the truck, pausing over the gas cap.

He knelt down and picked up a pebble. Unscrewing the cap, he dropped the pebble down the shaft and listened for the muted splash. Then he detached a grenade from his belt.

It was just slightly narrower than the tube going down to the tank.

The two boys began to scratch and bite at their bindings. They could see Lu Gao through a side window cut in the canvas. There were frantic mumblings in the truck bed as the wounded wrestled and rolled, trying to free themselves from the weight of so many tangled men.

Lu Gao pulled the pin out of the grenade, dropped it into the tank, and ran.

The Chinese scattered in the tall grass, throwing themselves to the ground.

The truck exploded in a giant fireball that rocked the earth and wracked the air. Shrapnel buzzed about, cutting blades of grass. The size of the explosion surprised Yuen, who had already moved well away from the blast. The intense wall of heat forced him to turn away and retreat farther.

Moments passed. Crouching men got to their feet. What was left of the truck was an orange cinder.

Yuen turned to the east and stared at the dark and distant hills. He could hear the screams and feel the inferno as it continued to burn—but far away in the hills the silence was deep, and the tips of the pines touched the stars, where ancient fires burned more fiercely than those on earth.

TEN

Chungking, June 1944

Katherine hurried to the mansion, trying not to work up a sweat. The muggy weather was already beginning to frizzle her hair, and her dress was sticking to the small of her back.

She wanted to look good for David, though she wasn't quite sure why. Her assistant and best friend, An Li, had been quick to voice her opinion when Katherine told her about David's invitation to the vice president's press conference.

"He's much too young for you," An Li had said as she helped Katherine get ready.

"You think so? Or do you just want him for yourself?" Katherine teased, fastening her brassiere.

"Me and a foreign devil? My ancestors would renounce me! My soul would wander for eternity!"

The two women giggled. An Li was a beautiful girl, with perfectly symmetrical almond eyes and a small mouth that reminded Katherine of a porcelain doll. She was Katherine's indispensable interpreter, confidante, and advisor regarding all things Chinese.

"He's just a boy trying to be a man," An Li said.

"He's still older than you," Katherine reminded her.

Katherine felt An Li pull her dress tight and she let out a wheeze. An Li then fastened the buttons down Katherine's back.

"Western men take a long time to grow up," An Li said. "They want only one thing." She reached around and cupped her fingers around Katherine's right breast.

Katherine lips parted in surprise.

An Li's hand lingered for a conscious moment, then she let go and laughed out loud. "And in China," she continued, wagging her finger, "a Westerner thinks he can do whatever he wants to whomever he wants."

Katherine crossed her arms over her chest, but she continued to smile. "You might be mistaken about David. He's a bit awkward at times. It's rather endearing, actually."

"You will see when he tries something," An Li replied. Then her voice became low, the laughter gone. "Maybe not tonight, but soon. You be ready. Trust me."

Katherine turned around and put her hand on her friend's shoulder. The touch seemed to soften An Li, and she closed her eyes a little as Katherine spoke to her. "Yes, dear An Li. I do trust you. I wonder what I would do without you?"

An Li opened her eyes wide. "You'd have had an affair with the British ambassador by now," she said mischievously.

At this, Katherine let out a playful squeal, and the two women dropped to the floor, laughing.

Still, Katherine couldn't help feeling An Li was wrong about David. He seemed unsure of himself, and she sensed he'd not been close with many women. His mission had made him a minor celebrity among the American and British expatriates, and she could see how some might consider him dashing and clever, but there was something equally innocent and vulnerable about him—his gentle touch and reticence to be intimate with her. This was what she found refreshing and irresistible.

Yes, he's too young.

But at the same time, she wasn't embarrassed by how often she thought of him.

The mansion came into view and Katherine slowed to a walk. *Just five minutes late.* She felt her brow. *Damn. Sweating all right.* The trail to the hilltop mansion wound past a rose garden and several topiaries. Two late-working gardeners bowed as they scurried out of her way near the wide, stone steps that led to the mansion's enormous front doors.

Entering the foyer, she realized that few others had arrived. David stood at the far end, between a pair of kneeling marble lions that flanked the entrance to the ballroom where Wallace and Chiang Kai-shek would officially meet. In a corner, a pianist played Chopin on a nine-foot ebony Steinway, practicing for his performance at the gala being held in Wallace's honor that evening.

Katherine's heels clacked, echoing across the tiled floor. "Sorry, I'm a bit tardy," she said to David.

"Not a problem, it seems we are unfashionably early." David waved a hand at the empty foyer.

"No bother, you're too kind to know that punctuality doesn't exist in this country," she teased.

They listened to the music for a few minutes. The pianist was middle-aged and Chinese. His hands and fingers clambered over the keys with remarkable agility. The music was intoxicating.

"You know there's only one grand piano in Chungking?" David said.

"Really? I thought I saw one at the British consulate."

"This is the same one. They moved it here this afternoon. Colonel Barrett jokes that the Japs have spies assigned to it in the hope that a well-placed bomb might erase our morale. So they try to keep it on the move."

"Sounds like an important job," Katherine said. "One for one of Chiang's generals, no doubt. I say, that fellow is quite good."

The pianist's fingers flew up and down the keyboard through a perfect cadenza.

"One of China's best," a rigid voice spoke from behind them.

They turned. It was Major Robert Enfield. "He studied with Cortot in Paris. I heard that he played for Mussolini in Rome and had quite a career in Shanghai ten years ago. I've seen him play twice now, and I'll be damned if I've ever heard a better Rachmaninoff Two."

Enfield's eyes traced Katherine up and down, flashing a devious grin as he gestured to the piano.

"That thing's a piece of crap though. All the play has worn down the felts. The keys don't stop. It'll be a perfectly muddy performance, but that's music during war, I suppose."

David felt uncomfortably warm in Enfield's presence. "You know a lot about music...sir."

Enfield grunted, self-satisfied. "Yes, yes, but the music here *does* leave something to be desired. You know, I recall catching a

Chinese opera performance a few years back in Peking. I have to say, it's all rather mystifying to me, with all the shrieking and fighting."

Enfield made a show of boxing the air. He chuckled to himself. "Lieutenant, perhaps you can explain to me how these people like fighting in their art, and yet they're so thoroughly inept on the battlefield."

Enfield took a carton of cigarettes out of his pocket, tapped one out, and lit it. He blew smoke at David's face, enough so that David had to fan it away with one hand.

"I'm not sure I understand your meaning, sir," David said, coughing.

"Come now. If we had just one regiment of U.S. Marines here we could drive these Japanese leftovers out of China single-handedly. And I'll be damned if we couldn't subdue this ragged country with even half that number."

Katherine cleared her throat. "So you'd like to create an American colony out of this place?" she asked, pointedly.

"Well Katie, my dear, now that you put it out there…What is *your* opinion, Lieutenant?" Enfield's lips drew into a sneer. "You grew up here, with these savages."

Katherine blushed. Enfield beamed, seeming to enjoy her discomfort.

"Forgive me," Katherine interjected, tugging at David's arm. "That was an impulsive comment, and now I'm afraid I desperately need to find the loo. David, would you help me find it? I've never been here."

"Answer the question first, Lieutenant," Enfield pressed. "Really man, have the courage to say what you think." He turned to Katherine and grinned. "Katie likes men who do that."

David gently removed Katherine's hand from his arm and squared up to the major. "I know Chinese who can fight, sir.

They died fighting and killed a lot of Japs, too. Not every Chinaman is as weak as you say."

Enfield's grin disappeared. Just then, the pianist finished his piece with a series of crashing but harmonious chords.

"Major Enfield," a new, thickly accented voice called out in English. A tall Nationalist officer approached. He wore pince-nez glasses and walked with a swagger—and a slightly sinister air of arrogance, David thought.

"My name is Dai Li. I am the generalissimo's chief of police," he said, acknowledging David and Katherine's presence with a nod.

Katherine elbowed David. David glanced at her knowingly. *Boss Dai. Juntong. Secret police.*

Enfield stood up a little straighter, affording the man greater respect. "Oh. How can I help you?"

"I came to thank you, Major, because you already have. I received the intelligence you supplied to my subordinate. I must say that I was taken completely by surprise by its contents."

Enfield stiffened.

The chief of police continued, "But I must ask you, where did you acquire this information?"

"Afraid I can't tell you the specifics. I need to protect my sources or else they wouldn't be much use in the future, eh? You understand. Let's just say it came from some good detective work."

"Major," Dai said, chuckling as if he were toying with Enfield, "I'm afraid you'll have to do better than that. You provided us with a very alarming list of names. Acting upon your information will have far-reaching effects. We need to know where it came from."

Enfield's eyes darted between David and Dai. "I think it'd be better if we continued this discussion in private."

The police chief gave a short nod. "If it would make you more comfortable."

Without looking at David, Enfield led Dai away.

"What was that all about?" Katherine asked.

David's mind spun. *That wasn't...? How could it be?*

"Well?" Katherine said.

"I'm not sure," David managed to say. *What the hell is going on?*

"More people are arriving," he said to her. "Let's go in."

They walked up a few marble steps and entered the ballroom.

"David, I'm sorry Robert is such a bastard. I mean, the nasty things he said." Katherine took his hand. "I'm sorry if me being here counts as some grudge against you. I...oh, dear—"

She pulled her hand out of his grasp. "Your hand..."

David looked down, confused.

"I'm sorry. It's just that...it's *very* moist," Katherine said.

David wiped his hands down the sides of his trousers. His heart was beating quickly, and now he realized this wasn't because of the heat, or the major, or from being close to Katherine.

"I'm sorry," he mumbled. "It's hot in here."

"Yes, it is," Katherine replied. She carefully took his arm again, but then her grip tightened.

David looked up to where she was staring. Zhou Enlai was approaching.

"Miss Payne," Zhou called out, gesturing for them to join him as he retreated through a pair of French doors to the side yard, which was flanked on one side by the mansion's towering east wall, and on another side by a steep embankment leading up toward the heights of the city center. Two tall, dark-suited men trailed behind.

As they followed, David whispered, "You know him?"

Katherine answered, "Well, I sought him out for an interview once last year. I didn't land it, but I met him briefly. He has a remarkable memory."

Zhou's face was expressive, with thick, dark brows and intense, brown eyes. He was shorter than his guards, about the same height as Katherine, but he moved with sprite-like quickness.

"Colonel, what a great pleasure," Zhou said in accented English, taking David's hand.

Embarrassed, David responded in Mandarin, "Oh, no. My name is David Parker, lieutenant to Colonel Barrett."

"Ah!" Zhou said in his mother tongue, responding with both pleasure and surprise. "Your accent is impeccable."

"As it should be," David replied. "I was born Chinese, in Tianjin. I lived there until I was seventeen."

"How fascinating," Zhou said, beaming. "So, you are a son of China! An American man with a Chinese tongue. Wouldn't it be fortune to us all if you also had the mind of the Chinese."

"I have no such mind," David said, surprised by his own candor. It was as if the language itself had loosened his tongue. "Sorry, I mean to say that I believe in nothing in particular as far as philosophy goes."

"Don't apologize. I like a man who speaks his mind. He has nothing to hide." Zhou's attention was so fixed on him that David felt incapable of looking at anyone else. Zhou's men stood around him with animal intensity, as if searching for something to dominate.

Zhou turned his eyes to Katherine. "She is your companion?" he asked David.

"What is he saying?" Katherine whispered out of the side of her mouth as she smiled back demurely at Zhou.

"Just a friend," David said to Zhou.

"A woman like this is not just your friend," Zhou said, still speaking in Mandarin. "Either you despise her or you are her slave."

"He says that you look well," David said to Katherine, frowning at his choice of words.

"Ah," Katherine emitted, dissatisfied.

"I've never met your colonel," Zhou said, directing his attention back to David with a voice that was softer but more focused. "I am hoping that he shares at least some of my enthusiasm for our meeting today."

"I have to be perfectly honest with you, Mr. Zhou. You should know that Generalissimo Chiang is not aware that you will be here."

"Actually Lieutenant, this doesn't surprise me at all. So don't feel unease. We suspected that the side doors might be both our entrance and exit for this evening."

Zhou's effortless smile allayed David's fears. He had indeed been prepared for a lion's den.

"Then you must be wondering why you are here…"

"These men," Zhou interrupted, pointing to the sullen men who shadowed him. "These men and I ran for our lives for years. We hid in outhouses and sewers. We slept more in the rain than I can bear to recall. We walked thousands of miles to get away from other Chinese who had it in mind to murder us. But all along the way, we found ordinary people who came out to feed us. I never asked them why. When you die a thousand deaths, watching all of your friends fall along the way, you stop looking for motives, because they don't matter. You take what you are given and you speak your mind. Does that make sense to you, Lieutenant?"

David nodded, absorbing Zhou's words. Though Katherine could not understand Zhou's speech, she was spellbound by the man's intensity.

"Should we see what an American vice president looks like?" Zhou said, clasping his hands together. He smiled and extended his arm to Katherine. Switching to accented English, he asked, "Shall we, Miss Payne?"

After leaving Zhou to stand with a group of Chinese reporters along the ballroom's side wall, David led Katherine to a seat in the front row of assembled chairs, near a podium that had been set up at the back of the cavernous room. David spotted his State Department friends, Ray Ludden and John Davies, standing along an opposite wall. He joined them.

"So where's Zhou Enlai?" Ray Ludden asked in a low voice.

"Over there with those Chinese journalists," David said.

"And the Russians," added John Davies. Davies was a bookish State Department journeyman who had been born in China, like David. He had an ever-present cigarette dangling from a corner of his mouth and considered it fashionable to tuck his tie into his shirt between the buttons.

Stretching his neck to get a glimpse of the famous guest, Ray said, "Wow, he's shorter than I expected."

A door opened. Flanked by Colonel Barrett, Vice President Henry Wallace emerged wearing a dark suit. He was tall and thin, with graying hair combed from a perfect part. He came to a stop beside the podium; a flag bearer with the Stars and Stripes entered and stood next to him and the colonel.

On David's side of the room, another door opened, and ten Nationalist officers marched out, single file, each bedecked with at least a dozen shiny medals. Behind them, Chiang Kai-shek appeared. His English interpreter waddled behind him. Chiang's uniform was perfectly pressed, his posture and gait impeccably military. His head was shaved, and his thin mustache displayed a few streaks of gray. The room hushed out of respect for the Supreme Allied Commander of the China Theater.

Chiang and Wallace shook hands. Chiang's officers lined up off to the side, while Chiang went to the podium with his interpreter.

Speaking from notes and in terse, unembellished Mandarin, Chiang began, "Dear friends of China, we welcome Vice President Henry Wallace and hope you will have a good visit. Thanks to our American allies, who have given us tools with which millions of Chinese soldiers are bravely fighting the Japanese invaders. The Chinese people have spilled much blood to fight our common enemy, and we will fight on to honor those who have fallen already, until all Japanese are driven out of China forever."

Chiang was already walking away before the few who realized he had finished began to clap. As the belated applause began to swell, some Nationalist officials rose, obliging the other seated guests to join the standing ovation.

David spoke close to Davies' ear, "Not much of an orator, is he? Shouldn't he be more grateful to us?"

Like a teacher addressing a student, Davies replied, "It's difficult for him to thank us—all of us are the very foreigners he thinks have humiliated China for decades."

Okay, got your point, David thought. He glimpsed across the room, hoping to see Zhou Enlai's reaction to the speech, but he couldn't find Zhou in the crowd.

Now Vice President Wallace came to the podium. Without notes, he began to speak in a more conversational manner: "Thank you, Generalissimo. I had the pleasure of meeting your wife, Madame Chiang, in the States. She made quite an impression on all of us, and I look forward to the opportunity to get to know you as well. The fight here in China is essential to our overall war effort. Every Japanese soldier here is one Americans don't have to face in the Pacific. All of our allies, working together, will succeed in eradicating tyrants from the face of the earth. I just traveled here from Russia, where our Soviet allies are fighting the Germans with incredible tenacity. I was impressed by their effort, and I hope to be able to report the same to the president after my visit to China."

The vice president spoke for a few more minutes. To Katherine's disappointment, there would be no questions from reporters afterwards. As soon as the speaking was over, David saw Colonel Barrett make a beeline for Zhou Enlai. David worked his way to Katherine, tugged her sleeve, and together they migrated that way. A small group was already gathered around Zhou, which included Major Enfield.

"...we want to do everything we can to defeat our common enemy," they heard Zhou say through an interpreter. Zhou's intelligent eyes darted to take in his audience. David imagined him cataloging the faces and ranks of those present. "So we invite all of you to Yenan for a visit, as several journalists have already done."

Barrett crossed his arms and said, "Yes, those journalists say some good things, but are they true?"

Zhou waited patiently as the question was translated. He responded, "You are wise to be skeptical, Colonel, so you should come and see it for yourself. The areas of China that we control, with Yenan as our center, are dramatically different from where we are now. In our areas there is no poverty, corruption, or banditry. Really, this is true. Though we receive practically no supplies from the outside world, we continue to fight a guerilla war that makes life very uncomfortable for the Japanese."

Katherine raised her hand, which held a pencil, and asked, "Mr. Zhou, is there any chance you could still work with the Nationalists, like you did in the past?"

Zhou had a glimmer of a smile on his face as he answered, "Let me answer your question this way. We are fighting for all of China. We would gladly join forces with the Nationalists under a fair agreement. We do not intend to waste our resources fighting our Chinese brothers. If Chiang betrays and attacks us, as he has done in the past, we will be forced to defend ourselves. But we will not provoke him."

Speaking more emphatically, Zhou went on. "Friends, let me be completely frank. Our goal is to bring China out of a thousand years of serfdom into modern times. If necessary, we would ally with those who would destroy us in order to resist the Japanese.

"After all," Zhou added, laughing lightly, "we must have a country left in which to practice Communism! By single-mindedly trying to eradicate us, Chiang puts the salvation of our country at risk."

Colonel Barrett cleared his throat. David and the others looked up to find Chiang Kai-shek approaching them. Chiang's gaze fell upon Colonel Barrett. From Chiang's perspective, Zhou Enlai was obscured behind a column.

Chiang offered a hand and spoke through his interpreter: "Colonel Barrett, thank you for arranging the press conference today."

Shaking hands, Barrett replied in Mandarin, "Of course, Generalissimo. We hope you have enjoyed it."

"Very much, thank you. It is unfortunate that General Stilwell could not be here to join us." Chiang's Mandarin was formal. His arms were now immobile at his sides, bent a little at the elbow, fingers aligned—the picture of a perfect soldier.

"Yes, well, as you know the general prefers to be close to the front lines with the fighting men in Burma."

Chiang considered the point, his expression suggesting that the idea was new to him. "I see," he said. "He does seem to be away from Chungking quite often. If you do happen to be in communication with him, please let him know how well our troops are holding the line against the Japanese in the east."

Holding the line? David thought. *Right now the Japs are overrunning your armies. Who knows when they'll stop?*

"Yes, sir, I will relay that," Barrett answered politely.

Courtesy dictated that Chiang greet all the others. David found the generalissimo's grip firm, his handshake crisp. When he arrived at Major Enfield, Chiang's eyebrows rose and he said, "You are the officer who supplied the list today?"

Colonel Barrett stood up straighter. *The colonel has no idea about this*, David thought.

"Yes, sir," Enfield said awkwardly.

"You've done us a great service. We are in your debt." Still shaking Enfield's hand, Chiang looked at Colonel Barrett and said to Enfield, "I hope you are rewarded for all of your efforts; thank you again."

Barrett, trying to hide his ignorance, offered Chiang a thin smile.

Enfield was visibly relieved when everyone's attention was drawn away from him to the person Chiang greeted next: Zhou Enlai.

Recognizing Zhou, Chiang's face registered a slight hint of surprise but only for a moment. Calmly, he said in Mandarin, "Hello Mr. Zhou. It has been a long time."

"It has indeed, Generalissimo. You look well."

"Thank you."

Chiang did not return the compliment but moved on to others in the group. David pondered how much raw emotion had been concealed in that briefest of polite exchanges. *Hate? Resentment? Condemnation?*

Chiang excused himself, and for a while nobody said anything. Zhou stood comfortably, not in the least self-conscious after the brief encounter with the Communists' archenemy. In contrast, Major Enfield stared at the floor and folded his hands behind his back.

Ignoring Enfield for the moment, Barrett said, "Mr. Zhou, if you would join me now, I'd like to bring you upstairs to meet the vice president and learn more about the disposition of your forces in the north."

Zhou, eyes bright, replied, "Yes, Colonel. It would be an honor."

—

"He did what?" Barrett bellowed. His voice echoed off the mahogany walls of General Stilwell's office. He and David were alone, the meeting with Zhou was over, and the vice president had gone off to rest. For the last fifteen minutes, David had been aware that his hands were trembling. He kept them shoved deep in his pockets.

"That's what I think happened, sir."

"But how in God's name did he get a copy of that list? I checked it last night; it was right where I'd left it."

"I don't know, sir. Maybe he got in there with some Chinese aide who copied it for him. We all work pretty closely; there isn't a lot of security…"

Barrett shook his head in disgust. "That son of a bitch stole it and just handed it over. What was he hoping to gain?"

"Maybe he's already gotten what he wants. Chiang gives him credit for this, and Stilwell's going to hear about it. The Old

Man's not going to care who provided the list, he'll just be pleased that Chiang is grateful to him. So Enfield probably expects Stilwell to reward him."

"Hell, I'm gonna do everything I can to make sure the opposite happens. That peacock would sell his soul to make colonel and do worse to make general. But if I have anything to say about it—"

Colonel Barrett was cut off by the opening of the office door. None other than Major Enfield strolled in. He stopped cold when he saw David with the colonel.

"You wanted to see me, sir?" Enfield said, eyeing David.

Glaring at Enfield and more than a little red in the face, Colonel Barrett said, "David, will you please excuse the major and me?"

A few minutes later, as David was leaving the grounds, something caught his eye in a second floor window above the mansion's front entrance. He looked up and found himself meeting Robert Enfield's piercing glare. The major did not waver; he stared at David with a hateful scowl that made David shudder. David turned and continued down the hill. He felt Enfield's eyes burning holes into him, but he didn't look back. As he stepped through the front gates and turned right, he heaved a sigh of relief.

But he could not escape the feeling that he had just made an enemy for life.

⌒

David needed a fix. Bad.

But his opium dealer had disappeared.

The loquacious Nationalist corporal who'd befriended many of the Americans—and probably supplied plenty of them with opium, too—had not come by the officer's quarters for two weeks. Since returning to Chungking, David had bought from him every week without fail.

The chills were bad enough to make him shiver, even as sweat ran down the sides of his face and neck. Now he felt on edge, and he understood why he'd had trouble sleeping, tossing and turning for hours, feeling his heart race like a running motor.

David walked home briskly and racked his brain for the next best place to get opium. He reached his apartment building and went through the front door. Then he heard a man's voice.

"*Lieutenant!*"

It was a whisper, staccato and edgy, coming from under the stairwell.

"Who's there?" David said, tensing his arms and legs.

"Sir." A thin Chinese soldier stepped out of the shadows. "It's me, Gong."

"Gong!"

David hugged the young soldier who'd paddled him to safety after their mission at the bridge. He looked worn out, with bloodshot eyes desperate for sleep. His dirt-streaked gray fatigues made David think he might have just come from working in a pit.

"What are you doing here? I thought you might have gotten captured in Changsha."

"No, no. I escaped, but just barely. I was ordered to the front line—it was terrible. The enemy came at us with tanks and planes. Our lines dissolved in minutes. They sent me back to headquarters in a jeep to deliver a message. Otherwise I'd be captured or dead."

David held him at arm's length. "Thank God you're alive. I—"

Gong interrupted. "I am sorry; I do not have much time. I came to warn you."

"What?"

David stiffened. *About opium?*

"The Nationalists are watching you," Gong said. "You and your friends. They have men following you, and your offices might be bugged. They want to know what you are saying to the Communists and what you are saying about them."

David felt anger rising in his throat. "They're spying on *us*? After everything we're doing for them? When I tell the colonel he's going to march over to Chiang himself and—"

Gong grabbed David's shoulders. "No! Don't do anything, sir. That would make it worse. Just watch out, please. They'd be crazy to hurt an American officer, but then again, they are capable of terrible things. You remember the spy we met?"

"At the river?"

"Yes. Remember how nervous he was?"

"Sure. So what?"

"I found out the secret police have got his family here in Chungking. The only reason he's still in Wuhan providing intelligence is because they'll kill his wife and kid if he stops. If he hadn't shown up that day to meet us, they might have done it, too."

"How do you know all this?"

A door slamming two floors up made both men jump. They froze.

No one came down the stairs.

"How do you know this?" David repeated.

"Because I'm one of them," Gong whispered.

"One of who?"

"I've been recruited into the Juntong."

The secret police? Gong? David couldn't believe it.

Gong looked at his feet. "You cannot refuse them."

"But why you?"

"I'm not sure...I don't really know. I thought it might be because I know you." Saying this, Gong looked up. "But don't worry. I'll never let them use me against you. I..."

David put his arm around Gong's shoulder.

"I know."

Gong wiped his eyes and glanced out the front window and back up the staircase. "I better go. I've already stayed too long. Just be careful."

"Thanks, I will."

"And..." Gong hesitated. He looked closely at David's eyes. "Are you...all right, sir?"

David averted his gaze. "Yes, of course. I'm fine. Please...be careful."

Gong nodded. Then he slid out the door and disappeared into the crowded street.

David stood frozen behind the door for a few moments, watching the passersby on the street through the small window. He realized his fists were clenched and his undershirt was soaked with sweat. Slowly, he backed away from the door.

Then he turned and ran up the steps to his apartment.

ELEVEN

Central Shanxi Province, June 1944

Heavy drops of sweat dripped from Yuen's chin; distant foothills quivered in the humid air. Knee-high wild grasses—uncultivated yet orderly in their uniformity—grew thick upon the flats, and a few maple trees broke the horizon left and right.

Yuen allowed his men to remove their shirts, though he did not. It had been two uneventful days since the ambush, two days in which the hot, humid weather had become oppressive. The land was sparsely populated, but as a precaution, Yuen spread out four scouts a quarter mile ahead to report on anyone they might encounter or wish to avoid.

They stopped at a stream. Some men began to fill their canteens while others rested in a small copse of trees that provided rare shade in the flatlands. Besides a few remaining packages of hardtack crackers, their pack rations were gone. Fortunately, the grassy terrain was home to pheasant and rabbit, and since they were plentiful, the Chinese would be living off the land from now on.

Bao, the hefty former stonecutter, lurched into the foot-deep water and belly-flopped. Curses flew at him for fouling the stream, but his friends Jou and Han laughed.

Jou walked a few yards upstream to find clear, unsullied water. He noticed Yuen sitting under a lone weeping willow, apart from the men and out of earshot. The tree's long, slender branches bowed low and touched the streambed.

Jou called over his shoulder, "Han, did you ever find out what Yuen did before the war?"

About to pour a canteen of water over his head, Han stopped. "Eh? No, I never did find out."

It wasn't unusual for Yuen to slink off at times. The men were used to his odd habits, like the way he spaced out during a march or walked off when he wanted to be alone so he could...that was another mystery. Think? Remember? Strategize? They wondered how much of their fate depended on Yuen's solitary interludes. His aloofness added to his mystique, his unknown past, his mercurial nature.

Jou said, "You should ask Lu Gao." He pointed at Yuen's second-in-command, who was cutting willow wands as a spit to roast pheasants.

Looking doubtful, Han shrugged and walked over to Lu Gao. Jou splashed closer as Lu Gao looked up from whittling the point on his wooden skewer.

"Comrade," Han asked him, "do you know what Comrade Lin did before the war?"

Lu Gao had known Yuen the longest. The creases of his sun-weathered face crinkled when he spoke. "Yuen? Well, of course I know. He was with Chiang in the twenties, like the rest of the Party. In those days, we were all fighting together against the warlords."

"No, before he became a soldier."

Lu Gao chuckled. He glanced at Yuen under the tree, lying on his back staring up at the sky through the tracery of willows. "That I do not know—even after all these years. I asked him once, but he didn't tell me." Seeing their disappointment, Lu Gao offered, "I *do* know he grew up in a very privileged place— Gulangyu Island. Have you ever heard of it?"

Han and Jou shook their heads.

"It's where the foreigners took over and built their fancy houses." Lu Gao stroked the stubble on his chin with his fingers. Turning back to his whittling, he added, "You know, maybe that's why he hates the Westerners so much..."

The turquoise sky and fluffy clouds seemed old and familiar friends to Yuen, like the skies over the sunny beaches of Gulangyu, the island that had been his ancestral home for many generations—long before the foreigners usurped it. Gulangyu was a short ferry ride from the bustling port of Xiamen, on China's southeastern coast. The Westerners had carved out sections of other port cities as "foreign concessions," but for Xiamen, they took the entire island of Gulangyu. In these gilded enclaves, complete with European mansions and manicured grounds, Westerners ruled and were exempt from Chinese law.

The sound of the stream's running water and the feel of glutinous air also reminded him of home, and the effect was soporific. He shut his eyes and momentarily permitted himself to doze. He dreamed of home—the home he hadn't seen for over two decades. Flickeringly, he glimpsed the view from Sunlight Rock, his favorite spot for climbing, and one of the few places on the crowded island where white society did not frown on the brown-skinned boys and girls as they played. For an instant, he saw his parents, and in the dream, wondered if they were ghosts. *Are they alive or dead?* Yuen did not know. Then, the dream brought back the memory of the last time he had seen his father.

The doorway was half open; light through it cast a narrow rectangle across the dusty wood-planked floor. Yuen hid, waiting for inevitable discovery by his father, the local Chinese doctor. He trembled. His father was not a violent man, but he was stern. On a normal day, Yuen's happiness hinged on a kind word or approving look from his father. He knew this would not be a normal day.

But he could not keep the secret any longer. He loved Yi Chen. They had courted in secret for four months. She was pretty and sweet, the first girl he'd ever kissed. But, she was the daughter of a dock worker. His parents were still arguing in the house. He clearly heard his father bellow he would never permit his son to marry someone so low.

Yuen had run to the small outbuilding that served as his father's examining room, surgical suite, and pharmacy. He crouched down, hiding behind the long, ancient exam table and beneath shelves crowded with jars of herbs and roots. For a moment, he wondered to himself why he was hiding. He was fifteen years old, practically a man. Yet his father held a power over him that almost made him forget that he loved Yi Chen. Almost.

His father's brisk footsteps approached the doorway. The doctor's shadow loomed on the floor, where Yuen stared. A deep voice filled the room.

"*You shame me, Yuen.*"

Yuen stood slowly but kept his eyes on the gaps between the floorboards. "*You are young and stupid,*" his father said. "*You fall for the first girl who looks at you. You do not know what this will do. Everyone already knows of this.*"

Doctor Lin wore a long, flowing, silk robe with knotted buttons. He had slender, deft hands, and a thin mustache. Yuen forced himself to meet his father's furious face.

"*You think they don't?*" His father's voice rose in pitch, and his right hand flashed across the empty air.

"*But father, I—*"

"*Silence! Tonight you leave for Peking. It is a year too early for you to start university, but I sent a telegram to my friends. They will take you as a special student until you can join the regular class next year.*"

The words stunned Yuen. He felt them strike his face like his father's bamboo cane. He was dizzy. He couldn't leave.

"*But father—*"

"*No discussion! You leave!*" Spittle frothed at the corner of his father's mouth. "*You forget this girl. You do not come back until you have become a man. Pack your things.*"

His father left. In the house, Yuen heard his mother crying.

He slid to the floor. He felt lost.

TWELVE

Chungking, June 1944

David held the brown paper bag close inside his jacket and under his arm. Already, his scalp tingled in anticipation of the satisfaction the opium would bring. Careful not to slip on the slick cobblestones, he wound his way back to his apartment. The afternoon sun failed to penetrate the thick mist that hung in the air beneath a blanket of fog.

The slums had been less threatening than he'd imagined. There was no other place he could think to get opium without risk of being known or noticed. So he went there, eyes wide and bloodshot, aching for an opium pipe, but also taking in the squalor he'd never seen before up close.

Navigating by instinct, David had negotiated several dark and unnamed alleyways, just a few of the hundreds that crisscrossed Chungking like latticework. Green slime coated the well-worn cobblestones under his feet. He turned sideways to avoid a stray dog lapping at a stream of sewage along the path. A woman tossed out a pail full of something brown from a second floor window, and the contents almost hit him on the head.

Most Chinese took one look at him and scattered. David couldn't help staring at the ones that didn't. Their eyes were hollow, glassy with hunger. One waifish whore startled him by yanking his sleeve. She had a pocked face, with sweat that made her mascara run. Her gaudy red slit gown stood out in the gray alley.

"Hello, Joe. Hello, G.I.," she said. "For one U.S. dollar." She opened the folds of her gown so David could see her flat breasts. Her ribs showed too. "You like, yes?"

David turned away, but then a fatter, stouter woman, with a large wart adorning the side of her nose, stepped into his path. She added, "For two U.S. dollars you get virgin—guaranteed virgin."

Her pimp. David stepped sideways and shook his head.

"For food?" the pimp asked. She added slowly, in accented English, "Ration?"

The proposal stopped David cold. If he had any food, he'd gladly give it away. But he didn't have so much as a Hershey bar, and so he looked at them as kindly as he could and shook his head apologetically. Then he turned sideways to shuffle past them.

Behind him, David heard the pimp cursing under her breath.

Then he had a thought and turned around.

"Yia pian?" he asked the pair. *Opium?*

A look of fear replaced the scowl on the plump woman's face. Her eyes darted from David's face to the U.S. flag sewn onto the shoulder of his green army jacket.

David held up his palms. "No trouble, no trouble. Where is there opium?"

The pimp gave the whore a little shove, prodding her to walk in the other direction.

"Wait," David said. He took out his wallet.

The pimp stopped.

David held out a dollar bill.

"Please...for me," he explained, pointing at his chest.

The fat woman searched David's face and seemed to recognize the signs of opium addiction, for she resumed an aggressive stance and snatched the dollar from David's hand. She held it up and smelled it, as if making sure it was real.

"Go to the end of the alley," she pointed. "See Tan, the rickshaw puller."

Then, both women turned and walked away.

Tan sat shirtless on a stool, facing away from David, in front of a one-room adobe hut. The hut's walls were crumbling, with large gaps covered by sheets of corrugated aluminum. Off to the side was a dilapidated cart whose wheels were detached. The rim of one wheel was bent, and David doubted that he really earned his living pulling rickshaws. The tattoo on Tan's back displayed the tail of a dragon, the body went around his side, and the head was presumably in front, on his chest.

David cleared his throat as he approached. "Do you sell opium?" he asked softly.

Tan turned around. When he saw David, he froze. He had a long face and a mustache. A dirty, brown bandanna was tied around his head.

"Do you sell opium?" David repeated.

Tan looked David up and down. Then he sat up straighter and said in a normal voice, "Five American dollars."

Certain he was being ripped off, David produced the money.

"Wait here," Tan said. He went inside the small hut.

A few minutes later, the transaction was done. David had a tennis ball-sized lump of opium wrapped in a brown paper bag.

Now at his door, he was already beginning to open the sack. Once inside, he sat down at his rolltop desk, below a smudgy window with copper framing that had turned green. He reached down and pulled an eighteen-inch-long pipe out of the bottom drawer. The pipe's bamboo stem had a wide, two-inch diameter. He pinched off a bit of the tarry opium ball and stuffed this into the pipe's ceramic bowl. Then he lit an oil lamp on his desk and held the bowl above the flame.

Soon, the heated opium began to vaporize, and the familiar aroma heightened his senses. David leaned back and took his first deep drag of the smoke, holding his breath as long as possible before slowly exhaling through his nose.

A few minutes later, he was relaxed. All tension gone, a sense of contentment suffused his body. He wasn't looking to overdo it, he wasn't interested in euphoric hallucinations today. Besides, these days it would take the whole bag if he wanted to reach that level. No, tonight he had a date with Katherine. He just needed enough to feel right when he was with her.

The room began to feel warm, and David undid his tie, tossing it on the metal-framed bed in the corner. A few minutes later, he put his head down on his desk and fell asleep.

David woke up with a start.

What time is it?

He glanced at his watch. *Five-thirty.*

He had to get moving. He looked in the mirror and noticed his pupils were pinpoint. *I hope she doesn't notice.*

Thirty minutes later, he was taking the stairs to Katherine's second floor apartment three at a time. The staircase was located outside, along the façade of a three-story building that was popular with foreign journalists; its proximity to the British and French consulates conferred a sense of security.

David knocked. He heard sounds of another door closing and the rapid patter of feet. David smiled as the door opened.

"Hello," An Li said, smiling. She held out her hand. "I don't think we've been properly introduced. I'm An Li, Katherine's assistant."

David stared at her for a moment. "I'm David," he said, obviously surprised. He took her slender hand in his, noticing her perfectly groomed nails.

"Well, well." Katherine said, walking up to the door.

She was unhurried, composed. Her lipstick and mascara were perfect. Her hair gave off a fresh, citrus-like scent. "Ready to go?"

"If you are," David answered. Katherine's white summer dress had a simple blue lace design along its hem. She closed the door partly to retrieve a wide-brimmed sun hat from the adjacent wall. Then she gave An Li a little hug and said, "I'll see you tomorrow morning?"

"Naturally." An Li looked at Katherine with a fey sort of smile. There was a glitter in her gaze that made David wonder about her.

An Li sighed. "I suppose I will go home, read a book." For an unmistakable moment she stared at David with crafty eyes that made her look foxlike. Her mouth was smiling but her eyes were not. Then she seemed to snap out of a trance. "Goodbye for now," she said.

"Bye," David replied.

An Li slid past them and left.

The day's humidity had slackened, and a gentle breeze cooled the back of David's neck as he and Katherine descended the stairs and began to stroll down the steeply sloping street. Several Chinese men and women turned to stare at the tall couple.

"Any news on visiting Yenan?" Katherine asked.

David shook his head. "We're still trying to work it out. There's strong opposition from Chiang, of course. Some people back in Washington aren't too thrilled with the idea, either."

Katherine squeezed his arm. "Oh, I hope they let you go. Anything to feel like progress is being made here. *Bloody hell*, it feels like this is such a backwater!"

She paused and took a deep breath. The color in her face was rosy and lovely in the light. She went on talking with sudden conviction. "Our men are fighting and dying in France right now! This very moment! God, what a sight the invasion must have been." She spoke with a sense of awe. "And what's going on here? *Nothing*." She detached herself from David and raised her slender arms in a gesture of futility and surrender. The movement surprised him, for there was something sexual about it.

"I know what you mean," he said. "When I heard about Normandy, I wanted to be there. I wanted to be in the Pacific. Anywhere but here."

They cut through a park with a large stone fountain, no water running. The steps past the fountain were steep and worn, and as they descended them, Katherine took David's arm and threaded hers through it for balance. She clung to him, and her closeness made David's heart beat faster.

"The peculiar thing is—it wasn't always so depressing here. When I first arrived, there was a spirit about this place, not dissimilar to the spirit in London during the Blitz, I'd wager."

"No way. You're joking."

"Not hardly. Think about it. The people who first came here were the strong and loyal ones. It would have been much easier for them to give up, to stay home in the east and accept life under Japanese rule. Why would anyone *choose* to walk hundreds and thousands of miles to *this*? They wouldn't, unless they harbored hope that Chiang could defeat the Japanese."

David looked at her, unconvinced.

She saw his reluctance to take her words at face value, and spoke even more forcefully. "It was the bombings that brought the people together, you see. They built those marvelous bomb shelters blasted out of the hillsides. They sorted out the air-raid warning system—with spotters ringing this city for hundreds of miles. There was a real sense of pride here; these people felt they were *resisting*."

"Well, those days are gone now," David commented. "I'm sure you agree."

"Oh, I definitely agree, darling, but it's all because *you* showed up." "Excuse me?"

"I mean you Yanks. *I* think that once Pearl Harbor got bombed, Chiang knew the war was won. He stopped worrying about Japan and started worrying about the Communists again. He's inundated with American supplies, so he hoards them. He holds back his best troops, saving them to use against Mao. Honestly, I'd venture to say that his strategy is quite rational— given the circumstances."

David frowned.

They rounded the corner of a building, and the ground opened up and went flat. Close to the river now, the wharves came into view, and a few desultory gulls cried and dipped in the breeze above their heads.

Katherine continued, "You have to stop applying your American standards to this country. *You*, of all people, know this culture is peculiar. Corruption is part of everyday life. Deals are made to be broken. People don't say what they think. All of it is dodgy to you, I'm certain. But just stop and think about what America *really* needs from China."

Katherine paused for effect, but David remained silent and stone-faced. He found himself annoyed at everything she was saying.

"All America *really* needs is for Chiang to keep China *in* the war," Katherine went on. "Who cares how many Japanese he kills, as long as he keeps a lot of them *here*? Believe me, it's always possible Chiang could make a deal with Tokyo and pull out. That's why no matter what he does, your president will keep supplying him with whatever he asks."

"No." David shook his head. "There's a point at which it becomes too much. You can't prop up a rotten government forever."

They were beside the docks now. A shirtless riverboat captain prodded his half-dozen workers, hoping to finish unloading before nightfall.

"You'd think so, but what's happening here is probably far from your president's mind. China isn't a priority, and it's easier to just maintain the status quo."

"So, you think that you, me, our friends—we're all just wasting our time here?"

"All I'm saying is that in the grand scheme of this war China doesn't matter as much as you think. The war is going to be won in Europe and in the Pacific. The Normandy invasion is the important thing now. Out here, we're just marking time."

Her words stung. David turned to face her. His expression was dead serious.

"Katherine, I'm *not* just marking time."

"You don't want to think you are, but—"

Katherine stopped, surprised by David's mounting scowl. She looked past him, across the river. Softly, she said, "You Americans always think of yourselves as so important—"

"Is that what you think?" David demanded. "We're just trying to win the war, you know, so Hitler won't invade *your* country. So you can keep your *empire*—"

Suddenly, Katherine was so furious she wanted to scream.

"You should listen to yourself, dripping with self-righteousness. You really have no blasted idea—"

She stopped short, red in the face.

David had raised his index finger to her lips.

She stepped back.

"Stop," he said. *Was this me or the opium?* he thought. "I'm sorry. I shouldn't have gotten upset."

A sprinkle of sunny rain pattered down on them. Katherine looked up and adjusted her broad hat. David accepted the rain on his face, not bothering to wipe it off; and then, as quickly as it had come, the silver rain stopped, and the air became hot and dense again. Far off, a riverboat bellman rang a brass bell, while close at hand a dizi player toodled a few notes with his bamboo flute, which was answered by a magpie's cry.

Katherine was used to debating and winning, but David didn't look like an adversary. Her eyes followed the gentle curve of his chestnut hair. His eyes were soft, apologetic. *He wants to make a difference. Wasn't I like that, at the beginning?*

"I'm sorry, too," she said.

They walked side by side in silence to their usual spot: a quiet dock that was also clean, away from the smell of fish, coal smoke, and diesel fuel. They sat and let their legs dangle over the edge of the dock, inches from the murky, brown water. Behind them, the setting sun cast an orange glow over the bobbing steamships and barges.

After several minutes, David reached across and touched Katherine's hand. She let him hold it.

"Why did you come out here to China, Katherine? I mean, in the first place?"

"Good question," she said in a normal tone that showed she'd put their harsh words behind them—at the same time, she gave her hair a nervous twirl that puzzled David. "I suppose I enjoy reporting here. I like being in an exotic place. There's not much action here, I grant you—"

"I mean," David clarified, "I'm impressed that you came here alone, trying to succeed in a man's profession. You really came all the way out here for the adventure?"

"I suppose so."

They watched the fading sunlight caught in the ripples of the current. The darkness brought silence, and the docks seemed almost deserted.

Spontaneously, David leaned in and kissed her, and though it was unexpected, she received it naturally and with every ounce of her lips and body.

After a few seconds, she pulled away.

David smiled at her.

"Goodness, you surprised me," she said, grinning.

"Can I do that again?"

Katherine laughed, and held his hand as they stared out at the city, whose brown, high-walled buildings became squat shadows on the hillside. Neither one of them seemed concerned by the growing darkness.

David's heart was pounding, but Katherine seemed so at ease, as if their intimacy had been the most natural thing. He was having a hard time overcoming the desire to take her in his arms.

"An Li warned me you'd try something like that," Katherine said, smiling seductively.

"What's she got to do with it?"

"Oh, don't mind An Li. She's my best friend, as you know."

"I didn't know—exactly. But now that you've told me, I wonder if she's got something against you having more than one friend."

"Truth is, I believe she's a little afraid of men."

"But she's so pretty."

Katherine's face fell, and David wondered if he'd offended her by calling another woman attractive.

"An Li's afraid of men—and I must say, by right—considering what happened to her."

"And that was…?"

"Well, she lived in Nanking. When the Japanese came they went house to house, searching for girls. An Li was only twelve or thirteen. Her mother hid her and her older sister in the attic. When the soldiers came, they demanded the daughters. Their mother kept saying there weren't any, but the girls' clothing was scattered around the house, and the soldiers started beating the mother. When the sisters couldn't stand it any longer, An Li's older sister went out to them. They took turns raping her, dozens of them, over and over, in front of her mother…"

Katherine's voice broke. "They raped her to death," she whispered, "and murdered her mother."

David could find nothing to say after this.

Katherine touched the corner of her eye with a small handkerchief and added, "Her sister sacrificed herself. An Li was never touched. It's amazing the girl still has so much spirit in her after all that."

David nodded.

Katherine reached out for his hand and held it in her lap.

In that instant, David saw a slim figure wearing a brown derby and black cloak duck behind the corner of one of the warehouses lining the riverfront. It was the quick movement that caught his eye, and he racked his memory to determine when he'd first seen the shadowy figure.

Was he there all the time? Am I imagining things?

Katherine tugged at his sleeve. "What's wrong?"

He kept his eyes glued to the spot where the person had disappeared. Nothing. No one. He scanned the area and realized how deserted the dockyard was. *We'd better get going. I don't like us being here all alone.*

"David?"

"What? Oh, it's nothing." He tore his eyes away to look at her face. He used the back of his fingers to wipe one last tear from her cheek.

"It's getting late," he said. "Why don't we head back?"

Katherine was silent on the walk home, but it wasn't because of what she'd revealed about An Li. She wanted to feel happy, like David, because of the kiss, but for some reason, she was haunted by something in her life—the *real* reason she'd come to China. Was it a kind of turning point? A threshold? Not like An Li's at all, but one of her own.

The memory of the night that changed the course of her life four years earlier was still fresh in her mind. She'd defied her parents' wishes by choosing a career rather than a husband. As an eager young reporter in London, she latched on to a distinguished editor, John Tarrington, who told her everything she wrote was magic. She came to adore the man as a father figure; he provided the affirmation her own father never had. She *thought* he was happily married, and he even had sons not much younger than her.

One moment changed everything.

They were both working late one night. Tarrington mixed a couple of drinks, and Katherine remembered feeling flattered that he considered her mature enough to drink with. As she reviewed the front page before sending the final proof to the presses, she thought it odd that he dropped a pencil in front of her, and as they both bent down to pick it up, he kissed her. Though it only lasted a second, it was hard, cold. Like being kissed by a dead person. Before she pulled herself away, she felt his teeth against hers.

Tarrington stood there with a half-smile, as if to say: "There, I've done what I wanted to do."

He waited a moment for Katherine to respond, but the shock in her eyes conveyed it all.

He was—to all who knew him—a man of some decorum, and it wouldn't do to get caught in a situation like this if someone were to appear around the corner. And so, without a word, he turned and walked out of the room.

The next day, Katherine found a letter on her desk from the editor-in-chief instructing her to go to China—that is, if she wanted to keep her job. Unwilling to return home defeated, she'd gone, and had stayed ever since.

Thirteen

Yenan, July 1944

From a mile away, the ancient, red pagoda resembled a dart—the feathered ends balanced upon a boulder the size of a mountain, the point aimed at the clouds. The pagoda atop Chaling Hill was Yenan's most prominent landmark, and it stirred a sense of home in the men. Emerging from a sinuous trail nestled between two craggy cliffsides, Yuen's soldiers spread out on the loess flats. Before them, the stunted mud and plaster buildings of Yenan lay low against the dusky horizon.

Yuen still couldn't believe their good fortune. *Not a man lost. Not one.* After three months patrolling and several skirmishes, every man was coming home alive. Even the one wounded man was lucky. *It was his own stupidity*, Yuen thought. *No matter how many times you've blown up tracks, you need to pay attention. Too close to the charge and too absent-minded.* He had initially thought the foot-long splinter in the soldier's back would be mortal; it was lodged deep between two ribs. But, to his surprise, the shard came out smoothly; it had miraculously missed the lungs and major arteries.

Yuen looked from the line of shambling soldiers to a figure that darted suddenly by the roadside. He dropped to one knee, raising his rifle in readiness, but it was only a woman with two children trailing her, he could see that now. They rushed to one of the men and embraced him. And now a handful of other women and children ran out from between the low houses at the city's edge—word of their return was already spreading.

Yuen formally dismissed his men and began jogging for home. He couldn't stop smiling; the thought of seeing Mei Fong gave purpose to each step. Familiar streets and old storefronts threw long shadows in the lowering sun, but Yuen only saw them peripherally as he kept up his strong, steady pace. He thought only of home.

A shrill voice came from inside a squat building with a swinging wooden sign that hung from a post. The sign's three characters read "Ying Shua Guan." *Print shop.*

"Comrade Lin! You're back!"

Yuen stopped reluctantly and turned to face the caller, a small man he recognized as Liu Shaoqi, the army's political commissar. As Liu hustled toward Yuen, the printer, a bald man whose ink-stained apron hung low to the ground, came to the doorway and called out to Liu. Turning around, Liu waved him back with a scowl, and the printer shuffled back into his shop.

"Tell me, tell me, how did it go?" Liu asked, animated and hungry for news. Yuen accepted Liu's greeting—a hard, well-meant slap on the back. Dust flew from Yuen's rough-cut cotton shirt, and Liu stepped back as if the dust was toxic. He nervously pushed his black wire glasses farther up the bridge of his nose and withdrew a handkerchief from his pocket. Feigning nonchalance, he wiped his hand thoroughly.

"So—it went well?" Liu asked again, now rubbing his hands together in anticipation of some positive news.

"Not bad," Yuen said. "Killed some Japanese, didn't lose anyone—all is well."

"That *is* a reason to celebrate," Liu said.

Yuen looked down the road. He was anxious to be off, but he couldn't risk being too impolite. *Liu's always been an odd fit for commissar. What does he do? I've never liked his job, nor fully understood it. A commissar "keeps us in line with revolutionary ideals"—what does that even mean?*

"Have you heard the big news?" Liu asked.

"What big news?"

The crow's feet at the corners of Liu's eyes crinkled, and his small, dark teeth were as brown as loess. "The Americans are coming! They've accepted Comrade Zhou's invitation and will arrive in a week. We're preparing to—"

"—Is that all?" Yuen said.

Liu's face fell and grew serious. "What do you mean, Comrade? This could be the beginning of something very big— American weapons and supplies! We could gain international recognition! We must make the best impression possible. Think of how this could help us!"

"I would not count on it."

"Why not?" Liu demanded.

Yuen imagined his front door; he yearned for it and nothing else. But Liu hung there, anticipating his next utterance.

Yuen inhaled and exhaled once, very loudly, as if about to address a bunch of school children. "Americans are no different from any other Westerners," he said. "They all want to use China, not help China. This is what I mean. And you remember what the Chairman says, don't you? 'The bird who jumps at the worm too quickly gets dirt in his mouth.'"

Liu smiled wearily as Yuen upstaged him, but his childlike zeal was undimmed. He couldn't pass up an opportunity to remind Yuen of his authority. Sternly, he said, "Best not to let your lack of enthusiasm show when the Americans arrive. Mark my words, Comrade, this will be a grand opportunity. Now, you must excuse me as I have to finish printing these pamphlets…"

Liu trailed off mysteriously, as if he had more important things to do than chat in the street.

Yuen smiled. He could see how he'd gotten to the man, pricked him a little bit. *Why not? He isn't getting guns pointed at his face. He doesn't lead men or face any danger here.*

Yuen resumed his jog down the lane, his booted feet making dusty thumps as he went past a pair of oxen chewing grass in their pen. He turned at an angle to head up the slanting, narrow ramp which led to his home.

"Ba Ba!"Yuen looked up and saw Mei Fong hurtling toward him. She landed hard in his arms, almost ramming her head into his chin. Yuen shed his pack, laughed, enveloped his daughter with both arms. A wave of joy swept over him. He was finally home.

"Mei Mei! My, you have grown, and in just three short months." He held her at arm's length and used the flat of his hand to mark her height on his chest. "Yes, at least a few fingers taller. How is your mother?"

"Mother is fine." Mei Fong nuzzled into his chest again. They both laughed. "We just heard you were back. She's making dumplings for you now. Oh, Ba Ba, I'm so glad you're home."

"Me too."

The door was the same, and the familiar patio was neatly kept. Small green radish leaves poked through the earth in the center of the vegetable patch. Laundry hung on ropes drawn between the window and a T-pole staked in the dirt.

Inside, Jiang Hong was spooning small mounds of ground meat and diced vegetable into round dumpling skins. Her wet fingers expertly formed each dumpling. Looking up, she grinned but didn't stand.

"Welcome home. We wish we had known you were coming. We would have had more food ready."

"No bother," he said as he sat down and began to remove his boots.

Jiang Hong dropped her hands and blurted, "Ai ya! Take those filthy boots outside! It's hard enough to keep this place clean!" Yuen's hands froze on his laces. Without a word, he stood up and went outside. Barefoot, he re-entered the room. Mei Fong sat on the floor in a corner, staring at him with warm, bright eyes.

"Did you hear the Americans are coming?" Jiang Hong asked, her eyes on the dumpling in her hands.

"Comrade Liu told me."

Jiang Hong's head popped up. "Liu Shaoqi? Now *there's* a man with half your courage who is moving up in the ranks just by sucking up to the Party leaders. You could be doing that, I—"

She stopped, watching Yuen drop wearily into a chair. Looking down again, she continued in a relaxed tone. "Yes, it's very exciting. Orders have gone out to clean up every street and home. Everyone is to be happy, cheerful, and orderly."

"Is that so much different from now?"

Jiang Hong looked at him again. *She looks at me like I'm a stranger*, Yuen thought. There was something unnerving about the passion in her eyes as she said, "Well, we can make it even more so. This could be *very* good for us."

Yuen didn't respond. He didn't want to talk about politics and risk a fight. It felt so good to sit down in the rough-hewn pinewood chair. He felt the tension seep out of his body, into the chair, and into the earth. No longer responsible for the conduct and safety of other men, he could finally relax.

Each dumpling sizzled as Jiang Hong placed them in the skillet of heated oil. A wonderful aroma filled the room, and Yuen felt himself become drowsy. He thought about going to lie down in the back room but saw the cotton-stuffed mat had not been rolled out.

Jiang Hong dashed a cup of water into the pan, raising a crackling cloud of steam. Talking to herself, she said, "I wonder what sort of men they will be sending."

FOURTEEN

Chungking, July 1944

"Guess what!" Jack said as he reached up with both hands to grasp the transom above the doorway to David's office. Swinging forward and back, he gave David a verbal poke. "Were you resting your eyes or nodding off on company time?"

David rubbed his eyes and tried to shake off a cloud of drowsiness and the dreamy images of a slow passage home with Katherine: across India by train, the long whiskers of barking seals off the Cape of Good Hope, the pitching and yawing of a ship at sea. It was a little too real, given the circumstances—and here was Jack behaving like an orangutan.

"You're going to Yenan with us," Jack said, letting go of the transom and scuffing into the room. "You *do* know that Chiang agreed to it after Wallace twisted his arm, right?"

David stared blankly, still under the spell of the dream. "What? Oh, yeah. I wondered what he'd promised Chiang. A fleet of B-29s? A Marine battalion?"

Jack shrugged. "Who knows? I'm sure Chiang's got some angle, but who cares? We're going!"

"But I saw the list. I wasn't on it."

"I know, I know. That was the *preliminary* list. You're on the new one. Barrett specifically mentioned you should come. There's going to be eleven of us in the first group, and we leave on the 22nd."

The news penetrated David's shrouded consciousness. *Yenan!* Sitting up straight, he blinked hard. "Really? You're not kidding?"

Jack laughed. "I'm serious, you're coming."

Just two days from now. I've got to tell Katherine.

Jack continued, "Yep, pack your bags. A few of us want to call this the 'Dixie Mission.' You know, since the Communists are the rebels in this country."

David grinned. "That's got a ring to it."

"We might be there for a while, at least five or six months, maybe longer. Barrett's going to want you to help assess their military."

Five or six months? Maybe longer? David realized this meant separation from Katherine.

But of course, you idiot, it's not a vacation. They don't let girlfriends tag along.

And I can't even call her my girlfriend.

"Aren't you excited?" Jack said, leaning on the cluttered desk.

"Of course I am!" David stood up and looked at the piles of paper that Jack—hands splayed and flat—was resting on. "I guess none of this paperwork matters much now," David said with a smile. "I better start getting ready."

—

After two sun-drenched days, the cobblestone alleys were uncharacteristically dry and David sprinted to Katherine's flat, confident of his footing. He thought about her more than Yenan.

It's what I wanted, but I won't see her for months.

Three nights ago, he'd taken Katherine out to dinner, and afterward they'd met three of her girlfriends at a Polynesian bar. Her friends, two nurses and one secretary, giggled and teased Katherine all night, certainly acting like David was her beau. He liked the way she stood close to him and held his arm while her friends watched. He liked the physical current that traveled through his limbs whenever she made body contact with him.

I'm finally getting somewhere. And now I've got to leave?

He came in sight of her flat and slowed to a walk, breathing heavily. *What's the use in worrying?* he scolded himself. *Are you going or not? Of course you are!* A young woman trotted past him, her face hidden by a parasol. The twirling parasol's twin blue and red phoenixes, vivid in white sunlight, caught David's eye. Their cheerful, spiral dance taunted him.

That's it, then, he decided. *She won't like being apart any more than I will, but she'll understand.*

For a long moment, he watched the phoenixes, imagining they were real and spinning up into the sky...

Inside Katherine's flat, An Li asked Katherine, "Do you love him?" She said this in an offhanded way as she sat on the small wicker loveseat in the center of the nicely decorated but spare one-bedroom apartment. The loveseat faced a broad, three-paneled bank of windows that looked out onto the street below. Katherine was seated at her desk, an arm's length away from her friend.

"Who?" she asked, not looking up from her typewriter. Her brow was furrowed in concentration. For several seconds, the only sound was the machine's clacking. A shaft of sunlight through the window illuminated myriad dust particles, stirred by a lazily turning ceiling fan.

"Who do you think?"

Katherine looked up. An Li wore a slender red gown. She had her hair up and looked like a model from one of the glamorous old Shanghai department store catalogs.

"David?"

An Li nodded. She neatly folded her legs, one over the other.

Katherine's brow relaxed, her face now a girlish smile. "I don't know…maybe."

An Li reached out and casually, but deliberately, brushed the back of Katherine's hand. The suddenness, the roughness of the gesture made the fine dark hairs on Katherine's forearm prickle. There was a lost, faraway look in An Li's eyes. "You are so lucky to be in love. Sometimes, I—"

She choked on the words. Then she sighed and turned her head toward the window where a trio of pigeons were flying above the red-tiled roof of a house across the street. She looked back at Katherine, eyes moist.

"What's this?" Katherine said as she slid onto the loveseat beside An Li. "Are you all right?" She embraced her friend. The two of them fit snugly together, like figures carved from the same stone. An Li buried her face into Katherine's shoulder, and for a long time Katherine held her while listening to her stifled sobs.

Finally, when An Li's breathing slowed, Katherine smoothed her long hair with her fingers. "Let's not talk about men. What can we do to make you feel better?"

An Li lifted her head and gazed at her. A lone tear rolled down her cheek. Then she bent forward and kissed Katherine on the mouth.

Katherine froze.

An Li's lips felt soft and alive. Her eyes were closed. Katherine had never been kissed so tenderly.

Katherine pulled away. A hundred images flashed through her mind. But the one image that stayed with her in that moment was how An Li had gazed at her with those beautiful eyes, for it was in that gaze that the faraway look disappeared.

An Li stared at her friend. "You're so beautiful," she whispered.

"Please don't—"

An Li kissed her again.

Suddenly, the door opened, and David walked in.

At first, David thought he had the wrong apartment. To him, at that moment, the scene seemed almost surreal: two women wrapped around each other—one Chinese, one white—kissing on the mouth. He took a step back, blinked, wondered if he should turn and go. But then his eyes met Katherine's. She was as startled as he was, and the three of them looked at each other in a kind of suspended animation for several seconds.

"What is this?" David's voice was toneless, barely above a whisper.

"David...what are you doing here?" Katherine moved away from An Li and stood up. She used her hands to brush down the front of her pleated, yellow skirt.

He didn't answer. His eyes moved from Katherine to An Li and back again. There was a shell-shocked look in his eyes. For a long time, the only sound was the whirring ceiling fan that clicked every few seconds.

"David? Please...say something."

He stood completely still, but his mouth closed, and his lips tightened into a thin line.

"David?"

"What do you want me to say?"

Katherine's gaze dropped to the floor, and she avoided An Li's stare. "You shouldn't barge in on me like this," she said quietly.

"I shouldn't...what?" He lifted his head up higher. "Why? So I won't find out what you're doing here? So I won't know your secret?"

"It's not at all what you think—"

"What is it, then?" David stammered. "What the hell is this?"

Katherine felt the surprise of sudden tears. She couldn't help it. She buried her face in her hands and began to cry softly.

At that moment, An Li's slender hand shot out at David, index finger aimed at his face. She glared at him and chanted like a Tibetan monk, her voice louder with each successive phrase.

"Wang ba dan." *Bastard.* "Gui dan." *Turtle egg.* "Wang ba dan!" *Bastard!* "Gui dan!" *Turtle egg!*"

David cringed as her insults compounded his consternation and embarrassment.

Katherine reached out to lower An Li's arm. "What's wrong? I can't understand what you're saying."

An Li looked hard at Katherine. Switching to English, she cried, "He's not good enough for you! He's got no right to come in here like this, like he owned the place. Let me tell you something, he's got a secret so big, that if you knew it you'd never want to see him again!"

Katherine looked at David, but her hands continued to hold An Li.

"What's she talking about?"

"I've no idea," David protested.

An Li stared at him with scornful, hate-filled eyes. "Ru guo ni bu gaosu ta wo hui gaosu ta." *If you don't tell her, I will.*

"Gaosu ta shenme?" *Tell her what?*

An Li emitted a visceral grunt.

"What are you saying?" Katherine asked. "An Li, tell me what you're feeling. Look at me. Tell me."

"Did your clumsy boyfriend ever tell you that he's an opium addict?"

David's heart jumped. He felt it pounding in a scary, elliptical rhythm.

"What? That's crazy!" Katherine looked at David. "Crazy— right?"

He started to say something, but the words caught in his throat. He tried again and came out with—"I don't know what in Christ she's talking about."

An Li shrieked. It made David's ears hurt.

"Pianzi!" *Liar!*

He took two steps back as An Li's hand shot forth again. Her words tumbled out. "He smokes opium. I know it. I *smell* it on him. I know what it looks like. His eyes"—she jabbed two fingers at her face—"tiny pupils. Like my worthless father. Opium killed him."

"David…is any of this even remotely true?"

"Of course not."

"Pianzi! I've seen you smoke, liar!"

What? David's mind scrambled for some refuge, but there was none. Truth was, he'd only smoked in two places—his room and down a dark, vine-choked alley one block from the U.S. headquarters—that was his daytime fix hideaway.

There's no way she could have ever seen me, unless she were some sort of ghost.

David forced a half-hearted laugh. Then, not knowing what else to do, he pointed his own finger at An Li. "You're the liar," he said. "And I think you're crazy, too."

Katherine searched his face for the truth, but he resisted her gaze by looking elsewhere. *Does she believe me?* Feeling trapped, he looked from one woman to the other: An Li's face a mask of hatred, Katherine's full of doubt.

It was more than he could bear.

David turned on his heel and walked out of the apartment.

He hadn't even told her about Yenan, and now he feared there would be no need to tell her.

—

The following day passed in a whirlwind of activity: clothes to wash, gear to stow, papers to be checked. There was hardly any time to think about Katherine. Every man was required to fill out a last will and testament.

David was surprised to learn that Major Enfield had been removed from the mission list. Jack thought Colonel Barrett might have had something to do with it. But this happy news was diminished by the fact that his friend John Davies had been ordered back to Washington and wouldn't be coming either.

David rushed through his errands. He began to feel calmer, and his thoughts turned to Katherine. *Maybe I overreacted. She didn't get a chance to explain. And then that witch started screaming. I must try to see her again.*

His mind made up, he began to make his way through the dusk-filtered streets to reach Katherine's flat before the light failed.

I know she loves me, he thought. *Why else would she have started crying? And she has to—because I still love her, maybe now more than ever. She's a skeptic, so there's no way she'd believe that witch without at least hearing my side of the story. I've got to patch things up before I leave Chungking.*

He was feeling almost optimistic as he lifted his feet into a soft jog. The air felt cool, and the scent of burning incense from a nearby temple awakened his mind as well as his senses. Yet, by the time he approached her building, he found his hands were shaking. His heart pounded like the night before when An Li had destroyed everything. He stood and took deep breaths to calm himself, and then he pictured Katherine wearing the same yellow skirt and flowery blouse as last night, and he imagined how things might have been different if An Li hadn't been there. Then that brought him to the fatal kiss, the two women, and his blunder. *What were they really going to do, make love right on the floor?* The thought disgusted him.

Almost at Katherine's flat, David paused in an alleyway and continued to breathe, eyes closed. After a few minutes, he walked into the lane in front of her building, in full possession of himself.

But he stopped—in mid-step—horrified.

There, on the steps leading to Katherine's flat, was Robert Enfield.

David wheeled about and backtracked, slinking into the alley.

A moment later, hidden in shadow, he peered out.

They were talking together, Katherine and Enfield. Enfield was smiling, laughing, and to David's dismay, Katherine seemed to be interested in whatever he was saying. She wore a tight-fitting, white cotton blouse and the same yellow skirt which swished against her knees. David noticed she'd put on makeup, and her eyes were accentuated. She was gorgeous.

David was sweating. His shirt was stuck to his skin, and there were wet wells beneath his armpits. He could smell the tension in his body.

Enfield and Katherine kept talking. Then, sort of awkwardly, Enfield gave Katherine a sudden muscled embrace. To David's surprise, she hugged him in return. Enfield seemed to ask a question, and Katherine opened the door to let him in.

Disgust and despair turned to ice in David's stomach. He slumped against a stone wall, and in a sudden and irreparable fantasy, he imagined Katherine and Enfield, naked, making love.

David bent over, wanting to retch.

What am I to do? Barge in there? For the second day in a row?

He was impotent, facing a horrible scene he had no control over, except to leave, to run away like a scolded child. He felt desperate, crazed.

Somehow, even An Li and her warped insults now seemed harmless—at least what she had said was true. But this, in comparison, was a nightmare. *Enfield, that...bastard! That...Gui dan! Turtle egg!*

He took a long and solitary route home, wandering between rows of plum trees and then beside a long adobe-looking wall enshrouded in kudzu. A passing summer shower drenched him but quickly ceased. Now his dress uniform was wet, but he didn't mind that, nor his mud-caked, spit-shine shoes, nor the foul odor of the sewers—none of it bothered him. He wished for a good long draw of opium, and he could already feel the smoke entering his extremities, tricking his conscious mind into giving up and letting go. Then the long rest would follow, the long, dark night of the soul where no pain, no feeling existed.

By the time he re-entered his apartment, night had come, and the crickets were singing.

⁓

The following morning, Jack and David took a jeep together to the airfield before dawn. The road was muddy from overnight rain, and Jack had trouble keeping the jeep on a straight course. David jostled from side to side. He'd not slept well.

As they neared the airfield, sunlight broadened over the horizon. A lone C-47 transport plane sat on the runway; other members of the group were already loading up their gear. Nearby, a pair of Nationalist sentries watched glumly.

In addition to David and Jack, there were nine other men in the group. Each had his own assignment to evaluate the Communists from a particular vantage point: political, economic, or military. One spoke Japanese and could interview enemy prisoners; another was assigned to set up a weather station in Yenan, which would provide reports to American bombers en route to Japan.

David threw his duffle through the cargo hatch and climbed aboard through the aft hatch. The pilot revved the engines, and the propellers blurred. Nearby soldiers pulled out the chocks, and the plane lumbered forward.

The bumps of the runway yielded to a smoothness that David had felt only a few times before. There was a sudden uplift, and they were airborne.

Chungking, wreathed in the morning mist, lay behind him now. The engines droned full throttle, and the last thing David saw before he slept was Katherine's face.

PART TWO

New Allies—Old Adversaries

July 1944 – January 1945

FIFTEEN

En route to Yenan, July 22, 1944

David craned his neck to view the wrinkled, beige landscape below over which the plane's shadow rippled like a swift, dark bird. Down below nothing moved: not a person, animal or vehicle. The cloudless, blue sky mirrored the infinite, brown blanket of earth that lay in folds from horizon to horizon. The eternal emptiness of China.

The C-47 Skytrain's droning engines made it impossible for David to sleep for long. He'd passed out for twenty minutes after takeoff but now felt wide awake. They flew over Xian, the ancient capital, which looked like a small desert ant colony from five thousand feet.

An hour later, the plane banked hard to the right. Through the window David saw a panorama of plateaus, valleys, and narrow gulches. There was pressure in his ears, and he felt the plane banking in its wide descent. They dove lower, into a craggy canyon whose walls contained cave dwellings. To David's astonishment, people at their level waved as they stood at their doorways. David waved back. Angling his head to glimpse forward, he saw a central plain out of which individual buildings, squat and bunched around a river, rose into view. He saw an airstrip; a small crowd was gathered.

The plane came down hard; the runway was rough. Seconds later, David lurched sideways as the plane struck something solid. Strangely, the plane kept moving forward. David bounced on his bench and clung one-handed to the overhead strap.

"What the hell?" someone shouted. The plane dropped down on the left. The left wing and propeller scraped the ground. David lost his grip on the strap above his seat, grabbed for it again, and missed. His hands found the front lip of the bench, and he gripped it hard. Through the window opposite him, he saw a fountain of sparks dancing off the engine cowling.

Whump!

Something hit the plane forward, close to the cockpit.

Someone shooting at us? David thought.

The plane slowed.

Twisting to the left, skidding and stopping, there came a pinging of gravel against the undercarriage plates.

David exhaled.

"Everyone all right?" Colonel Barrett shouted.

There came a volley of yays and nays and murmurs and moans.

Apparently, no one thinks this plane is about to blow up but me. Let's get out of this thing!

No sooner had David thought this than Colonel Barrett opened the rear hatch and jumped out.

Stooping, David followed the others aft. The floor slanted down and right at a steep angle. Bright sunlight blinded David as he bent through the hatch. Then he jumped down to the welcoming earth.

Fifty yards behind the plane, men were gathering around a small hole in the ground. A trail of plowed-up earth and metal debris littered the space from there to the plane. He heard Barrett cry out near the cockpit.

"Holy cow! You all right, Champion?"

Captain Jack Champion, the pilot, looked pale. "My God, that was close!" he said, shaking his head. "If I hadn't been leaning forward to cut the engine, I'd be dead."

There was a jagged, gaping hole cut into the side of the cockpit. *How did that happen? No one was shooting at them.* David looked from the cockpit to the mangled wing. *The propeller!* The left propeller had broken off, and one of its props had knifed into the cockpit, ripping it open.

"What the hell happened?" shouted Colonel Barrett.

An Army captain came jogging up and pointed down the runway. "Looks like the left wheel dove into some hole on the runway back there. I don't think it was visible from the surface."

Colonel Barrett knelt down to examine the damaged wheel strut. Cap off, he was practically bald, and he scratched the crown of his head as he inspected the mangled metal. Then he stood up, taking note of the four-man Communist reception that approached. Barrett jammed his cap back on, stood straight, and met them head on.

Mao Zedong was unmistakable from the photographs David had seen. He was taller than the others: Zhou Enlai, Peng Dehuai—who David knew was vice-commander of the

Communist army—and Yeh Chien-ying, the army chief of staff. The Chinese seemed perplexed at what to say after the bizarre landing. Barrett shook Mao's hand, pumping four or five times. He moved to Zhou, who said in English, "Colonel, your men, is everyone—"

Barrett waved his hand dismissively and replying in Mandarin said, "Nothing to worry about. Everyone is fine."

Mao glanced at the hole in the runway, where a few Americans were poking around. He looked embarrassed but not unnerved. A young Chinese man ran up and whispered into Mao's ear. The words were barely audible to David, but he heard "sunken grave." Mao's face fell with displeasure.

"Please, please," Barrett said to Mao. "Everything is fine. Thank you for inviting us to come."

Mao looked up at Barrett and smiled. In a rustic, Hunanese dialect, he said, "Thank you for coming. We hope you will enjoy your stay." Mao decided to make formal introductions. "You know Comrade Zhou already. May I introduce Comrade Peng and Comrade Yeh..."

It took ten minutes to introduce all of the American and Communist officials to each other. A small crowd of about forty people was assembled at the edge of the airfield. Both men and women wore the same cotton-wadded gray shirts and pants. Several wore caps with visors, which they cheerily waved to the assembled guests.

David scanned the airfield. There were no other planes. He could not see any hangars or buildings, not even a wind sock. The only other machine was a covered truck with the words "Donated by the Chinese Laundryman's Association of New York City" painted on its side.

Colonel Barrett accompanied the Communist leaders in the truck, which crossed the river ahead and drove toward the city.

The rest walked. After the harrowing landing, David enjoyed the firm ground underfoot. A few minutes later, he was surprised by the veneer of dust on his re-polished black shoes.

Yenan seemed more like a town than a city—though it was like no town David had ever seen. The dozens of doors and windows cut out of each hillside brought to mind the cliff dwellings of Mesa Verde. Darkly tanned women, most looking cheerful and hardy, waved to him while hanging out their wash or tending small vegetable gardens. Many freestanding buildings were bomb damaged, which explained why they looked oddly flattened from the air.

The procession of Americans and their Chinese guides ambled down a street with small shops on both sides. The quiet, arid atmosphere was a welcome change from wet, noisy Chungking. Nearby, a man hitched two horses to a cart filled with straw; the horses clomped the dusty ground with their hooves. A woman prodded her young sons to stand up and bow to the passing visitors.

The group approached a low, mud-walled complex. Passing through the gate, David saw two long, adobe-style buildings whose roofs were camouflaged with sod and weeds. A small wooden outhouse stood apart from the larger buildings, its fetid smell hanging in the breeze.

"Are we going to stay here?" he asked a nearby guide.

Shaking his head, the smiling man said, "No. These are buildings you will use for dining, meetings, and other activities. You will be housed in the caves over there." He pointed to a nearby hillside with a single row of doors across its breadth. "After all the enemy bombings we endured, we learned it was better to live in caves," the guide explained.

In front of their new quarters, David chose a door and opened it. The cave was a single, tunnel-like room, about fifteen feet deep with an arched ceiling. The floor was gray brick, arranged like a cobblestone street. He walked the length of the room and felt the cool, bare wall opposite the door. The wall's texture was hard-packed and grainy; sand particles came off on his fingers when he pressed them against it. For the first time, he noticed the strong earthy smell and a sense of being underground and close-walled that unsettled him.

"Mind if I join you?" Jack asked, stepping into the dimly lit room.

David dropped his pack on one of the two beds, each made of boards set on sawhorses. Comforters stuffed with straw and cotton lay folded on top. With his back to Jack, David reached inside his pack to shove the brown paper bag—his stash of opium—down deeper inside. "Sure. Haven't had a roomie in a while. I snore—be forewarned."

"No problem," Jack said as he sat down on one of two rough-hewn pine chairs. He set his bag next to a small round table, also made of unfinished, rough-cut wood.

"Look at that thing." Jack pointed to a charcoal brazier in the corner.

David nodded. "For heat, I suppose...and look! We'll be reading by candlelight," he said, holding up one of the tallow candles set on the window sill next to the door.

"This is going to be like summer camp," Jack said, chuckling.

The Americans were invited to spend the afternoon resting or exploring at their leisure before attending a banquet in their honor that night. After stowing their gear, David and Jack walked toward what seemed to be the center of town.

Men and women smiled at them, some glancing away if the Americans met their gaze. Most seemed busy with chores such as sweeping out their doorways or tending to their gardens, children, and animals. David saw a few men reading books and newspapers.

"Hello...friends?" A male voice called to them in accented English.

They turned to see a young man and woman approaching. They seemed to be in their mid-twenties, like David. The man who had spoken wore spectacles and had an earnest, inquiring face. The woman was plain and even a little homely, with long, braided hair that hung down to the middle of her back.

"Hello," Jack said.

"If please, would you practice English with us?" the man asked.

"Sure, we'd love to," David said.

"My name is Sun Fong, and this is my wife, Wai Ling. May I ask, where are you from in United States?"

Jack answered, speaking slowly, "I am Jack, and this is David. I was born in Sichuan, but I did go to school in California, near San Francisco."

The man was surprised. "Ai ya! You born in China, in Sichuan? Why?"

"My parents were missionaries. They ran the YMCA in Chengdu."

"I know the Young Men's Christian Association," Wai Ling interjected proudly. "A nice lady from the YMCA in Shanghai first taught me English when I was a child." She spoke more correctly than her husband.

"And you, friend?" Sun Fong asked David.

"Believe it or not, I was born in China too, in Tianjin." The Chinese couple now showed more shock and delight.

"Are you happy living here?" David asked.

"Yes, very happy. Here I farm and grow food for the people. Wai Ling helps me." He smiled at her. "All women work with us."

Looking closely, David saw the dirt under their fingernails and their thick callouses.

"What about you, Wai Ling?" Jack said.

"Oh yes, I love it here. I am originally from Shanghai, where I worked in a factory as a seamstress. The Communists helped us organize so we could fight for better working hours and pay. When the Japanese came and we all fled the city, I decided to follow them here." Wai Ling spoke with confidence, and she was clearly comfortable talking to men.

David had never met Chinese who conversed like this before. Their friendliness and earnestness struck him as almost...American.

They chatted as they walked and later reached the end of the road, the outskirts of Yenan. Before them lay a vast and empty land punctuated by craggy mountainsides. David was beginning to wonder if they had discovered a completely new China, one that few Westerners had ever seen.

Before turning around, he paused and let the dry wind lick the sides of his face. Images of Katherine and Enfield making love crept back into his mind. He tried to purge the thought, but kept seeing flashes of Katherine's silky, white skin and then Enfield's hairy back and his hands groping, prying. He was smearing himself all over her, and David, all at once, clenched his fists in anger. A wave of heat and frustration washed over him.

As an antidote, David tried to think of the war and his place in it, but the barren landscape offered no inspiration.

I've come all this way. Am I going to get another chance to fight?

Enfield on top of Katherine, Katherine panting, whimpering with pleasure—the thoughts intruded again, and they, like the opium, made him hate himself for being an impotent fool. What could he do but boil with an inner rage that was useless in the present? It could only distort things, get him into deeper trouble. But what could he do to stop the lovers from rolling around lasciviously in his mind?

SIXTEEN

Yuen was struggling to balance too many pieces of firewood when he heard the yelping. There was laughing and shouting too, the voices of more than one boy.

He shuffled quickly toward the sounds, which came from behind the Reception House, a sturdy, square building made of yellow bricks and red roof tiles that stood out from its more ramshackle neighbors. Jiang Hong had mentioned the welcome banquet for the Americans had gone off well there last night.

The yelping was definitely from a dog, and its cries grew so wretched that Yuen dropped his armful of logs and rushed around the corner.

Three boys, not yet teenagers, spun around to face him. One had an arm raised, ready to throw a rock at the mutt cowering against the wall. Another boy had a crude wooden slingshot. The dog's limp hindquarter and inability to run away told Yuen its leg was broken, or worse. Its gray coat was darkened with blood around the head and flank, and in some places, the fur was ripped away so that red, meaty flesh was visible.

"What are you doing?" Yuen bellowed at the boys.

The one holding the rock dropped it. For a moment, all three stared at him, eyes wide.

Then, all three ran in different directions.

One of them, a little chubbier than the other two, tried to cut back the way Yuen had come. Yuen made a quick shuffle to his right and grabbed the boy's sleeve just as he rounded the corner. He clenched the boy's shirt and pushed him up against the wall. They were at the front of the building, but Yuen didn't care if others could see.

"You boys get a kick out of stoning helpless dogs?" Yuen shouted, trying to scare the boy but also venting his own anger. "How many dogs have you three killed? There's been reports of a few more dead ones, as I recall."

The boy stared at Yuen. He didn't speak, but the way he narrowed his brow to go with the smug look in his eyes gave him away. Yuen knew this one wasn't going to apologize.

"What is your name?" Yuen demanded.

The boy remained silent. The dog's whimpering made Yuen look around the corner at it. It wasn't moving. It was going to die.

He shook the boy and tried again. "Who are you?"

"He's my son," came a new voice from behind, deep and authoritative.

Yuen turned his head around. A heavyset Chinese man, balding, with a long drooping mustache, scurried toward them. Yuen had seen him before somewhere.

"Let go of him!" the man demanded, fist raised and red in the face.

Yuen released his grip, and the boy darted to his father, who held him with both arms.

"Your son and two others just killed a dog; they were stoning it."

"A dog?" the man sputtered, still furious. "You were abusing him over a dog?" The man's rage surprised Yuen. He looked fat and slow; he was certainly no match for Yuen physically.

Yuen squared up to the father. "Yes. I'm sorry to say it, but your boy needs to be taught a lesson. He—"

"My boy?" the father shouted. "My boy? You presume to discipline my son when you should be begging forgiveness for manhandling him? Do you enjoy beating up little boys?"

"What? Of course not—"

"Do you know who I am?"

Yuen took a step back, surprised. *I've seen him.* But he couldn't recall where, so he said, "No."

This seemed to make the man even more angry. "I'm the deputy political commissar. Comrade Liu Shaoqi relies on me every day to root out counter-revolutionaries!"

It was a naked threat, but one that made Yuen irate. The boy was now hiding behind his father like a toddler. Yuen wanted to raise his voice to match that of the other man and scream, *So what? Sons of arrogant jerks like you can be cruel anytime they want?* But he bit his tongue, knowing how foolish it would be to win this fight.

The deputy commissar took a deep breath, preparing to launch a verbal barrage, but at the same instant, both men noticed there was someone watching them. Yuen turned to his left and saw an American officer standing not ten feet away.

The deputy commissar gasped as if wounded. His puffed-up chest deflated. For a few seconds, the three men just stared at each other. Then the deputy commissar shuffled back, pulling his son along. He made two short bows to the American and tried to smile, but only succeeded in contorting his swollen, red face so that he looked like a drunk. Quickly, he turned and walked away.

Yuen was so surprised by his adversary's abrupt departure that he failed to react to the greater surprise, that being when the American said, "Dui bu qi, da raole." *I'm sorry for intruding.*

Yuen didn't speak.

The American walked closer and held out his hand. Continuing in Mandarin, he said, "My name is David Parker."

Yuen shook his hand. "I am Lin Yuen."

"I hope I didn't scare that man," David said, trying to make a joke.

Yuen remained expressionless. He stared at David's wavy, brown hair and wide, friendly eyes. It had been a long time since he'd seen a white man, and to meet one who spoke Mandarin so well was a real shock.

David felt the need to explain. "I'm one of the Americans, visiting from Chungking. We just arrived yesterday."

Yuen nodded. "I know."

"I noticed you were carrying all of this firewood. Can I help?"

Yuen looked at the half-dozen logs scattered on the ground. He shook his head. "Please, no. That is not necessary. Thank you just the same."

"Nonsense," David said, bending down to pick up a log. "I insist."

Spending more time with the American was the last thing Yuen wanted to do, but he couldn't think of a way to refuse. Once all the wood was gathered up, he pointed the way, and the two of them began to walk down the dusty street.

"What is your job?" David asked.

"I am a soldier," Yuen answered.

"Really? Can I ask you some questions?"

Yuen shrugged. He was getting the impression this American was very talkative.

"What's your opinion of the Japanese you've come up against?"

Yuen looked at David, searching his face to see if there might be an ulterior motive to his question.

After a moment of silence, he stated, "The Japanese are poor soldiers. But their modern weapons make the difference in a lot of battles." He let this sink in for a second or two and then added, "Because even a poor, fearful soldier can pull the trigger of a machine gun."

Thinking Yuen meant this as a joke, David chuckled, but his mouth grew taut when he noticed Yuen wasn't smiling.

They walked for a while without talking. Then David thought of another question.

"How long have you been fighting?"

Yuen stared straight ahead. "From the beginning," he said.

—

The Americans' first week in Yenan was filled with lectures on the Communists' military capabilities. Each day, David and the others gathered beneath a corrugated tin awning that fronted a ramshackle hut—what they learned was the Red Army headquarters. The scene—sitting on too-small wooden stools out in the open air with Chinese soldiers strolling by, stopping to listen, sitting cross-legged on the ground—gave David the impression of a bizarre, grown-up kindergarten class.

Red Army leaders like Yeh Chien-ying (chief of staff), Zhu De (commander-in-chief), and Lin Biao (a commander in the Eighth Route Army), gave hours-long talks on the Red Army's strategies, strengths, and weaknesses:

"We inflict damage on the Japanese through a war of movement—not engaging them in set battles but by giving ground, attacking weak points, harassing behind enemy lines, and conducting sabotage. As Chairman Mao says, 'Fight when you know you can win, don't fight battles you may lose!'"

"We lack artillery, engineers, transport vehicles, and battlefield communication. Our guerilla tactics make it difficult to save wounded soldiers. Casualties are particularly high among junior officers, who are trained to lead from the front. Ammunition is always in short supply."

"Our advantages include high mobility, high morale as a volunteer army, the ability of small units to operate independently, and good leadership from a strong cadre of officers with over a decade of combat experience."

By the end of the week, the Communists had offered a frank and comprehensive review of their military disposition. In two-and-a-half years, the Nationalists had never offered a similar assessment. And to David's surprise, none of the Communists asked for American aid. The closest thing to a request had been General Yeh's comment that the Communists were not embarrassed by what they had accomplished with the tools available to them, but they knew they could inflict far more damage on the enemy with more weapons and equipment.

That's one thing I have no doubt is true, David thought. *But how to get more? Something that could be so simple but will probably be maddeningly difficult.*

It was a question that David wanted answered.

SEVENTEEN

At the close of the last day of briefings, David walked back to the barracks with Jack. Hands in pockets, he nodded toward a park where a dozen laborers were reading newspapers. "You don't think this whole place could be staged for us, do you?"

Jack chuckled. "The thought did cross my mind, but I don't believe they could orchestrate all this." He spread his arms out. "It's too perfect. There's no way."

By the roadside, a bunch of laughing kids ran after a ball one of them had kicked.

"I did see two men having an argument," David said, "and one of them looked real embarrassed that I'd seen it. But I agree, all this would be too hard to fake. You know, if I hadn't known what Mao looked like, I wouldn't know who's in charge. They all dress the same, no trappings here."

"Can't believe we've been here a week," Jack said, running his hand through his hair. "Seems like a month."

"I feel the same."

They passed the now familiar landmarks: the former rich merchant's house at the foot of Phoenix Mountain, the Red Army University, the reception center where the welcome dinner had been held, and a school with a small bell tower. Looking up one of the hillsides they saw an office Mao used; they'd been shown it on a walking tour. It was a simple cave room with one desk, one chair, and a stone-tiled floor. They saw light from several candles flickering in the window.

"Got anything going back on the first plane out?" asked Jack. The army was sending another C-47 with a group of mechanics to repair the first one, which the Americans were now calling the "Wounded Duck." The so-called Dixie Mission was to be supplied by a weekly flight from Chungking.

"Thanks for reminding me," David said. "Guess I could write a letter tonight."

"For Katherine?" Jack asked with a grin.

"Maybe…I haven't decided. Actually, I'm trying hard not to think of her."

If Jack thought his friend's comments were confusing, he didn't let it show.

Later that evening, as he pushed the small gold U.S. pin through the collar of his khaki dress shirt, David debated whether he should wear his tie. He'd only brought one and was unsure how formal the occasion would be. He decided to wear it and tried to gauge the knot and length without the help of a mirror, for there was none.

He felt good. Jack had been out for an hour to eat supper in the home of a local family, something the Party had arranged. This had given David a chance to smoke opium. He'd already done it once since arriving in Yenan. Both times he'd smoked only a small pinch, because he was worried Jack would pick up the smell and because he was rationing it. He had no idea where to get opium in Yenan, or if it was even possible.

Alone in his room, he danced a few steps to imaginary swing music, moving, then spinning in a gawky fashion until he landed, butt down, on his bed. He felt a little giddy but still in control.

He heard footsteps outside the door.

Jack was back.

David smiled at his friend, enjoying the gentle cloud that had settled on his brain and the feeling of optimism for everything around him.

Jack looked at him curiously. "I see you're excited to get going," he remarked.

"Uh-huh," David replied. Then he had an alarming thought and jerked his head to make sure he'd re-stashed the opium back in his duffel. He had.

"Then let's go, it's already started," Jack said.

From what they'd heard, the Saturday evening dances were an important part of Yenan's social life. Though they were often held in the Reception House, the new guests and fine weather warranted an outdoor party, in a grove of fruit trees some of the correspondents called the Pear Orchard. The Americans had already introduced their own contribution to the nightlife: a movie projector. In the first week there had already been two screenings of *Modern Times*, starring Charlie Chaplin. The Chinese loved it.

David and Jack approached the grove after sunset. Red and orange lanterns strung from tree to tree illuminated a small clearing. To one side, a traditional Chinese band comprised of four erhu—two-stringed Chinese fiddles—and other players with mouth organs, flutes, and a mandolin, played lively tunes—including "Yankee Doodle"—in honor of the guests. The cheerful melodies were not conducive to dancing, and small groups of Chinese and Americans stood about staring curiously at one another.

Suddenly, the scratchy sound of a phonograph sputtered through an amplifier. Familiar strains of Glenn Miller's "In the Mood" gave David a start. To hear this song here, in a pear orchard in rural China, was anachronistic, bizarre. He'd last heard it years ago, stateside, during Ranger training. Pairs of energetic Chinese started dancing swing—and quite well, David thought. A small Chinese girl with short-cropped hair approached Ray, who had come with the second planeload of Americans, and asked him to dance. With a hoot and holler, Ray spun on his heels and danced off.

A girl with a slender face and short hair, wearing a gray cotton shirt tucked into gray trousers, walked up to David. She gave a short bow and said in English, "Please to dance with me."

David was charmed—a girl asking him to dance. Her innocent formality was sweet as was her manner of asking. David glanced at a pair of her friends watching him from across the clearing. He smiled warmly and took her outstretched hand.

Dancing felt good, and David threw his body into the rhythm and movement. His world shrank to the space between him and the girl.

"Atta boy, David!" Ray called out.

The song ended. David smiled at his partner, who bowed and skipped off in the opposite direction, giggling again.

"I hope you weren't watching," David said, walking over to Ray as the next song started up. "I've ten feet and none of them know how to dance."

"No worse than me or poor Barrett over there."

David glanced at Colonel Barrett dancing with a middle-aged Chinese woman in the center of the gathering.

David couldn't help but laugh.

"What the colonel lacks in talent, he makes up for in enthusiasm," Ray said.

David threw his head back and breathed the cool night air. He saw a twinkling star, then another. There were crowds of stars glimmering in the velvet blackness. Ray tapped his shoulder. There, not twenty feet away, was Mao Zedong—and he was heading toward them.

Dressed in a white shirt and dark brown pants, Mao was almost as tall as David. Though not fat, he did give an impression of gravity and weight. He had a round face with a high, wide forehead and rich black hair that he parted down the middle. His handshake was damp and light, yet his smile exuded calm self-confidence.

In Mandarin, Mao said, "Welcome friends. How are you enjoying yourselves?"

"We're having a wonderful time," Ray replied in Mandarin, with a nod of the head that was almost a bow.

"I am glad. We are very happy you are here. I saw that you enjoy dancing."

Ray laughed. "Please forgive my ineptitude."

The corners of Mao's lips turned up, his round cheeks swelling in a beatific smile. "Please, please. We dance not to please each other. We dance because it is a way of expressing our happiness, our love of life."

David had seen Mao dancing with at least three different girls, and his talent level was close to Colonel Barrett's.

Mao pointed to a short wooden table next to Ray and said, "Would you share a drink with me?"

"Of course!" Ray replied.

With a grin, Mao picked an uncorked, unlabeled bottle from the table and poured clear liquid from it into three small porcelain teacups. He handed one each to David and Ray.

"A toast," he said. "To friendship."

"Here, here," Ray said.

"To friendship," David said.

David raised his cup and drained the shot. The liquor went down like acid, and he had a ringing in his ears so loud that he couldn't hear the laughter around him.

"Whoa!" he squeaked. He glanced at Ray, who was having a similar reaction. Mao doubled over with laughter. "Turpentine!" David croaked.

"Please forgive," Mao pleaded. "I should have warned you. Our wine is difficult to enjoy. It is made from distilled millet, which we grow here ourselves."

Millet? David thought.

Mao continued to laugh as David and Ray regained their composure. After few moments, he asked them, "So, will you tell me your impressions of Yenan?"

Ray coughed once more, then answered, "Very impressive. Everyone seems very happy."

Mao nodded twice, his small mouth set in a catlike look. "Yes, there is a spirit about this place that anything is possible. Together, we can move mountains, but only if we stay true to our principles."

This said, the cat smile went away, and Mao's face became serious.

"How do you do it?" David asked. "I mean, how do you manage to *thrive*, not just survive, in this barren land?"

Mao emitted a troll's chortle. "The Nationalist blockade was devastating at first, but it was a blessing in disguise. It forced us to become self-sufficient. Now we produce the crops we need to survive. We make our own paper. We make do with and recycle the modern equipment that we do have." With each sentence, Mao's right hand chopped the air in front of him. "Without Chiang's blockade, we might still be reliant on foreign assistance…like *he* is."

Mao seemed younger than David had imagined him and so alive and changeable in his demeanor. He in no way resembled the drab photos taken of him. He was animated when he spoke, but when he listened to others he was as still as a stone. He did not have Zhou's sophistication, but he certainly seemed at home with the common man.

A young Chinese girl confidently approached them and faced Mao. She bowed low and said, "Chairman, please dance with me."

Pleased, Mao nodded. "Please excuse me, gentlemen." He took her outstretched hand and went off.

David grinned at Ray, who surprised him by pouring himself more millet wine.

—

Yuen stood alone on a small hillside at the edge of the orchard. He did not enjoy these social dances, but his wife always insisted they come in order to be seen. He also knew Mao encouraged participation so he consented to attend, though he refused to dance. His pretty wife mingled on her own. For his part, Yuen felt equally comfortable talking to others or standing alone; he was never insecure. He'd not felt self-conscious since he was a teenager. A life of war had forced him to grow up fast and made such vain emotions seem irrelevant.

Yuen saw the tall American who had helped carry his firewood begin to climb the hill and walk toward him. Yuen watched the man closely: his walk was gangly, a shuffling amble rather than a confident stride. His face was smooth, no stress lines or scars. A tuft of hair on the crown of his head stuck up and made him look perhaps a little younger than he was.

"Hello," David said in Mandarin, extending his right hand, "Nice to see you again. Yuen, right?"

"Yes."

"I'm David Parker."

"I remember."

Yuen looked away and watched the dancers, hoping that his reticence might make the American lose interest in him.

"Are you here long or will you deploy again soon?" David asked.

"We will go out again when we get orders."

"When might that be?"

Yuen sighed, resigned to having to converse. "It could be a few weeks or a couple of months. We've recently come back, just before you arrived."

"Really? What was your last mission like?"

Yuen followed David's eager eyes. *A glory seeker,* he thought. *Another naïve kid who fights for thrill rather than survival.* Though he considered sidestepping the question, he decided there was no harm in being honest.

"I took thirty men to the east, about a two-month stretch behind enemy lines."

"Did you run into any Japanese?"

"We came upon a village they had burned out, killing everyone."

David's eyes widened. "What did you do?"

"We punished them."

"How?"

"We ambushed them," Yuen said. He didn't want to relive it. By all measures, it had been the least eventful patrol he'd led, and yet the American looked mesmerized.

David didn't pursue it further.

Doubtfully, Yuen asked, "Have *you* seen any action?"

"Yes. I led a small group to destroy a bridge near Wuhan."

Well, thought Yuen, *that's at least something.* "What happened?"

"We had all the charges ready to go, but I decided to wait for a train to pass over. When one did we blew the bridge, and it came down, but it was a troop transport and they came after us…I lost two men."

To this, Yuen made no comment. His gaze drifted down toward the dance area, where Ray was leading a dozen Chinese in a conga line.

"Now I'm anxious to get back into the field," David said. "Do you think I could go with you on your next mission?"

Yuen's head snapped up. The request caught him off guard, and he searched for a polite way to refuse. He had no interest in pleasing this American. Playing tour guide in a war zone could jeopardize a mission and put everyone in danger.

He gave David a quick surmise. *He's white. He's big. He won't be content to just lie down and hide if he's told to. He could be a serious hazard.*

"I am not sure that would be possible," Yuen responded.

David, saying no more, eyed him blankly.

Several seconds passed.

"Perhaps we could discuss it with the leadership," Yuen said at last.

David, relieved, said, "Yes, thank you. Let's find out what they think of the idea."

The two parted with Yuen feeling ill at ease. He hoped there would be a gracious way to deny the request, or that David might not be truly serious about it.

It was a terrible idea.

EIGHTEEN

Dear Katherine,

I am in Yenan. Maybe you already knew that, maybe you thought I just disappeared. I've been so confused ever since the last time I saw you, and I still don't know what to think. I am sorry things went so badly. I came to tell you I was going to Yenan—I was so excited, that's why I burst in without knocking.

I also came to see you the night before we left, but I saw you with Robert Enfield. After that I got mad and just left.

What you do is your business. I don't know if I've been wrong about the feelings between us. I know how I've

felt, and I thought we might have had a chance to be
something more.

I don't know why I'm writing you all this. I may go into
the field with a platoon of men here. I'm actually desperate to
go. I'd rather be fighting than anything else right now.

Goodbye,

David

David pulled the single-spaced, half-page letter out of Jack's
portable Underwood typewriter. Jack was already asleep. By the
light of several candles, David read the letter over. For a
moment, he considered shredding it with his fingers. A moment
later, he folded it, jammed it into an envelope and, leaving it
unsealed, flicked it on top of his green canvas duffel. The thing
that bothered him the most, aside from having to include
Enfield's name, was his closure. How could he end a letter to the
one he loved with "goodbye"? It didn't suit him—or her. Yet,
once again, he didn't know what to do about it.

The request to join Yuen had been an impulsive move too,
but now the thought of joining him quickened David's heartbeat.
What are you getting yourself into? Are you so anxious to get into a
fight that you'd beg to go with someone you hardly know, with
soldiers you've never met? He stared into the blue center of the
flame of the candle closest to him. *Yes. You are.*

Before blowing out the last candle, David picked up the
letter again. He sealed and addressed it, but then he held it close
to the flickering flame for a moment. *Why should I bother? I'm not*
going to see her for months. She's not one to sit there just waiting for
me to come back. I'm a fool.

But he didn't burn it. Finally, he put on the table, resolved to just let it be.

Yuen was in bed long before David. He lay in the comparative comfort of his handmade, cotton-stuffed mattress and reviewed the day.

He and Jiang Hong had walked home from the dance, and he'd told her about the odd American wanting to go bivouacking with him. The thought still made him jittery. The moon, like a white chrysanthemum, had risen over the barren highlands. Suddenly, a red wolf raised its large head and loosed a howl commensurate with the huge moon.

Jiang Hong, as alert as Yuen or the wolf, turned and looked at her husband. "This man you're talking about...is he dangerous?"

Yuen laughed. "He would be a liability but maybe not a disaster. I want to put my feelings aside and consider it clearly. He's had little experience—some, but not much. He is accustomed to modern weapons, not ours. We'd be unable to hide him—how could we disguise a six-foot tall foreigner?"

Jiang Hong pursed her lips and stared into the moony night. "Could you teach him if you took him along?" Yuen grimaced. "He seeks adventure. This type of man may do anything—especially under stress. Perhaps he will run off under fire? Or worse, get himself into a bad situation where we'd have to rescue him."

"You need to ask the Party leaders. Would they grant such a request just because he's an American?"

"Perhaps so. With the Americans they may think 'I heard' is good; 'I saw' is better."

Inside their home, they tiptoed around Mei Fong, who was asleep on the floor. In the adjoining back room, he and Jiang Hong faced opposite walls and undressed. Yuen looked over his shoulder and caught a glimpse of her bare back in the candlelight. He sat down on his cotton-stuffed mat to remove his dust-caked shoes and pulled on a pair of thin cotton pants. Then he moved to Jiang Hong's mat. Drawing close to her, he gently stroked her arm. He ran a finger slowly down her spine, into the small of her back—a gesture that was his way of suggesting lovemaking.

Jiang Hong turned away and covered herself with a blanket.

Rejected, Yuen rolled back onto his mat. They hadn't had sex for almost a year, and although he refused to whine about it, he found it was hard to stifle his resentment. He felt his mood begin to darken, but there was nothing he could say or do that would change his wife's attitude, so he stewed in silence.

Jiang Hong had no trouble sleeping. She'd long ago lost any sense of obligation to Yuen. She knew he was a good man, a man of honor, a person quite better than herself in some ways, but she'd stopped showing him certain deferences. In truth, he was nothing like the promising, ambitious man she had married. That man intended to rise in station, to be something more than a common foot soldier. Now it was clear that Yuen no longer possessed the desire to rise in the Party, and so Jiang Hong's own hopes for distinction had been ruined.

Although she didn't think about it consciously, on some level, withholding sex was a way of getting back at him. She knew she was still beautiful. In the early years, when she could have attracted anyone, she chose Yuen because he was a born leader and others respected him. For a time, she'd been genuinely in love, but presently she couldn't remember the last time she'd felt that way—many years at least. These same years of strenuous combat had sapped Yuen's idealism and his cheerful good humor. He'd once been tender and sweet, sometimes picking flowers for her and always sharing little secrets. Now, except for the time he spent with Mei Fong, he was dark and melancholy, and he usually kept his thoughts to himself.

It irritated Jiang Hong that Yuen appeared not to notice that she was still attractive to other men. She'd learned how to capture their attention at a young age, with a coy smile or an innocent touch. And though she was older now, her breasts were still ample, and her figure was trim. She could tell male comrades admired her, but their respect for—and fear of—Yuen stopped them from anything more than politeness.

All this had changed six months earlier, when Yuen's immediate superior, Chen Zhen Guo, offered to carry Jiang Hong's buckets of water home from the well. At the time, Yuen had been gone for three months, and perhaps that was why Zhen Guo felt bold enough to make the gesture. In the old days, offering to help another man's wife in this manner would have raised eyebrows, but in Yenan, it could be seen as one comrade simply helping another. She did not think much of it, until she noticed Zhen Guo staring at her. Nothing else happened that first day, but he began turning up often during her chores and errands. She liked him. He was very good-looking, and he was *definitely* a rising star—he stayed in Yenan planning grand strategy with the generals. She liked to hear him talk, and it pleased her that he seemed interested in all the ideas she had for the Party. He had never been married, and he was a horse. The tiger—her sign—and the horse always make a lucky pair.

So she was not displeased when one morning, after Mei Fong had gone to school, Zhen Guo came by to visit. She invited him in, and they sat at the small table and talked over weak chrysanthemum tea. While conversing, she saw a flicker of desire in his eyes, and then, without warning, he drew her close to him and kissed her. She returned the kiss, and as he brought her to her feet, they pressed their bodies close.

Yuen might have come into her thoughts but he'd been gone for so long that she didn't spend more than a fleeting moment thinking of him. Mainly, her darting thoughts, like fish in a pond, were of who else might see...who might come to the door...

The two repeated their mid-morning meeting several times, and finally Jiang Hong gave in to his desire to make love. It surprised her how much she enjoyed it. Zhen Guo was gentle, yet confident and strong. She felt desirable and feminine again, something the years of manual work and hard living had not taken away. How quickly she remembered what she'd forgotten—what it was like to be caressed by a passionate man who did not close himself off to her feelings or his own. She gave herself completely to the lovemaking and blossomed in the breath of love.

—

The next morning, Yuen found out that Jiang Hong had been completely right.

When he reported his conversation with the American David Parker and said that Parker wished to accompany him on a mission, his superiors could hardly contain their excitement. He was seated in Peng Dehuai's office. He spoke succinctly, in a low monotone, yet the mounting enthusiasm of Mao, Peng, Zhou Enlai, and Chen Zhen Guo was present the entire time. They all agreed the American should go along. Yuen's heart sank.

Zhen Guo walked up behind him and put a hand on his shoulder. "I understand your concern," he said, "but this is a great opportunity for them to see us in action. You will greatly impress him. I, personally, would not have chosen anyone but you to take him out."

Shaking him gently, Zhen Guo declared, "Comrade, we have full confidence in you!"

Yuen glanced at Peng, who was seated at the desk in front of him. Peng bit off a piece of chewing tobacco and then put the tightly braided piece into his front shirt pocket. Mao stood by the window, hands behind his back, deep in thought, while Zhou paced a small, circumscribed space opposite him.

Yuen said, "I have concerns about concealing the American. There may be times when—"

"Just avoid the cities and keep to the backcountry, like you always do," Peng said, before spitting tobacco juice into a can that he held in his right hand.

"Comrade," Mao said, "if he gives a favorable report the Americans might arm us. Think of this. Just as the American revolutionaries succeeded only after obtaining aid from the French, our success could be much swifter with American aid. And the better the Americans regard us, the more pressure they will put on Chiang to come to terms with us."

Yuen listened to this without comment. *You aren't the one who will be risking his neck—or the American's for that matter. This could end badly if the American gets hurt—or worse, killed. And then there are my men to think about too.*

Yuen sighed almost imperceptibly and knew he had no choice but to accept it. *If the first words fail, ten thousand will then not avail.*

When he was dismissed, Zhou walked with him out onto the small porch. The bright sunlight made Yuen squint.

Yuen spoke first. "I will do what is needed."

Zhou smiled. "I know that."

They heard Peng and Mao laugh at some joke inside, and then Zhou said in a low voice, "Yuen, you must try to impress the American, but you must do this safely."

"Safely?"

"I mean keep *him* safe."

Grimly, Yuen nodded. *What does that mean? What do they expect me to do—stage mock battles? Am I supposed to protect the American in combat and also fight a real enemy? No horse can wear two saddles.*

Satisfied, Zhou, bestowing one more benighted smile, turned and walked back inside the building. Yuen heard him join the laughter of the others, and he bristled.

Man's schemes are inferior to those made by heaven. There will be no special consideration for Lieutenant Parker. He will see us in action, and he will share the danger. Who can say whether he, or any of us, will return?

Nineteen

"I think it's a fine idea," Colonel Barrett said, much to David's relief. "Hell, I wish I could go on a Communist guerilla mission myself."

They were seated in the Colonel's room. Jack and Ray stood just inside the doorway. Both men's heads almost touched the arched ceiling.

"Are you sure you want to do this?" Jack asked. "If you get captured by the Japs, who knows how they'll regard you—maybe as a spy out of uniform."

Ray interjected, "In any case, the Japs won't take you prisoner; they don't respect those who surrender. After they interrogate you…" Ray drew a finger across his throat. "But don't get me wrong, it's a grand idea. Wish I'd thought of it myself. I'm not an *Army Ranger* like you, God bless ya, but I'd love to see some action."

Jack glared at Ray and said, "You'll be hard to hide, and you won't have any backup out there. You heard what they said in that briefing: you get yourself wounded, and you likely won't be coming back."

David had to admit he hadn't really considered the downside. Still, the more he thought about it, the more desperately he wanted to go. He was a soldier, not a diplomat.

"Thanks for the concern, Jack, but I want to go, and I can't think of anyone else better suited to do something like this. Let me bring up a B.A.R and some M-1s, show them how to use proper equipment, and see what they can do. Grunts all over the world are risking their necks, why shouldn't I? Sometimes we forget that we're in a shooting war. The Japs bombed Pearl Harbor! I want to go help kill some of 'em."

"Hell yeah!" cheered Ray, punching the air.

Barrett clapped his hands together decisively. "Okay. If they agree, you'll go. We'll be here waiting for you to regale us with your adventures when you get back. Happy hunting, Lieutenant."

—

Yuen received marching orders two weeks later. They were to penetrate deeply, past Peking to the coast, where the Communists hoped to strengthen their influence in Shandong Province, the probable location of any future American landings in China. He was instructed to link with resistance fighters, provide new orders for them, and raise hell for the Japanese along the way. He handpicked thirty men for the mission. Of all the lives in the group, Yuen admitted that he valued the American's the least—despite his orders to do the opposite.

Yuen kept his men sharp. Though he let them off for the first week of their furlough, he conducted daily training exercises thereafter. The day he introduced Lieutenant Parker to the group was comfortable and sunny. They assembled on a flat, open field just outside the city. Nearby, young boys peeked at them from behind trees and the corners of buildings. The Communists dressed in typical gray civilian clothes, but David wore a clean and pressed khaki uniform. All in all, he stuck out like a flamingo in a flock of cormorants.

Some men snickered whenever David spoke Chinese. Most had never seen a white man speak their language so well. None seemed to disapprove when Yuen announced that David would be joining their mission, though. Yuen searched their faces: there was not one look of concern or dismay that this American might slow them down or endanger them. *Typical*, he thought. *It's my job to worry.*

The next day, Yuen saw David and nine Chinese soldiers carrying large wooden crates to the field. There were three rectangular crates, three smaller boxes, and one longer, more narrow crate. Stenciled letters forming the words "U.S. Army" were painted on the crates in black.

As the men fell in, David approached Yuen, saluted, and asked, "May I show the men something I've brought?" He was beaming.

What's he so happy about? And he's got to learn to stop saluting.

Yuen nodded.

David used a crowbar to pry the top off one of the large crates. The Chinese gathered around. The sight of beautiful, new

American rifles prompted a chorus of "oohs" and "ahhs" from the men.

Laying his hands on the rifles, David announced, "I've been able to requisition some weapons."

"How did you bring these?" Yuen asked.

"Technically, they're for us—us Americans. We asked for them." David's voice dropped a little, and he added, "But we didn't tell them that we'd be taking all of them with us on our mission."

The men smiled and began to murmur excitedly to each another. Yuen could not help but be impressed. The American had delivered in at least one way.

"I've also got a Browning Automatic Rifle, or B.A.R. for short," David added, pointing at the longer, narrow crate.

"First…" David said as he lifted a brand new rifle out of the box, "this is the M-1 Garand rifle. It's a very reliable semiautomatic weapon with few moving parts that are easy to replace." He took a moment to open a smaller crate, which was filled with rifle cartridges.

"This rugged and forgiving weapon can withstand being dropped, thrown, drenched with water—even pissed on." David looked up and grinned.

Urinating on your weapon? Yuen said to himself. *What is he talking about?*

His joke fallen flat, David next passed around a clip. Each soldier seemed impressed. More than one caressed the shiny new bullets inside.

"Each clip holds eight rounds," David instructed. "Gas propelled from the previous shot expels the shell casing, and the next round comes into position." Out of habit, David checked to make sure there was no round in the chamber. Then he demonstrated loading a clip.

He had tacked up a paper target to the crumbling wall of a bombed-out building thirty yards away. David brought the rifle up, flipped the safety, and sighted down the barrel. He fired three shots in quick succession, and each hit the center of the target. The men let out a collective gasp of admiration. David flipped the safety back.

With a confident smile, he turned toward the Communists. Holding the rifle out with both hands, he said, "Now let's have each man take a turn."

The men didn't move. Yuen thought some of them might have actually stepped back.

"Come now, don't be shy."

He does not know that to us ammunition is too valuable to waste, Yuen thought.

David seemed to realize this, because he said, "Please, we have plenty of ammunition here." He gestured to the boxes. "We can't possibly carry all of this with us. Let each man fire a few rounds."

Yuen beckoned Han to step forward. Han accepted the rifle. He handled the weapon gingerly at first, and then he hefted it up and down a few times in his arms. David pointed out the safety then stepped back.

Han slowly raised the rifle, aimed, and fired.

The bullet clipped the edge of the paper target.

"Good! Well done," David praised.

Han beamed. He handed the weapon back. David wanted him to shoot again, but Han wouldn't. As each man took a turn to fire, the men began to cheer. Yuen, too, couldn't help smiling at the new American toys. He had to admit that David seemed a likable fellow. But despite the new weapons, he still hated the idea of bringing an American tourist on patrol.

TWENTY

Yenan, September 1944

Dawn lit the plain at the city's eastern edge, dew sparking on the patches of wild grass and low scrub. The morning wind tumbled a tiny torrent of red and orange leaves off a row of chestnut trees to the ground below, and just for a moment, the level of light shifted from gray-dark to silver-gray as the sun crept up a notch higher on the horizon.

David shivered in the chill wind as he watched the women and children bid their men goodbye. Tired eyes in every face—up all night, tearful partings, and now long, lingering hugs in the early morning. He noticed the older children said farewell with silent pride. They knew, some of them, that this could be final.

For his part, David asked his friends not to see him off. He tried to close up the front of his gray wool jacket but had trouble getting the knotted buttons through the stiff little loops. As usual, his fingers were too eager. *The opium? Nothing I can do about that now.*

He adjusted the coat; it fit squarely on his raw-boned body, as if the material were cut for a block of wood rather than a man. Nonetheless, Communist uniforms were warmer than U.S. Army khakis—but then again, the coarse wool was itchy around the neck and made him sweat.

At the moment of departure only one woman cried openly, and it was to the chagrin of the two men beside her. She clung to the younger of the two, her tears wetting the collar of his jacket. The older man stared at his feet, embarrassed by her display of emotion. David recognized this man as Yang Lu Gao, Yuen's second-in-command. The woman released their son, Yang Gu Ying, a baby-faced eighteen-year-old. This would be Gu Ying's first mission. David liked the boy's manner and his skill as a quick learner; he could disassemble and reassemble the M-1 almost as swiftly as David could. And Gu Ying could easily outsprint every other man in the platoon.

Without a word, Yuen started to walk east, the men following here and there in small groups of five or six. As he walked, David tapped his breast pocket, listening for the sound of the crinkling paper folded inside. It was a letter from Katherine that had arrived the day before. Written in longhand on a gossamer, four-folded aerogram, David had read it seven times already.

Dear David,

I must say, your letter upset me. You are grossly uninformed. I never had the chance to explain what you saw, and we never talked about what An Li said about you. Can I trust you? I'd like to, but I've never known her to lie.

There is nothing between me and An Li but friendship. You saw something foolish, nothing more than a game. I'm sorry for the way it might have surprised you—but you needn't let it offend you any further.

I shall tell you now that Robert Enfield and I saw one another for a time before you ever arrived in Chungking. I shan't try to defend myself as to why I fell for him. He called on me that day, and I saw no reason to put him off, as you were behaving like such a fool.

I do care for you, I really do. But I'm confused right now, and I need time to sort things out. We need, more than anything, to talk. If what An Li accused you of is true, then I need to know the whole story, not just a little part of it. You have a way of dismissing things. You must be honest with me—fully and openly—at any cost.

I hope this letter reaches you with all speed before you embark on your new mission. In any event, I will pray for your safe return.

Fondly,

Katherine

The letter made David feel elated and depressed at the same time. He took out the aerogram and pressed his face into it. The paper was infused with her fragrance. He breathed it into his lungs as if it were a heavenly tonic. As if it were his own blend of opium. He smiled. *Would that work? Could I kick the habit by smelling Katherine's perfume?*

And for the first time in a long time, he felt a contentment that he didn't owe to opium. Katherine had written him; she wanted to talk. He wasn't imagining it. She'd offered him *hope*.

They made almost twelve miles by midafternoon, on familiar roads that snaked between the escarpments of craggy mountains. By this time, David's only thought was to keep pace with the others. He wasn't unfit, but the march was his first sustained exercise in months. After nine hours of marching, his thighs were spongy, and the arches of his feet felt tight and were beginning to hurt. Moreover, his stomach grumbled, working on the unpolished brown rice and dried radish slices from the midday meal they'd eaten on the move.

David fell in step with Yuen, who carried the B.A.R. slung backwards over his right shoulder so that it rested on his forty-pound backpack. Two small black scorpions skittered out of their way and scrambled into a crumble of rocks at the roadside.

"Want me to carry that thing for a while?" David asked.

"No," Yuen replied, staring ahead, quickening his pace.

"It's a pain to carry around but a clincher in a fight."

Yuen grunted his agreement.

"Have you ever ventured beyond Peking before? On a mission, I mean?"

"No, I have not."

"I went into the city once. I was seven. I remember seeing the Temple of Heaven. Ever been there?"

"Yes." Yuen hesitated, then added, "I was a student in Peking…a long time ago."

"Really? Where'd you go to school?"

"Peking University."

David whistled at the mention of the premier university in China, but Yuen did not elaborate further. The B.A.R. *was* heavy, and he wasn't in the mood to talk.

"And where are you from, originally?" David asked.

I'm not going to get rid of you, am I? Yuen thought.

"I grew up on a small island off the coast near Xiamen."

"Xiamen? Then you must have seen a lot of Westerners growing up. Did you ever meet any Americans?"

"Yes," Yuen said. "I did meet some Americans. But I didn't like them."

"Why not?"

Yuen sighed. "Would you like anyone from a country that had invaded yours? Perhaps not militarily, but economically and socially, all the while loathing your people and humiliating them?"

At first, David thought Yuen was joking, and he almost expected him to break out laughing, but Yuen's blank expression did not change.

"That sounds like the British you're talking about," David said.

"Americans are no different. They just haven't been here as long."

David cinched the strap of his pack and fairly trotted to keep up with Yuen.

"But...it's the other countries that have taken advantage of China," he said. "We're here to help. We don't take over places; we don't make colonies like—"

"The Philippines?"

"But that's different—"

"When I was seven, an American sailor raped a Chinese girl on our island. When the girl's brother later punched the sailor in a rage, the sailor's friends killed the brother. The murderers were not subject to Chinese law, and the Americans let them off with a reprimand. They paid the family sixteen American dollars. How do you think that made us feel?"

David didn't know what to say.

"It's a feeling you would never understand."

David's eyes searched the dusky horizon, as if seeking some inspiration from the brown and yellow hues of the land. He didn't want to give Yuen the last word, but all he could think to say was, "Well, we're helping China now. We're all fighting against the Japanese, aren't we?"

Yuen responded in a deep but quiet voice. "America is helping only because this is in her interest. It is important to America that China does not crumble and that the Japanese armies stay here. But your government is misguided. By supplying Chiang, it is propping up the rotten shell of a corrupt government." Yuen glanced at David. "Surely you know all of this."

They walked in silence for a while. David's legs felt a bit rubbery but he nevertheless stayed beside Yuen. Even if he had wanted to disengage and move away, he could not do it in a natural way. The other men were several yards behind them.

Then Yuen surprised him by asking, "What about you and your background? Are the Parkers a renowned American family?"

David searched for a hint of sarcasm but didn't detect it. Yuen's eyes were locked on the horizon.

"Sorry, no celebrity here. My dad started a missionary school and church in Tianjin, where I grew up. My people came from Philadelphia, but I had never been there until I was seventeen."

"And where are your parents now?"

"My father's in New Haven, Connecticut, back at the church that originally sent him to China. I haven't seen him in years."

"Why not?"

David stiffened. "We didn't get along. I thought he was a hypocrite. He came here to serve himself, trying to be holier than anyone else. It's because of him that I gave up religion."

Yuen nodded. "All religion is myth—just another form of opium. There is no God. Your father wasted his life and probably ruined the lives of a lot of Chinese—like all missionaries."

"Hold on," David interjected. "My father may have been like that, but I've known many missionaries who were good men." He added, "And I wouldn't say there is definitely no God."

"Look at the suffering in China and ask yourself—how can there be a God? What deity would create people and then permit them to rape, kill, and enslave other people?"

"Well, there are a lot of good things in the world too."

Yuen's eyes narrowed. "You are naïve to say something like that. You know what the Japanese did at Nanking." He glanced at the group of men behind them and added, "Some of us were there!"

Hearing this, David felt any reverse argument turn to water.

"Where was your God? Or maybe he's just a God for white people?" Yuen exhaled loudly. "Let me say it this way—for the Chinese, there is no God."

What can I say to that? David thought. He was beginning to think Yuen had it in for him—and maybe for all foreigners.

"What did your mother think of China?" Yuen asked.

"My mother…" David felt a thickness in his throat. He didn't want Yuen to see him tear up, so he looked away. After a long pause, he answered, "My mother was killed in a riot in Tianjin."

Yuen's eyebrows lifted.

"There was an anti-imperialist riot in '25. I was with her. We were caught outside the concession and attacked by a mob that was trying to kill all the white people they could find. They knocked us down, and she covered me with her body. The soldiers came in time to save me but not her." David's voice quavered. "She died protecting me."

Yuen slowed and turned to gaze into David's eyes for the first time. He nodded gravely as if acknowledging that David might indeed have some idea of the realities of life in China. Then he regained his stride and this time, David dropped back and let Yuen go ahead, alone.

Twenty-One

The days on the trail merged into weeks, and the men welcomed the change in terrain from flat, yellow loess to green, rolling hillsides. They crossed the Yellow River, the border between Shaanxi and Shanxi provinces.

"China's Sorrow," as the river was called for its unpredictable floodplains in the east, was thick here with erosive and airborne silt. The snaking river lagged and meandered, dotted with sandbars and shallow pools, making it almost unnavigable. This, along with less than average rainfall in the spring and summer, made the river easy to cross on foot. They stayed well north of Taiyuan, just south of the Great Wall.

One morning, David awoke sweating and shivering. He'd lain awake most of the night, staring at the Milky Way, unable to stop his mind from churning, his heart from racing. Although he'd hardly eaten anything for two days, he wasn't hungry.

He'd not smoked opium for almost a week.

He'd shortened his pipe by sawing it in half, making it easier to hide in his pack, and he'd succeeded in slinking off to smoke a few times in the first weeks when they'd overnighted in villages friendly to the Communists. But now they had not seen a village in several days, and there was no private way of smoking on the trail, no way to avoid the notice of the ever-present comrade standing watch at night. In desperation, David had tried eating a small piece of dried opium, but the taste of it was so horrid that he spat it out. A day later, he managed to swallow a piece whole but found that it did little to alleviate his symptoms.

David sat up on his thick wool blanket and worked to get his right foot into its boot, the leather hard and rigid from the cold night. He struggled to quiet his shaking fingers long enough to tie the laces.

Rapid footsteps rustling through fallen leaves caused him to look up.

Jou came into the clearing out of breath. He'd had night picket duty, and now he jogged up to Yuen, who was within earshot of David.

"We saw three comrades approaching our position, so I hailed them. They look like they have a prisoner, a Japanese soldier. Gu Ying is waiting for them to catch up. I ran ahead to tell you."

"Could you tell if they are regulars or militia?" Yuen asked.

"They look like militia—no uniforms and I didn't see any rifles. Maybe from the village we passed yesterday."

Yuen nodded. He saw David listening and said to him, "We're at the borderlands between us and the Japanese. Most villages are loyal to us and send out militia to patrol locally."

A short time later, Gu Ying emerged at the edge of the clearing leading three Chinese peasants and a short, thin Japanese soldier whose hands were bound behind his back. The prisoner looked around the Communist camp and then stared at the ground. His tan uniform was clean, but his hair was mussed and his face was bruised. One captor had an outdated Russian pistol while the others carried machetes.

"Who are you?" Yuen asked the peasant with the pistol, who had a broad face and flat nose. His scraggly hair hung over his ears.

The man's words tumbled out of his mouth. "We are glad to find you! We are farmers from a village one day's march to the west. We suspected a man in our village was working for the Japanese as a spy. Two nights ago, he snuck away, and we followed him all night and the next day. He stopped at a deserted village. Then this Japanese soldier arrived, and we saw the spy give him this..."

The peasant handed over a few pieces of folded paper. David couldn't see the characters scrawled on them. Yuen looked over the papers, then handed them to Lu Gao.

The farmer continued. "When we showed ourselves the two of them began to run. We had to kill the spy, but we captured this soldier. We might have killed him too, but we thought it might be better to bring him back as a prisoner. Now we pass him on to you."

Yuen gazed at the Japanese soldier. He was defeated but did not seem afraid.

"Han, see if he knows anything," Yuen said.

Han questioned the prisoner in Japanese and David was surprised that he seemed to answer Han's questions without reluctance.

After ten minutes, Han reported, "He says he is a private, and that he deserted the Japanese army. He claims he was heading west to defect to the Communists, and that he has a lot to tell us about Japanese positions and strategy. He wants to be taken to Yenan."

Yuen considered this information. Rubbing his chin, he said, "Ask him why he's still in uniform."

Han asked and was told. "He says he didn't have any other clothes to change into."

Yuen shook the papers in the prisoner's face and said, "Ask him why he was given these papers that reveal Chinese forces and their positions." Yuen's face was hard, unrelenting. "It even says here that there are Americans visiting Yenan right now! Wouldn't the Japanese like to know that!"

Han translated for the prisoner, whose eyes were now wide with concern. Through Han, the prisoner said he had no idea what the papers said, he couldn't speak or read Chinese, and that he had never met the accused spy before.

Yuen took a little notebook out of his pocket. "Ask him to make a map of the Japanese forces in the area and add anything else he thinks is valuable information."

After Jou untied his hands, the prisoner spent twenty minutes writing. He worked assiduously. A bead of sweat trickled down the side of his face. Meanwhile, the rest of the Chinese began to gather their packs and prepared to move out.

When the prisoner finished, Han translated the paper for Yuen. David overheard the names of a few towns, figures of troop strength, but it was hard to hear it all. He wondered if Yuen might assign a few men to escort the Japanese soldier back to Yenan. That would be a setback, for they were a small force already, and every man was valuable. David finished packing his gear and walked across the clearing to be near the other men who were preparing to leave.

Yuen, Yang Lu Gao, and the prisoner stood close together, facing each other.

Speaking Mandarin, Yuen said to Lu Gao, "Shoot him."

The prisoner gasped.

Lu Gao drew his pistol. He took aim at the prisoner's forehead.

"Bu yao!" *No!* the Japanese soldier shouted in sharp, clear Mandarin. He tried to grab the pistol barrel, but Lu Gao took a step back and dodged the man's grasp. Then he raised the pistol again and pulled the trigger. David, whose back was turned, jumped at the sudden shot.

The prisoner's hands covered his face. His legs danced robotically, without neural input, and his hands fell revealing that his face was gone. Flecks of pinkish-white brain matter and bone chips were all over his uniform and littering the ground. Almost as an afterthought, the dead body obeyed the law of gravity and caved to the earth with a loud thump.

David blasted in English, "What the hell was that?" He dropped his gear and ran to face Lu Gao.

Yang Lu Gao stared at David blankly. He shrugged and holstered his smoking gun.

David turned to Yuen and switched to Mandarin. "Why did you do that?"

Yuen said matter-of-factly, "He was the enemy, so we shot him."

David spoke through clenched teeth, hissing the words, "He was a prisoner!"

"He was a spy."

"He was wearing his uniform! He wasn't a spy."

"He lied about not understanding Chinese. Kill one to warn a hundred. Besides, we couldn't spare anyone to guard him. If the Japanese captured any one of us, we'd be tortured first, *then* killed!"

David shook his head. His hands began to get the shakes, and he shoved them in his coat pockets to hide them. "This is wrong," he said, searching the indifferent faces of the Chinese. *No one's listening to me. Is there any code of conduct? Are they just a band of vigilantes?*

Yuen turned to walk away. Then, as if he could sense what David was thinking, he whirled around and said, "We were fighting these invaders long before you arrived. We did not ask the Japanese to invade our country, but they did. Every Japanese we kill is one less who will rape our women and kill our children. You cannot understand our war."

"I heard Japanese prisoners were brought back to Yenan and offered the chance to defect. I saw some of them in Yenan," David said.

Yuen's annoyance was in his eyes, not in his words, which came out with monotone precision. "Of course, if we were close to Yenan I would have considered sending him back, but we aren't. He gave us all the information he was likely to know. We can't waste men to watch prisoners—he might have escaped or even killed these villagers." He opened his mouth to say more, then hesitated. He looked hard at David's eyes. The two of them stood at arm's length.

Then, Yuen raised his voice an octave and his tone had an edge. "I do not have to explain myself to a foreign devil," he said, "especially one who is an opium addict."

David opened his mouth, but no words came out.

The men in the clearing watched David and Yuen silently.

"Don't bother to say anything," Yuen said. "Touch black paint, have black fingers. Your eyes tell the tale so well—and even though it's freezing cold, you look like you're roasting in hell. Do you think I haven't seen this before? Can you possibly think I don't know these symptoms of yours?"

David averted his eyes, looked at his boots, then glanced toward his pack lying on the ground.

"You have some with you? Go ahead and use it for all I care." Yuen gestured to the men around him. "We have no use for you like this. Go ahead, no one's going to stop you. After all, you are an *American*."

Yuen sneered at David before stalking off. Although his words had come off as cool and deliberate, his body said otherwise. Slowly, the others turned away and resumed preparations to leave. The three villagers departed, entertained by the surprise drama and completely satisfied with the ending of their odyssey.

David burned inside, his indignation turning to humiliation.

Everyone knows.

The Communists began moving east, but David stood in place. He stared skyward through the skeletal tree branches. He thought about leaving, walking away, but that would be foolish and would prove Yuen's point—that he was a coward, and that this was the real reason he was smoking opium.

He went to his pack and opened it. Reaching down, deep inside, he felt for the crinkly brown paper bag. He pulled it out and opened it. The golf ball-sized mound of dried opium had the consistency of clay.

The sight, smell, and feel of the gray-black substance set off bells inside his skull. All at once, his mind was alert, on edge, ready to be sated. Then he made a sudden, hard decision.

Grasping the ball, David raised his arm and, with an under-the-breath oath, he hurled it at the nearest tree.

The opium ball bounced off the tree and landed with a thump in the dirt.

Quickly, David cinched up his pack and shoved his blanket under his arm. Afraid he might still retrieve the drug, he sprinted after the last of the Communists who were leaving the clearing.

The broken, face-shattered Japanese prisoner lay where he'd collapsed, dead and disjointed.

Up front, Yuen seethed in silence as his mind took apart the situation. He didn't care what David thought, for he had little respect for the man, but he did not like to lose his composure in front of the men.

Never mind the opium, he reasoned. *The true problem is more dangerous: this boy has no understanding of war. Questioning my judgment—as if he knew something I did not.*

The Party leaders will not be happy he saw the execution—so what? Any other responsible commander would have done the same and would feel just as I do now.

Yuen marched on ahead of the others and put a good thirty yards between them and himself. While he walked alone, he began to feel better, but for one nagging thought. How *would* the Party leaders react to this? They seldom behaved in a predictable way.

That's the only thing I know for sure: they're never predictable. Make that the rule.

Will they hold this against me?

Twenty-Two

Chungking, September 1944

Katherine scurried away from the apartment, flustered and confused. Her shoulder bag danced against her back. She turned; An Li stood watching from the doorway, her eyes veiled in repose.

Why did she do that? Didn't she already understand?

Katherine jogged down one alley and emerged on to a narrow street packed with pedestrians. She froze just in time to avoid colliding with a large, spinning rickshaw wheel.

"Zou kai!"—*Out of the way!*—shouted the shirtless coolie who wrestled the rickshaw through the crowd. The silk-robed, silver-haired passenger was oblivious to Katherine or any other obstacle. The dark, circular lenses of her sunglasses reflected the brown-skinned faces in the crowd and also kept her at once removed from them.

Bewildered, Katherine retreated back into the alley and slid down to the ground, her back against a wall. She rubbed her forehead and replayed the last five minutes in her mind.

"Are you missing him?" An Li had asked as she set down a cup of tea for Katherine. Her tone was soft, almost apologetic.

Katherine sighed and sat back from her typewriter. An Li was visiting every day now. The two women loved working and laughing together. They'd not spoken of David or the argument.

Or the kiss.

I suppose she wants to talk about it now, Katherine concluded. She decided to be honest. "Yes, especially when I've had no news."

"He went on a mission with the Communists?"

"Maybe. I think so." Katherine looked at An Li. "You know, I don't think I ever told you about that."

An Li blushed. "I think I heard about it somewhere else." She turned away and looked out the window. "I hope he will stay safe."

"Do you really? I don't believe you." Katherine reached out and grasped her friend's elbow. "Why do you dislike him so?"

An Li stared at her. Katherine felt she could dive into her dark, beautiful eyes.

"Don't you know?" An Li said.

They sat in silence for several seconds. Steam from Katherine's teacup curled. The grandfather clock in the corner ticked on and mimicked a cricket in the hearth.

An Li kept staring at her.

Katherine turned her head. "Please don't look at me that way," she said.

"But you're so beautiful." An Li moved behind her and began to rub her shoulders.

Katherine closed her eyes involuntarily. The kneading felt good.

"You and I," An Li said softly, "we're 'you yuan qian li neng xiang hui.' It means, 'meant to be together.'"

Her hands slid down from Katherine's shoulders to her breasts.

Katherine was slow to react. "Please..."

"Please—what?" An Li whispered.

"Please," she said more forcefully. "Stop. Leave me alone. I need to think about...things."

"Think about...us?"

"No, damn it!" Katherine shouted, immediately wishing she could take the words back.

An Li shrunk back.

"Just...leave me alone. *Please.*"

A tear ran down An Li's face. She stumbled into the bathroom and closed the door.

Katherine let her head fall into her arms on the desk. She'd never felt attraction to An Li or any other woman, and yet, she did not understand why the idea of kissing An Li was not revolting to her.

Am I just starved for affection?

She tried to think rationally, but her mind was fluttering.

Not knowing what else to do, she stood up, grabbed her shoulder bag, and ran out the front door.

An Li had waited for Katherine to disappear from sight. Then she went back inside the apartment and closed the door. She stood still, leaning with her back against it. She knew she had to work fast, in case Katherine came back, but she gave herself a moment to wipe her eyes and get over her disappointment.

It was a short cry—only ten seconds—for even as Katherine's rejection made her want to die, she knew that if she was going to live, she needed to be more cunning than ever.

Now her life was truly in danger.

"You're attracted to her, aren't you?" her handler had said to her weeks ago. He was a thin-limbed, bald Cantonese peasant who had somehow worked his way up the ranks. The sight of him usually made An Li want to retch.

"What? Of course not."

The scrawny man smiled. "Don't worry, your secret is safe with me."

"I don't know what you are talking about."

Out of nowhere, the haggard peasant's palm whipped across An Li's face. Her cheek burned like fire, but she forced herself to keep her hands at her sides. She glared at her handler with a look of pure hatred. Her own hands thirsted for retribution, but she held them behind her back to keep her intention secret.

"You whore," he said, spitting on her. He shoved her against the brick wall and pressed his body up against her. He smelled of sweat and dung. The small, windowless room was in the basement of Juntong headquarters. An Li knew no one would hear her scream. And if she got the better of him, she'd pay for it. Still, she wanted to gouge out his eyes.

"You won't let me screw you. You'd rather be with some foreign devil woman!" He shoved her again, harder this time, and An Li hit her head against the wall. She fell to her knees but kept her wits about her. She must not let him know she was hurt.

The man stood over her. He started to unzip his fly. An Li closed her eyes. The nightmarish images of her sister's rape flashed across her mind.

The door opened suddenly.

"What is going on?" boomed a voice.

The old man fumbled with his pants. "Nothing, Chief," he muttered to Dai Li.

An Li drew a deep breath. The chief of Chiang Kai-shek's secret police was a hard man, but he wasn't a rapist. She was safe. For now.

"Stand up," Dai said. She did.

Dai paced in front of her. Wall to wall. Five paces one way; five paces back.

"You are a talented agent," he said. An Li knew not to reply. "But I fear your usefulness may be at an end. I've reviewed your reports for the last three months. You may have the English woman's confidence, but the intelligence you report is trash."

An Li kept her mouth shut. Speaking would only make things worse.

"It's always the same old things: pathetic stories about peasants and refugees. Nothing about the military, the Americans, the Communists. Nothing from their embassy." Dai punched his right fist into his left hand. "She is not...well-connected."

An Li stared at Dai's boots. He was now standing still.

"Perhaps she isn't worth working on anymore," he said conclusively.

An Li felt a cold stone of fear lodge in her throat. After working with Katherine for two years, the security of her position was something she'd taken for granted. She'd grown complacent, distracted by her own lust for her target. Now everything might change and could only be worse. The

Nationalists did whatever they wanted to women with no family. An Li could not cook; she could not clean. She'd always relied on her pretty face. Now she cringed at the thought of becoming a laborer—or worse, a prostitute for soldiers.

"Wait!" she shouted. "She *is* important." An Li thought fast. "She wants to go to Yenan as a reporter, and because her American boyfriend is there. If she goes, I'll go too. Then I'll provide loads of information on the Communists. You'd like that, right?"

Dai started to pace again and began rubbing his chin. "You think she will really go?"

"I know she will, first chance she gets."

He stopped and stared at the wall to An Li's left.

"All right. Continue with her. Report anything you hear, and I want to keep closer tabs on you. Come here once a week with an update."

An Li nodded.

Dai looked at the peasant who had stood in the corner, head bowed and completely still the whole time.

As he walked out, Dai said, "I think I'll get you a new handler, too. Someone a little less...corrupted."

But now An Li had botched it. She had needed Katherine's body so badly—as much or more than she needed food or water—and as she rifled through Katherine's desk, searching for new dispatches, letters, anything that might show what the British were thinking, she fought to hold back a flood of tears.

She won't want me around now. There's no way I'm going to Yenan.

Desperately, she searched for a shred of something significant, something to mitigate the news of her failure.

There was nothing An Li hadn't already seen.

Ten minutes later, she left the apartment.

The sky was bright blue with big, fluffy clouds, a beautiful day that seemed to taunt her. It took her almost two hours to reach her neighborhood on foot. The sun was beginning to set when she got to her house: a ramshackle hut a stone's throw from the slums.

Suddenly, a figure emerged from the shadows and stood next to her. An Li froze.

"An Li?" the man asked. He was young, like her.

"Yes?"

"Hello, my name is Gong. I'm your new handler."

An Li exhaled slowly. The man was thin, gaunt even. He had the body of a teenager but the glittery eyes of an old man.

"May I come in?" Gong asked.

His old world politeness surprised her. Perhaps this was a man she could control or manipulate. Better than another bully whose only thought was to get her into bed.

"Come inside," she said.

The hut was made of wood planks. There were no windows, just small round holes where the knots had been poked out of the wood. She sat down on her cot in a corner. Gong stood next to a small wood-burning stove with a chimney spout that went through a too-big hole in the ceiling. He looked up and tried to guess how much water must come in when it rained.

"What do you want? Why did you come here?" An Li asked him.

"I like to meet my contacts outside of headquarters, in places less likely to be watched by other spies."

An Li nodded. She hated going to headquarters. Sometimes she thought the Nationalists had no common sense.

"Is your British lady making progress toward going to Yenan?" Gong asked.

An Li sighed. *I might as well tell him. He seems nice enough. Maybe he can smooth things over for me.*

"I've lost the contact."

"What?"

"She won't want me around anymore."

"What happened?"

She shrugged. She wasn't about to tell him the truth. After a long silence, she said, "We had a fight. About a man. I don't think I'll be able to get anything more from her." Now for the plea. "Do you think Dai will find something else for me to do?"

Gong was still registering the momentous news. An Li was one of his best-placed spies, and now she was useless.

"Perhaps we should go to headquarters right now. I know Boss Dai will want to hear about what happened today."

An Li's face fell. This man was not going to be her savior. She shook her head. "No. I don't want to."

Gong held out an arm, a sympathetic gesture. "It's for the best. Let's find out what job he'll have for you next."

Reluctantly, An Li let Gong pull her toward the door. "Do you really think it will be all right?"

"You're a talented girl," he said. Then he looked away and lied, "I'm sure everything will be fine."

He hated himself for saying it. He hated his job. He knew what happened to girls who outlived their usefulness, who already knew too much.

Gong followed An Li out the door. He noticed she didn't look back at her house as they left and he wished she had.

Katherine was late for the reception. The arrival of Brigadier General Patrick Hurley, a former secretary of war under Hoover, was the biggest story Chungking had seen since the vice president's visit. Word had it that Hurley was FDR's Band-Aid for the "China problem." As the president's emissary, he was charged with getting Stilwell and Chiang to start working together. How he would attempt to mix oil and water, Katherine didn't know. But she did know the news conference was going to be crowded.

As she hurried, she tried to put An Li out of her mind. In doing so, she began to feel very alone.

There'd been no word from David since she'd sent her letter. She knew he must have gone on the mission, but she still checked her mailbox multiple times a day hoping for a response.

Now, more than ever, she realized how empty life felt without David; she'd no idea what an impact he'd had on her until this moment. The monotony of her current life—meals with the same boring women, hours at her typewriter covering subjects she'd written about more than once—showed her what a lift she'd gotten from David's cheerful optimism. *He's so typically American*, she thought wistfully. *Unlimited resources, never having known defeat, the belief that anything's possible. So different from us Brits.*

And worse, with David out of the way, Robert Enfield had shown renewed interest in her. Being left behind by those who went to Yenan incensed him. Katherine knew he had no love for the Communists. In fact, it was clear that he loathed them. But he obsessed over his exclusion and in his boredom chose to channel his energies toward Katherine.

It started with flowers and requests to join him for dinner— he'd shown up at her door uninvited three times now. So far, she had managed to come up with excuses, but it was becoming harder to remain polite. Lately, she'd made a habit of looking over her shoulder when she walked home, intending to avoid him if she spotted him nearby.

She finally reached the long, gated drive that led up the hill to the American headquarters. The cooler weather felt delightful when Katherine recalled the summer's insufferable humidity. She smoothed her pleated, beige skirt with her hands, forced herself to walk not run, and—almost as an afterthought—smiled at a pair of Army captains who tipped their caps at her.

The foyer was empty. *They've started.* Her hard-soled shoes clacked across the tiled floor as she headed for the ballroom doors and the same room where Wallace's press conference had taken place. Inside, about thirty journalists and onlookers huddled around a podium at the far end of the room.

Katherine joined the fringe of the crowd and stood on her toes to get a glimpse of the podium. General Hurley was unmistakable: a tall, grandfatherly Oklahoman with glowing white, wavy hair and a large white mustache. He wore a perfectly tailored olive green uniform with more than a dozen campaign ribbons over his breast. Katherine found these colorful rectangles of his ironic, since she suspected Hurley owed his rank more to political connections than to military accomplishment.

Hurley was finishing a statement: "...here to bring the Chinese and Americans together in common effort to defeat the Japs."

A reporter raised his hand. Hurley signaled him with a bony index finger.

"Sir, what's your plan for improving cooperation here in China?"

Hurley slapped his hand down hard on the wood podium. "Heck, son, work's already mostly done. We're on the same side, ain't we?"

Hurley turned to eye some of General Stilwell's staff, who were lined up behind him standing at attention. Stilwell wasn't in Chungking, but protocol required proper respect be paid to the visiting dignitary.

"We may have some differences," Hurley said, turning back to the audience, "but nothing we can't work out with some plain speaking."

A flashbulb went off. General Hurley beamed in the burst of light. Another reporter raised his arm, holding a pencil high. Hurley nodded to him and the reporter said, "Sir, have you learned to speak any Chinese?"

"Not a lick!" Hurley proclaimed. "I speak the common language of man: common sense talk. No substitute for it—in any language!" His wide eyes surveyed the crowd. A few reporters chuckled while scratching at their writing pads.

The same reporter followed up. "Sir, may I ask, do you have any previous experience with a situation such as this? I mean, the cultural situation here is complex, and—"

Hurley chopped the air with his hand. "Listen son, I've got a hell of a lot of experience for something like this. I grew up working with Choctaw Injuns, that's 'bout as foreign as you can get! Since this war began I've been everywhere from New Zealand to Afghanistan. Heck, I've just come from Russia! The president *asked* me to come out here to help the generalissimo and good ole' Joe see eye to eye, and that's what I intend to do."

Members of Stilwell's staff cringed at Hurley's all-too-casual reference to their superior.

"Now listen, folks," Hurley said, as if he were seated on a fence back home. "I'm sorry to cut this short but I've got to start settlin' in. We'll talk again real soon, and don't worry, you'll start seeing results lickety-split."

Hurley pointed his finger at the collective group of reporters and service personnel. "And I expect you to write accurately about every one of our expedient actions," he said with a mock seriousness that ended in a flashy, toothy smile. After that, he marched out.

Katherine walked home. A cool breeze lifted her hair, and her deep breaths summoned the aroma of fallen leaves. *I wonder where David is at this moment,* she wondered. *Marching? Eating?* The delicious smell of roast duck wafted into the street from the open door of a restaurant. This scent reminded her of dining with David and how much they'd enjoyed eating and talking.

"Man yi dian! Ting!" *Slow down! Stop!* A squawk from behind startled Katherine. Two small boys brushed past her, their short, squat mother chasing them. The boys brought tight-knuckled hands up to their chests and spun around like they were gripping machine guns and shooting each other.

"Dow! Dow! Dow!"

Katherine felt a jolt of fear.

What if he's fighting right now?

The thought struck her hard before she convinced herself the chance of this was small.

But he's sure to see action on patrol.

For a moment, she tried to imagine what she would do if David were killed. *I wouldn't even know how to reach any of his family. They wouldn't know about me; they wouldn't know about the two of us.* She shuddered.

Robert Enfield was seated on the stairs leading to her flat. His back was to the building, and his long legs took up three of the short-measured Chinese stairs. Seeing her, he got to his feet smiling his usual sheepish but crafty grin. He wore civilian clothes, and his smooth, brown linen shirt rippled in the breeze. He'd left the top three buttons open to give himself an easy-going, impromptu look.

"Evenin', Katie," he said.

"Hello, Robert," Katherine replied, cringing inside at the old, familiar nickname he'd used for her in the past.

Turning gracefully, she slipped by him and unlocked her apartment door.

Enfield watched her.

Hands in pockets, he smiled. "Are you going to invite me in?"

"Oh, well, I'm really quite weary, Robert. Had a rather long day…"

Enfield settled his hand on her shoulder, gave her a gentle squeeze. "I had a long day, too. I'd appreciate a chance to unwind with some civilized company."

Katherine dropped her shoulder and slid away from his hand.

Then, sighing noticeably, she said, "All right. But only for a moment…"

Enfield brightened. "Thanks, darlin'."

She opened the door and put her shoulder bag on the floor just inside the threshold. Then she walked to the apartment's kitchenette. There was no sign of An Li. Her favorite teacup—an old gift from Katherine—was gone from its place on the counter.

"Would you like a cup of tea?" Katherine called, watching Enfield out of the corner of her eye. He'd closed the door and was stalking the room like he was looking for something.

"No thanks, I brought my own drink."

Enfield took a silver-colored flask out of his pocket and held it up. Katherine smiled weakly and set the kettle to boil.

"How's work?" she asked.

Enfield sauntered over to the wicker loveseat, tossed an old newspaper from the couch to the floor, and sat down heavily, raising a small cloud of dust from the fraying seat cushions.

"Oh, same old stuff," he said, slouching sideways. "Mountains of paperwork."

"What about the men in Yenan, how are they faring?" she asked pleasantly while pretending not to be too interested in the answer.

Enfield whistled through his teeth. "Those buffoons are wasting their time up there. Commies can't fight. Why, they live in caves! They're like a bunch of cavemen." He took a hard swig from his flask and sighed with satisfaction. "But those State Department boys, Jack Service in particular, have become quite enamored with them. From their reports you'd think that Mao was the Messiah and the Communists live in Shangri-La."

"Oh?" Katherine's slender fingers touched the loose hair at her neck. "Surely they're most interested in how the Communists can help us defeat the Japanese, perhaps that's why they're so impressed? I've heard they're very effective."

Enfield snorted and swigged again. His cheeks were turning a little red. "That's bull. The Commies aren't fighting the Japs any harder than Chiang's people. I'm not sure why those men seem to love 'em so much. Their reports are mighty unpopular in Washington, I'll tell you. In fact, just to help 'em out, I've kept some of their dispatches from being sent to the State Department. I don't want them to get into trouble back home," he said, making a face.

"You haven't been passing on their reports?"

"Oh God no. I've had to send a few, but if you read any you'd see how blinded these fellows are. They're just trying to make a name for themselves, inflating the importance of the Chinks." He grinned at Katherine. "You know, with Stilwell and Barrett gone, I'm practically running this place. The Nationalists come at me with all kinds of favors. I know everyone important. If you like, I could give you an interview."

The kettle whistled.

Katherine readied the tea and came into the living room with the teapot and cups neatly arranged on a lacquered tray. Enfield moved to one side of the loveseat and patted the other cushion. Seeing no alternative, she sat down and placed the tray before them on a brass tea table.

The loveseat creaked as Enfield shifted his weight closer to her. There was a presumptuous look in his eyes. It repulsed Katherine to think that he believed himself to be so familiar with her.

He took another flamboyant drink from his flask. Wiping his mouth with the back of his hand, he chortled, his eyes moist with memory. "Katie, we had some fun times, didn't we, girl?"

Katherine quivered at his choice of words. "Those times are over, Robert," she said. She sipped her tea and glanced at him.

"Haven't you been lonely?"

"Not really."

His eyes wandered about the room, pausing over the books on her shelf and the photo of her parents on the windowsill. Coming back to her, his eyes traveled up and down her body before resting on her face. "Well, I can't stop thinking about that unforgettable night we had. I'm sure you haven't forgotten it either."

Katherine's stomach tightened. *How could I have been so stupid, making love with such a boor? I certainly wasn't in love...but I didn't want to lose him either, so I just let it happen. I must've been out of my mind. The only good thing—that's when I knew I had to end it.*

All at once, Enfield reached out and grasped Katherine's wrist. He held it so tight it hurt her.

"I just don't see why we can't pick up where we left off. I mean, we deserve each other, decent people like us, way out here in this god-awful place."

Enfield leaned in and put his arm around her. Katherine tensed, tried to get up, but now his weight was pressed upon her, and he was pushing her down. Somehow, he managed to land a crude kiss on her lips—too hard and too sudden—and his breath was bitter with the smell of recycled alcohol.

She twisted her face away and tried to stand, but she was pinned.

Enfield hesitated, surprised by Katherine's reaction. "Tell me you're not thinking about that adolescent lover boy who went to Yenan with the other Commie-lovers."

Katherine looked away.

"Damn it," Enfield growled. "My dear, you have no idea what you want or need…and I think I need to show you."

He grunted, eyes all over her. Then he shoved her right hip with his hand in a primitive effort to straighten her legs out. Katherine struggled to rise. Enfield ducked low and kissed her again, harder than before.

"Stop it Robert!" Katherine cried, jerking her head from side to side. "You're hurting me!"

This seemed to excite him, and he came at her for another dive-bomb kiss, but this time Katherine moved her head forward and down and Enfield's teeth collided with the top of her forehead.

Amazingly, it hurt Enfield more than Katherine. He howled—"Ow!"

Recoiling, he reached for his lip, which was bleeding. Still holding her down with one hand, he rubbed his sleeve against his mouth. The sleeve came away bloody.

Katherine froze.

Enfield sucked on his bleeding lip, and a deviant look crept into his eyes.

He's enjoying it, she thought—and she panicked.

He had both of her elbows—it was no use trying to get free. But by wriggling, she opened a small space between them, got her knee up just enough, and with it nailed him in the groin as hard as she could.

Enfield came off her. Doubled up and groaning, he fell to the floor.

Katherine rolled off the loveseat, stood up, and ran into the kitchen.

"I'm hurt, damn you!" Enfield cried from the floor.

Katherine found what she was looking for—her large chef's knife. Gripping it in her right hand—point down for plunging—she returned to the living room. Her eyes showed steely resolve.

"Get the hell out of here!" Her voice trembled but her intent was vicious.

Grimacing and groaning, Enfield realized how defeated he was—unable to even stand—and crawling on his knees, he got himself to the door and whimpered to be let out like a beaten dog.

Katherine opened the door and with her foot gave Enfield a kick. That was all it took. He scuttled through the opening, moaning in pain.

When his body was free of the doorway, she slammed the door, and the sound made him cry out one last time. She locked the door and leaned against it, listening as Enfield gathered himself and unsteadily got to his feet. She heard scuffing, dragging footfalls. Fading, fading. Gone.

Katherine collapsed, dropping the knife, which clattered on the tile beside her. Holding her knees close to her chest, she rocked back and forth. She had no idea how long she stayed there, sobbing. But after what may have been hours, she got up, went into the bathroom, and stripped off her clothes. She looked at herself in the mirror. Her shoulders already were purpled with finger marks, and there were red scratches on her neck. She went into the shower and covered her body with soap, cleansing every part of her, wiping away every trace of her attacker.

David, I wish you were here.

But how will I ever explain this to you?

Twenty-Three

North of Taiyuan, October 1944

The land was pitted and scarred from recent burning—flames intentionally set to deprive the Japanese of food. Elsewhere, fallow fields—burned long ago—were choked with weeds and saplings. The fifty-mile-wide strip of land running north to south was an undeclared border between the Japanese and Communists.

Though none complained, all the men were hungry. They had carefully rationed their remaining preserved turnips, cabbage, and precious salted pork jerky, but now the group's supplies had run low. Yuen had anticipated this stretch of no man's land, where it would be difficult to live off the land and impossible to expect help from local farmers. But he had never seen it quite so barren, so desolate. Hunger and fatigue showed on every face. They would need to find food soon.

The worst of David's withdrawal symptoms were over. The nausea and insomnia had lasted almost a week, the cold sweats and gnawing anxiety a few days more. His ordeal was private in the sense that the others ignored it and looked the other way, but in every other sense, his struggles were on full display. He was always exhausted. He lost ten pounds. His legs and hands wouldn't stop trembling. And now that he was coming out of it, the sense that he'd lost the respect of his fellow soldiers weighed heavily on his mind. He'd never been so unhappy.

On the trail, Yuen's shoes stuck a little with each step in the soft ground. A "V" of geese flew south overhead. The sun, still hanging a few hours over the western horizon, hid behind a cloud, and the land darkened dramatically—the effect almost eclipse-like.

Looking up, Yuen saw Yang Gu Ying running toward them from the denser tree line ahead. *He's seen something.*

Gu Ying sprinted to Yuen, eyes alive and alert. "Comrade..." he said, breathing heavily.

"What is it?" Yuen asked.

"There's a blockhouse on the other side of these woods."

"What kind of blockhouse?" The other soldiers gathered around.

"In a clearing, made of concrete. I didn't see any big guns, just the building," Gu Ying said.

"Manned?" Yang Lu Gao asked his son. "It could just be a leftover from the fighting here years ago."

"I saw three men. And they have a radio."

"So, a perimeter outpost," Han concluded.

Yuen stepped away from the gathering and faced toward the woods. He leaned against a large birch. *Should we attack or just steer around? If it goes badly and they radio in, Japanese patrols will search the area. It's not worth the risk.*

He knelt down, picked up a yellow leaf, and crinkled it in his right hand. *But they will have food, maybe enough supplies for several weeks—winter is coming.*

Yuen turned and saw all thirty men watching him. He searched the eyes of a few, looking for reluctance or fear. He gazed at David, who wore a sullen expression.

"Let's go take a look," Yuen said.

They walked a mile into the woods. It was dusk by the time they reached the clearing. The rectangular bunker had a heavy metal door at its rear and several horizontal gun slits. A tall antenna reached from the roof to the height of the surrounding trees. A thin web of vines had grown up the walls and was climbing the antennae.

An old communication center or strongpoint in the Japanese line, Yuen thought. *This place has not been important for a long time.* Fifty yards of open space surrounded the blockhouse in all directions.

Three Japanese soldiers sat around a fire outside the bunker doors. They were smoking, their cigarettes dancing like small wands of light. One of them threw a small carton into the fire. Another wiped a pair of chopsticks on his sleeve and put them in his shirt pocket.

Yuen was contemplating whether they could pick off all three with a volley when the men stood up and went into the blockhouse. The metal door clanged shut.

Now how to get at them? He thought again of bypassing the outpost altogether. *Was it worth the risk to get some food?* He tried to ignore his hunger pangs. They could hear the Japanese talking inside, their voices echoing in a rapid, staccato beat, harsh to his ears.

Han translated, whispering in Yuen's ear.

"No, you go!"

"Oy! Why bother?"

"Get out there you lazy fool!"

The door creaked open again, and a man straggled out dragging the butt of his rifle on the ground. He crouched near the fire. Shivering, he pulled his thin cotton jacket close.

We don't even know how much food they have, Yuen thought. He had almost decided against an attack when he heard the throaty rumble of an engine coming from the woods. On the opposite side of the clearing, Yuen saw a narrow dirt road. A dark green Japanese army truck came into view, its tailpipe puffing dark smoke. The Communists sunk low behind the trees.

There were two men in the cab. The truck came to a stop, and the blockhouse doors whined open; two soldiers came out.

One called to the driver, "What took you so long? We expected you yesterday."

"Ay!" the driver climbed down from the cab and rubbed his behind. "That road's a mess. We crawled the whole way."

"And you're a whole day late!" the soldier snapped. Then, glancing suspiciously at the bed of the truck, he added, "We'll have to check over everything."

The passenger climbed down on the other side of the truck and said, "Shut up and stop your bellyaching! Be glad you're getting any supplies at all. You know everything's scarce. Help us unload the crates and we can enjoy a good meal."

Yuen watched the five men unload the truck and reconsidered his decision. There were at least two dozen crates, which were sure to hold plenty of rations and maybe even weapons. He squinted, trying to gauge the five enemy soldiers by some measure—their strength, their confidence.

The men finished unloading quickly. Then, three of them went into the blockhouse while two stayed outside by the fire.

Yuen decided it was worth the risk.

"Listen," he whispered to Yang Lu Gao. "We can do this, but it must be silent. We must get them all before they can use the radio. This means we *must* get into that blockhouse."

Lu Gao nodded. So did the men within earshot.

"I'll go myself. Han? You too. I'll need you to speak Japanese and get them to open the door."

Lu Gao frowned. "Why just two of you?"

Yuen stared at the blockhouse and marked off the fifty yards in his mind. "They cannot hear us—I *need* to know we'll have them by surprise."

"Perhaps one more? That would be wiser. Let me come," Lu Gao said.

"No, if something happens to me we need you to lead."

"Let me go," David said.

All eyes turned to him. Yuen's unwavering stare gave David the impression that he was under the deepest scrutiny, not only as a man or a soldier but perhaps as a human being.

"Don't worry, I can do it. I'm ready."

"Very well," Yuen said. "You'll have your chance. We sneak around and take the sentries from behind. David kills his man. I take the other one, and Han makes him call out to his buddies to open the door. The rest of you stay back until you see the door open—then hurry. If we get locked out, put grenades in the slits and take down the radio antennae on top. Questions?"

There were none.

David, Yuen, and Han circled in the secrecy of the second-growth trees to the other side of the bunker. The blush wine-colored sky darkened, and the sound of crickets wove in and around the bursts of occasional laughter among the Japanese soldiers.

David's hands were clammy. He wiped them on his pant leg. Yuen looked at him and held up a foot-long knife, a simple hunting blade whose hilt was rusted. He whispered to David, "Have you ever killed a man up close?"

David shook his head. "I've never killed a man, period."

Yuen stared into the gathering dusk. "Remain calm. We have the advantage of surprise." He pointed the tip of his knife at the dagger hanging from David's belt. "That is more reliable than a gun. Now is your chance to use it."

David's lips tightened as he removed the blade from its tight leather scabbard.

The three men crouched low and scurried across the clearing to the blockhouse wall. Han held a pistol, with orders not to fire unless absolutely necessary. Yuen and Han went left around the building, and David went right. Yuen would wait for David to make the first move and immediately follow, so that their attack on the sentries would be nearly simultaneous.

David crept under the gun slits and made his way around the blockhouse. The concrete felt cool. Clinging vines tickled his neck. He could hear the men inside talking and he was tempted to glance inside but didn't.

He took up position at his corner of the blockhouse. A peek around the edge of the building showed both Japanese soldiers at the fire, facing away from him. They were mere boys—maybe seventeen—not exactly emaciated but far from well-nourished or strong. Nervous seconds passed in the twilit silence. David's heartbeat pounded in his ears. He couldn't see Yuen but knew he was where he said he'd be, waiting for David to make the first move.

David rushed out, covering ten yards like a broken-field runner. Out of the corner of his eye, he glimpsed Yuen coming on. His field of vision was now limited to his target's back, neck, and stringy black hair. He stepped on a dry leaf, which made a crunching noise. The second soldier looked up just as David's hand clasped the mouth of his friend from behind.

David cocked back his victim's neck and punctured his windpipe at the same time. The knife thrust was blind, path uneven, but David felt the sharp tip of the blade slice through muscle and cartilage as a rooster tail of scarlet blood sprayed across David's hands and arms. The soldier made a gargling noise, bubbling at the throat. His hands came up and clawed at David's forearm with surprising strength, while his body writhed and spasmed. David dropped the dagger to restrain him with both arms, and for a few interminable seconds, they were conjoined in a ghoulish hug.

Then the soldier's arms went soft. David tried to lay him down but he ended up falling clumsily on top of him. Blood pooled on the ground, black in the light of the fire. The soldier's bowels let go, and the smell of foulness went up David's nose. For a moment, he thought he was going to be sick, and then he remembered Yuen—and saw him with Han standing at the blockhouse door, shoulder to shoulder, watching him. David glanced toward the fire where the second sentry lay face down in the black dirt, the back of his shirt dark-soaked.

David got to his feet and joined them at the door. He didn't know why Yuen had killed his man rather than forced him to cooperate, but he figured there was a reason. The whites of Yuen's eyes glowed in the new risen moonlight.

David drew his pistol as Yuen gave the rusting door a gentle push. Locked. There was no sound from inside the bunker. Haunted seconds passed. Finally, they heard a voice, unalarmed and drowsy, from within the chambered walls. Relief showed on Yuen's face; Han exhaled. The only other sound was the crickets and the sobbing tremolo of a tiny mountain owl.

Yuen nodded to Han, who gripped his pistol and called out in Japanese, "Hey, come out, I've stolen a bottle of rice wine!"

A voice from inside the blockhouse: "Fushida, that you? Rice—what?"

Han answered, "Rice wine! Bring cigarettes!"

There was scuffling in the blockhouse. The door did not open. David looked at Yuen, but the moon was hidden in a cloud and he couldn't see his expression. Clipped Japanese words followed. More shuffling of feet. David imagined them peering through the rifle slits at the empty firelight.

Can they see the bodies by the fire? He prayed it was too dark. More seconds passed. *They aren't going for this.* David had one grenade. He fingered it, ready to un-clip it from the suspender strap near his left shoulder. *Will it fit through this gun slit above my head?*

The door opened a crack.

Han fired point-blank into the chest of the man who opened it.

"Hayaku shimero!" *Shut the door!* cried a voice from inside.

Han thrust his arm through the closing door space. The metal door slammed. Han screamed as the bones in his right forearm were crushed. A shot boomed inside the blockhouse.

Han staggered, hit.

Yuen dropped his pistol and used both hands to shove against the steel door. It flew open and Yuen, off-balance, stumbled in and grappled with a Japanese soldier.

David burst through the doorway.

The chamber was dark and musty; firelight from the outside swam on the walls.

He couldn't see anything. *Where's the other soldier?*

A gunshot ripped the air and roared against the concrete walls. David didn't feel the bullet strike him, but his ears rang from the concussion in the close room.

Now he saw the soldier crouched in a corner loading another round into his bolt-action rifle. He was stocky, and his movements were purposeful, swift, but not hurried. The soldier looked up just as David began to raise his pistol. Instantly, the soldier dropped the round and charged forward with his bayonet aimed at David's belly.

There was no time to squeeze a round. David twisted on his heels and dodged the bayonet by a fraction of an inch. At the same time, he dropped his pistol to grab the hot rifle barrel with both hands.

The two men wrestled over the rifle, each trying to gain control of it. The Japanese soldier was short but strong, and it was he who took control of the weapon, but not before David kicked his left foot out from under him. The stocky man lost balance and went back like a sack of sand. David landed on top of him with both knees, punching the wind out of him and making him pig-squeal in pain.

David reached for his knife, but it wasn't there—he'd left it outside. The Japanese soldier thrust his rifle upward with both hands, and the barrel caught David hard on the jaw. His hands shot up to his mouth where he'd bitten his tongue. He came off the smaller man, who sprang to his feet and hurled himself at David.

The two fell back to the ground, with the Japanese on top. He drew a knife from his belt and plunged it down toward David's chest. David caught the knife hand at the wrist.

For several seconds, the dagger was frozen in space. The Japanese man bent forward, all of his weight focused on the point of the blade.

The knife inched lower. David felt his resistance waning. He couldn't stop the dagger's slow but relentless descent. *Oh God! This isn't happening!* The tip was three inches from his face. He prepared himself for the mortal wound, the pain, the humiliation of letting this smaller man kill him. Sweat from his adversary's forehead dripped on his face. The Japanese soldier gritted his teeth, preparing for the final thrust.

David glimpsed a blur in the far corner of his left eye. The blur grew large and tackled the soldier. There was instant relief from the weight on his chest. He gasped.

Dazed, he rolled to one side and watched Yuen plunge his knife into the soldier's chest again and again. The man's eyes grew huge. His hands floated up in a kind of underwater dance, feebly trying to deflect the knife thrusts. Then his arms dropped, and his head rolled back.

With one wide-arcing swipe, Yuen opened the soldier's throat.

Twenty-Four

A single kerosene lamp with a blackened glass chimney was the only light in the small, dim room, now crowded with Yuen's men. Three Japanese soldiers lay dead on the blockhouse floor. Thick smoke from the lamp hung in the air along with the close smell of blood, cordite, and sweat.

Yuen wiped the blood off his knife and sheathed it. Then he looked down at his torn, sweat-soaked shirt and dragged it up and over his head. After this he walked to the dead man Han had killed. David watched him unbutton the man's shirt and hold it up to the lamplight. There was surprisingly little blood, and a single bullet hole at the heart, which Yuen poked his finger through. Then he slid his arms through the sleeves and put it on.

David rose, legs shaky, and stood close to Yuen. "Thanks for saving my life," he said.

Yuen looked surprised. "Saving your life?" He went back to fastening buttons. "You sound so dramatic." Then he grinned and said, "Forgive me for not arriving sooner."

The Communists rifled through a stack of papers on a table next to the radio set. They pried open the crates and rejoiced when they found over a hundred ration tins, as well as packets of dried fish, ready-to-boil noodles, and cigarettes. One heavy crate held rifle ammunition, but there were no additional weapons.

David moved to a corner and sat down. All around him, the sound of men opening tins and eating hungrily. An unseen voice came from near the radio table, exasperated—a soldier who said, "Damn it, *of course* it's all in Japanese."

The words reminded David that Han was no longer there. *Poor Han!* He got to his feet and stepped out into the night of ratcheting insects. Han lay dead on the ground, face tight and teeth clenched, as if still waiting for the mortal blow to fall. Jou and Bao knelt beside him. Jou straightened Han's glasses. Bao took some papers from his shirt pocket: a letter, an identification card. A couple other men spoke softly about where to dig the grave.

A sudden noise—David looked toward the truck. It was Lu Gao, kicking a tire in anger. David watched him walk to the back and glance into the truck bed. "It's huge," Lu Gao said. "Poor fortune—none of us can drive it."

"Wait a second," David said, walking over. *A little bigger than a deuce and a half.* He opened the cab door, noting: *standard tranny, probably eighteen gears, one of them a low-low for pulling heavy loads up a mountain…*

"I can handle it."

At the same time David said this he remembered the driver had been the first man Yuen had knifed in the blockhouse. He went back in the kerosene-stinking building. The body was still warm. David rolled the corpse over; it was heavier than he expected. In the pockets, his fingers happened upon metal—the keys. He returned to the truck and jingled them at Lu Gao, who gave an obligatory nod that said, *Why didn't I think of that?*

Yuen assented to driving the truck down the road leading southeast, until daylight or the gas ran out. Surprisingly, all the men huddled together fit in back. There had been no official ceremony for Han, but now, before leaving, Yuen stood at the mound of dirt at the edge of the moonlit clearing. He knelt and sunk his hands into the loose soil. His eyes were clear and dry.

Goodbye, my friend. At birth we bring nothing; at death we leave with the same.

David watched Yuen's crouching figure. Then his eyes angled up into the sky where he saw the Milky Way. He searched for the Big Dipper, but his focus blurred. He felt exhausted.

Though he hadn't driven a truck in years, David found the vehicle fairly easy to maneuver. Yuen sat beside him in the cab, along with two other men who were soon asleep. The cramped quarters barely gave David room to shift, so that each time he jammed the gearshift forward and up, Yuen got bludgeoned on the knee—and then the same thing downshifting as the road narrowed and dropped, or a huge bump or tree root was traversed.

During a smoother stretch of road, David felt himself becoming drowsy.

"It might help me stay awake if we talked," he said to Yuen.

Yuen's eyes opened. "So talk," he responded.

"Find anything useful back there?"

"Besides food? Nothing special. It was only an outpost. I have some papers in Japanese, but we can't read them, of course. And Han is gone."

David nodded soberly. "You want to lose the truck at daybreak?" he asked.

"Yes. To be caught unprepared in this truck—that is a sure way of getting us all killed at once."

The dirt road dwindled off into inky darkness. Naturally, David didn't use the headlights. Both men kept their gaze on the road ahead, dimly illuminated by the moon.

"How did it feel…to kill that man?" Yuen asked.

How did it feel? David asked himself. *Raw terror when I thought I was about to die. Otherwise…emptiness.*

"It doesn't feel like much of anything."

"It is not a simple thing," Yuen commented.

After a pause, David added, "I thought *I* was the one who was going to die back there."

"You were afraid?"

"Terrified."

"That feeling never leaves us, but you must control your fear. If you do not you are already dead."

"You don't seem afraid."

Yuen sighed and rubbed his eyes. "There were many times when I thought I might be killed, but each time I lived. Each time I was grateful and saw my remaining days as a gift. If that happens often enough, you do not fear death, because of all the times you could have—maybe even should have—died. But I hope you will not experience the same trials in order to learn this."

"It's that easy for you? Not fearing it?"

"I do not fear my own ending. If I had died tonight, the only thing I would have missed would have been my daughter."

"What's her name?"

"Mei Fong."

David stole a quick glance at Yuen, whose eyes were wide awake and staring into the black hole that was the bore of the road ahead of them. Then Yuen spoke again. "No, there's one more thing that also makes me want to live."

"What's that?"

Yuen pointed to the back of the truck. "Those men. We have had many years together, many battles. I do what I must to complete the mission, but I also must keep them alive and help them return home. Maybe someone else could do it as well—maybe better than me—but the task is mine."

"How long did you know Han?"

Yuen was silent for a few moments. The speedometer needle trembled near thirty kilometers per hour. The fuel gauge had dropped below the halfway mark.

"For eight years," he said. "I remember when he came to Yenan, shortly after we settled there." Yuen chuckled over the memory. "He reminded me of myself at his age, and he came from my old school, Peking University, where he studied literature, like me. He was a good boy. Very smart."

Yuen paused, lost in thought. Then he said, "Did you know it was at Peking University that I met Mao for the first time? He was working in the library."

"Really? The library? I never would have guessed."

"He did not impress me much at the time; he seemed like a country boy. But that's all changed now."

They drove on for three more hours. The truck ran out of gas close to six in the morning. The men sleeping in back dismounted the truck wearily. They slashed the truck's tires and tore out the carburetor.

Into the rising sun, they trod on.

TWENTY-FIVE

Hebei Province, November 1944

The grasslands of central Hebei made for monotonous hiking, the homogenous land broken only by a distant tree or occasional jumping water deer. Yuen so completely avoided towns and villages that, outside of their men, David failed to see another soul for two weeks. Sometimes, Yuen held up the march up for hours waiting for scouts to find the best way across a roadway or around a village. He had never taken men this deep into Japanese-occupied territory. He stayed on edge—praying to avoid an unlucky encounter with a Japanese patrol or Chinese collaborator.

They reached a point within a week's walk of Peking and proceeded to dip south toward Shandong Province and the coast.

A spate of thunderstorms brought drenching rain for three straight days. Tired and filthy, David dreamed of dry socks. The Communists didn't wear socks, and their canvas shoes seemed to dry out quickly. Nor did they seem bothered by their collective body odor, which curled David's nose downwind of them.

The rains stopped, but the ground was soft. They passed through gaps in the layers of hills surrounding Baoding. Yuen resolved to avoid the empty plains close to the old, historic city, no matter how tempting a more direct route might be.

From one ridgeline, Yuen spotted a village in the elbow of a gently sloping valley. While a friendly village could mean a clean bath and hot food, he couldn't take the risk and decided go around it. Then, even from a distance, he sensed something amiss about the place. No people moving around. No smoke from cooking fires. He led them closer. The village was large, about thirty mud huts. He squinted into the sun glare. Through the dry air he heard faint shouting—distant but unmistakably Japanese.

"Jou, Gu Ying, go down there and find out what's happening," Yuen ordered. The two men scrambled and slid, zigzagging to find the fastest route down the steep hillside. Meantime, Yuen and the others backtracked to the well-trodden, sloping trail that descended into the valley.

Jou and Gu Ying returned to them fifteen minutes later.

"The Japanese are here!" Gu Ying reported. "They have all the villagers bunched up at the far end."

"How many?" Yuen asked.

Gu Ying wrinkled his brow, guessed, "Probably around fifty."

"Japanese?" Yuen said, surprised.

"No, villagers. About ten Japanese—that I could see. They've got at least three machine guns."

"But why are they here?" Lu Gao asked.

Jou and Gu Ying shrugged. Yuen crossed his arms and stared at the ground.

"I think…" Gu Ying said, "I think they're going to kill them all."

The men were startled by a single gunshot from the village. Yuen gripped his gun, expecting more shots to follow, but they didn't come.

Should I risk my men for this?

Those civilians will be massacred, I'm sure of it.

He stared at the scrub brush at his feet. Two ground doves took off with a small whir of wings. The men watched Yuen to see what he'd do.

Yuen gritted his teeth, the decision made.

"There is not much time. Split into two groups, half with me, half with Lu Gao." Yuen waved for Lu Gao to go right. "Move out."

They closed on the village, crossing a low wall of mud and stone. Moving as swiftly as they dared, they dashed from hut to hut and sprinted past a fenced enclosure with a half-dozen pigs inside.

Yuen got close enough to see the villagers at the intersection of two dirt roads, huddled close like a crowd of koi at feeding time. There were three machine guns: two mounted on truck beds and one set up on the ground nearby—all facing away from the approaching Communists.

A red-faced Japanese officer screamed demands at the crowd, but Yuen could not understand what was said, and he doubted the villagers could either. One Chinese man lay dead already, face down in a pool of blood. A little woman caught Yuen's eye. She rocked back and forth on her knees holding a baby who looked oddly serene at the center of the macabre scene.

Yuen reached for Gu Ying, who was crouched behind a row of barrels.

"Get this message to your father," he said. "Take out the machine guns first. Fire after you hear me fire first."

Gu Ying nodded and dashed off.

Yuen waited precious seconds for Gu Ying to deliver the message. The Japanese officer sounded a single command and put a hand on the barrel of one machine gun. With a metallic snap, all three gunners drew back their bolts, chambering rounds. The crowd uttered a collective gasp.

There's no time, Yuen thought. They were forty yards from the intersection. *Closer. Hurry.* He ran for the cover of another hut. The men followed. Thirty yards. Twenty. An old man—one of the villagers—lifted his head and saw past the Japanese. He caught sight of Yuen and said something in surprise. The two soldiers in the closest armed truck turned to see what the old man was looking at.

Yuen quickly dropped to one knee, shouldered his PPS-43, and fired a burst into the truck bed. One Japanese toppled over the side, hit in the shoulder. The gun's recoil took Yuen's shots high. As the other soldier began to swing the machine gun around, Yuen re-aimed and fired once. The bullet thumped into the soldier's chest. He staggered back and glanced down in disbelief at the widening circle of blood oozing through his shirt.

The villagers flattened themselves on the ground. Bullets whizzed past Yuen as the comrades behind him began to open fire.

The two other machine guns turned toward the attackers. Before one could fire, Yuen saw a grenade blast contort the gunner's body, lifting him up and out of the truck with his arms flailing like a jack-in-the-box. The third machine gun opened up, spraying the village with an arc of fire. Yuen dove for cover behind a wooden water trough.

He lay flat for a few seconds. Then he peeked out from underneath the trough and saw a small boy—four or five years old—break away from his mother and run into the field of fire. A hail of bullets seemed to chase him as he ran rabbit-like through the grass. Yuen lifted himself to peer over the trough just as the top of it splintered from a sudden volley of lead.

He ducked down low. He couldn't do anything for the boy. Then he saw Gu Ying dart out, weaponless, and scoop the boy up. To Yuen's amazement, it seemed that Gu Ying would carry the child out of danger behind the nearest hut, but the machine gunner found them at the last possible moment. Gu Ying's body folded as he and the boy took the hits.

The other Japanese began to fall back behind the huts on the far side of the intersection. Yuen tapped David and Jou, who followed him around to the left. Now alone and exposed, the two Japanese manning the last machine gun were cut down by Chinese rifle shots.

Yuen flanked the Japanese and took up position on the enemy right, unseen by three nearby soldiers who knelt behind a low wall, steadily firing at the main Communist position. Yuen signaled Jou and David who to shoot.

Yuen's target looked to be a boyish fifteen. His uniform was dirty and several sizes too big for him. Yuen was close enough to see that the boy closed his eyes when he fired.

Yuen took aim and squeezed the trigger. The boy dropped his gun and swooned backwards, arms flung out.

Jou hit his man in the back, the body lurching forward before falling over the wall.

David's quarry pivoted and began to run. The man took two steps before David fired—the bullet struck the side of his head and blood rained red on the mud wall as the Japanese soldier pitched lifeless to the ground.

The sound of concentrated rifle fire drew them to the outskirts of the village. Five remaining Japanese soldiers were running away, across an open field. A new, repeating sound thrummed the air—*tat-tat-tat-tat*. Lu Gao was firing the B.A.R., propped up on a wooden fence. The Japanese dropped like pigeons, one by one.

A sudden and unnatural silence came over the village. The smell of burnt powder clung to the air. Then an isolated wail rose from some of the villagers at the intersection. Shouts. Moaning. A mix of sounds: of agony, relief, hysteria, and sorrow all thrown together in a cacophony of voices. This crescendoed to a chorus that reached Yuen's ears, and he ran to it. He saw Lu Gao at Gu Ying's body, weeping. More villagers began to rise from the muddy ground, shell-shocked, hardly able to believe they were still alive.

"Thank you! Thank you! You saved us, they were sure to kill us!" cried an elderly woman.

Yuen held the sobbing woman and asked, "What happened here? Can you tell us what happened?"

The man next to her said, "Yesterday morning two Americans landed in a farmer's field, half a mile from the village."

"Americans?" David said, thinking he had heard wrong.

"What do you mean they *landed*?" Yuen asked.

A wiry fellow elbowed his way through the crowd. His cheeks were hollow, his clothes muddy. "It was my field," he said.

He then pointed to the sky. "They were airmen; they parachuted down. One of them broke his leg on a hard landing. They woke me up—it was still dark out. I brought them into my house and sent my boy for the village councilors."

"Where are they?" David asked impatiently.

"The council decided to send them west, toward Fuping, hoping to find a Communist safe house in one of the villages."

"So they've gone?" Yuen asked.

The farmer nodded. "We made a sedan chair and sent four men to carry the crippled one."

As Yuen and David absorbed this, sounds of a commotion rose from a side street. Following the shouting, they found a small crowd gathered around five villagers who were beating two men and a woman with wooden rods. Other villagers darted in to land a hard kick or to spit on the three. The male victims wore blue silk robes and hard-soled shoes, signs of wealth. The young woman's face was red and swollen. A rivulet of blood from her scalp ran down the side of her face. Her panicked eyes darted at the faces in the angry crowd.

Two dozen voices rose in a chant. "Mai Guo Zai!" *Traitors!*

So they were collaborators, Yuen realized. *Collaborators who might have collected the grain tax or served as informants.*

The Japanese rarely came to rural villages like this one, but the ever-present possibility that they might appear generated enough fear to keep the populace in line. After their close call with death and the spilling of enemy blood, Yuen reckoned the villagers viewed the day as a liberation of sorts. They were probably venting years of anger against these people. The Communists stood back as the crowd began to lose control. Other young men brought metal hoes and shovels. A hard blow cracked one man's neck, opening the skin so that the tendons showed white through the blood. His head hung flaccid, his body motionless on the ground.

Someone shook Yuen's shoulder from behind. It was David.

"What are they doing? Why aren't you stopping them?" he shouted.

Yuen gestured toward the victims. "They were collaborators. They helped the Japanese."

"We have to stop this!"

David made a move toward the victims, but Yuen forcefully pulled him back. "We cannot know what these peasants have been through! You, of all people, cannot imagine what they've experienced!"

Yuen's angry retort shocked David into silence. He wrenched his arm away from Yuen's grasp but stayed where he was.

The other man now lay face down in a pool of blood; his legs twitched randomly. Villagers stomped on the body.

The woman lay on her side in the mud. Her clothes were torn wide open, revealing her small breasts. Bone showed through a deep laceration on her back. Her arms dropped, lacking the strength to defend against her neighbors' vicious blows.

Suddenly, a new cry emerged from the crowd.

"Ba ta shale! Ba ta shale!" *Kill it! Kill it!*

Three men stormed into the center of the circle. One held a small girl, who looked to be little more than a year old. She was wailing. Seeing the little girl, the dying female collaborator moaned louder as she took her last draughts of air.

David accosted the men with the child. Above the din of chanting villagers, he demanded, "What are you doing?"

Surprised to meet a white man who could speak Mandarin, the three Chinese were speechless.

"What are you doing with her?" David glared at the man holding the child.

Composing himself, the villager explained, "This is a bastard child. That whore"—he pointed at the dying woman—"had it with a Japanese soldier."

Yuen looked at the woman again. Even after the disfiguring blows, he could tell that she'd been pretty. Another villager yelled, "That whore was a bitch! She never did any work! She slept with any Japanese who wanted her. She acted high and mighty, so now she gets what she deserves!"

Yuen saw it clearly. The woman either had been raped or had willingly given herself to the Japanese. Though the villagers may have disliked her for any number of reasons, the threat that the enemy might return to her for sex was a morose form of protection. No one would risk harming or evicting the mistress of a Japanese soldier.

David wrestled the crying toddler from the man's arms. Taken by surprise, the villager let go of her.

David's voice cracked as he shouted, "You won't harm this girl!"

At first, the three villagers appeared more shocked than angry. Then one of them laughed nervously, waved a dismissive hand at David, and stalked off. The others scowled at David, still eager for revenge.

Yuen said to David in a cold voice, "You have no idea what you are doing."

"I'm saving an innocent girl."

"Don't you see? Look around." Yuen gestured at the villagers. "No one here is going to care for this girl. They consider her the product of evil. Already a girl is practically worthless to them—who would stick up for this half-breed, take care of her, and share what little food they have with her? You should just leave her here." Yuen pointed at the ground where they stood.

"What are you saying? You said yourself no one here will care for her!"

Yuen crossed his arms.

"What kind of people are you?" David said. "You would actually leave this girl to die?"

Yuen wanted to scream at him, for his insolence, his ignorance, but he caught himself just before the tipping point. Instead, he turned on his heel and marched away, as David fought to keep the flailing child from falling out of his arms.

TWENTY-SIX

The Communists buried their dead and were then ready to search for the American airmen. Grateful villagers ran to their huts and emerged with arms full of turnips, flat breads, and clay jars of water. The soldiers ate on their feet, waiting for Yuen's order to move out.

For the moment, Yuen put the mission to Shandong out of mind. The Americans were valuable; rescuing them would be an important—and tricky—accomplishment. He twisted a thin, wet branch with his hands. White-knuckled, he wrapped it around itself until the sinewy cord splayed, then tore. He stared at the five small mounds of stone under a copse of pear trees at the edge of the village—the men he'd lost in the battle. They'd made quick work of the grave digging, which was easy in the soft, damp soil. He glanced at the dirt under his fingernails, his chapped palms, and wondered whether to tell the villagers or to just leave.

Yuen had learned more about what happened from an old man he'd found sitting on a barrel, a man who seemed less shell-shocked than the others.

"What happened here before we came? I need to know everything."

The old man turned to Yuen, and in a voice that almost seemed like water running over stones, he told his version of the story.

The Japanese had come from the east, about an hour before the Communists arrived.

"Have you helped any Americans?" the Japanese officer bellowed at the front line of kneeling villagers, his voice carrying to the whole crowd. He was unusually large and muscular for a Japanese. His words were translated by another soldier. Eyes roving the black heads, he stroked his thin mustache as he spoke. "The wreckage of their plane was not far from here. Already we've found two of them, and we know there are more—that much they told us"—he drew a samurai sword out of its scabbard, sunlight sparking on the blade—"before we cut their heads off."

A lone baby wailed. Muffled cries among the kneeling villagers, huddled together, their understanding delayed by the translation.

"Whether you are guilty," the officer told them, "is not in question. But, if any one of you would admit to helping the Americans, that person would be spared."

Murmurs in the crowd. Heads tilting toward one another, furtive glances, eyes darting back to the ground. After a few moments, one man stood up. He was fatter than the others and wore a black silk cap, a sign of relative prosperity. His hand trembled as he raised it.

"It's true," he said. "They left yesterday, two of them, going west. One had a broken leg."

A few villagers cast the informant dirty looks; the rest feared to lift their heads.

The officer's forehead relaxed as he heard the translation, and he smiled thinly. "And where are they going?" he asked, climbing down from the truck bed, walking up to the fat man.

Face to face with the officer, the man removed his cap and rubbed his bald head nervously. He stared at the officer's shiny black boots. "I don't know where, they just said it would be good to go west, toward the…I mean, away from here."

The officer drummed his fingers on the black-checkered grip of the pistol holstered at his hip. "And is that all?"

The man looked up. "Yes, I swear. That's all I know."

"Fine," the officer said, smiling. He addressed the crowd. "Do any others have more information to add, so that they can be spared like this smart fellow?"

The fat man exhaled and his shoulders sagged. The officer rattled his sword, the scabbard drumming against his leg with rhythmic consistency. When no one said anything, his face hardened. "Is there no one else who wants to be saved?"

"Please sir, mercy," a young woman pleaded, kneeling at the edge of the crowd with a baby in her arms.

"What did you say?"

The young woman's eyes were wet, her hair straggly. "Mercy," she whispered.

The officer smirked. In one smooth motion he un-holstered his pistol and pointed it at the woman's head, cocking it. The man next to her gasped. The woman clutched her baby and buried her face in its hair.

"Mercy?" the officer said with a chuckle. "Chinese dogs don't deserve mercy."

He lowered the pistol, turned abruptly to his left, and fired from the hip. The bullet caught the fat man just under the chin, blowing out the back of his head. Amidst horrified cries of villagers, the dead man's body slumped backwards, hitting the soft earth with a heavy thud.

The officer smiled, pleased with this flamboyant execution. Barrel still emitting smoke, he holstered his weapon. "Thank you very much for the information," he said to the corpse lying at his feet.

Then he turned on his heel and walked back toward one of the trucks. "Radio it in," he said to a soldier. Climbing up into the truck bed, he clenched his jaw and addressed the villagers. "You people don't understand," he said, jabbing the air with his index finger. "Japan and China are *friends*. We are here to *help* you, to *liberate* you from Westerners who are a plague on our continent. If only you could see that," he pointed to the dead man, "this loss of life would not be necessary."

His diatribe went on for several minutes. It was near the end that Yuen and his men arrived.

A sudden, stiff wind chilled Yuen. Brown-yellow leaves swirled at his feet. The men were ready. He had to decide. *Somewhere, there are Japanese who were radioed about this village and the Americans. It is only a matter of time before they go after the airmen—and show up here.* He looked once more at the damaged trucks and dead Japanese bodies. *There's no hiding what happened here. Before long, all these people will be dead.* He heaved a sigh, resigned to speak, though feeling he might regret it. He motioned to the elderly man from the barrel, who shuffled up to him with a benevolent expression. "Please gather the villagers quickly," Yuen said. "I have something to say to them."

Yuen's men fidgeted as the villagers assembled. Fifty civilians crowded the narrow street. Yuen climbed on a wooden bench and spoke in a calm voice.

"You people have done an honorable thing in helping the Americans. We are going to follow them and help bring them to safety. But you must understand. You are all in grave danger. Soon, other Japanese will come here, and they will certainly kill you all. You must flee."

Renewed fear struck the villagers' faces.

"No! You must help us!"

"You must defend us, you cannot leave!"

"Please take us with you!"

Hands outstretched, Yuen said, "We cannot assist you. We must move quickly to reach the airmen."

A woman collapsed, sobbing. Mothers clutched their children. Men shouted at the Communists and at each other. Lu Gao waved his arms, trying to calm the crowd.

Yuen felt a twinge of impatience in his gut. Not yet noon, the sun was still climbing in the sky. *The smart choice is to abandon these people. How can I help them?* He looked one old man in the eye. Embarrassed to hold his gaze, Yuen looked down and saw the man's right leg was shriveled. He was leaning on a cane.

Yuen shook his head. *Dividing my force would be a mistake— the worst thing I could do.* He looked at David, who stood off to the side with the little girl in his arms. Amazingly, he had managed to quiet her. He'd also gotten a bottle of milk from somewhere, which the child was now eagerly sucking. Yuen noticed two other children: a brother and sister hugging each other, eyes anxious and fearful as their parents argued above their heads. *They won't be able to move anywhere fast. They'll be picked off right away.* Without his help, their death was certain.

And even with his help, there was still a good chance they'd all be killed, including the American airmen.

Yuen saw David staring at him. David's forelock of curly hair had grown past his eyebrows, and he pushed it away with his fingers. There wasn't any anger in David's eyes, no distrust or disappointment—just expectation.

He would have to make his decision now. Yuen's shoulders slumped; he took off his bulky pack, dropping it to the ground. This sudden move brought a new attentiveness to Yuen. The crowd grew quiet.

"If we help you," he said. "We would have to split my force, some to follow the Americans, others to hide you in the countryside until others can come back for you."

"Please take us!"

"Where?"

"Winter is coming."

The villagers' cries multiplied and morphed into a cacophonous drone of unintelligible speech, until a middle-aged man with bulbous cheeks and a bellowing voice shouted for attention. The crowd quieted, and he said, "I know of some hidden tunnels near the remains of a village outside Hunyuan, but they are hard to find. A relative showed it to me years ago. The tunnels are deep and long and large enough for all of us."

"That's at least a week-long walk from here!" a man exclaimed from the edge of the crowd. He threw his arms up in the air. "How could we possibly make it?"

Yuen replied, "That depends on how long it takes for the Japanese to follow us. Your chances are fair—they will first try to capture the Americans and will think punishing you is far less important. Still, you *must* get as far from here as possible, and Hunyuan is to the northwest, so you'd be moving toward Communist territory."

An old woman pointed her cane at the bulbous-faced man. "But what happened to the village that made those tunnels?" she questioned.

The man's face fell. "The Japanese wiped them out before they could even get into them. I know because two of my cousins lived there. The enemy came at night and killed almost everyone."

The woman stabbed her cane into the ground. "These tunnels—maybe the Japanese have already discovered them. What if we get there and they've been blown up or filled in?"

Yuen said, "If you make it that far you'll be closer to safety and can continue westward. If you stay here, you'll be dead by tomorrow."

He stopped talking, and after some deliberation, most of the villagers decided to flee. A few families wanted to stay, and several young men chose to leave in groups of two or three. Yuen hated to see it end this way, for this left fewer able men to help with supplies and the elderly.

Yuen reluctantly divided his men. Half would stay behind with Yang Lu Gao to help the peasants pack supplies, load up the elderly, and get moving as quickly as possible. Yuen and the others would strike out immediately.

Ready to leave, Yuen took two village councilors aside, both elderly men with white-streaked beards, and asked, "Are there any among you who could care for the child?"

One elder spat on the ground. The other shook his head sorrowfully. His was a kind face, and he said to Yuen, "Please understand that the child's mother was a mean-spirited woman. Over the years she toyed with the affections of many young men in our village. Then she curried favor with the Japanese by sleeping with them."

The old man looked past Yuen to the trees bowing in the wind. "She looked down on the rest of us. She only stayed here because of her grandmother..." He pointed out the crumpled body of an old woman who'd been hit by a stray bullet in the battle. It lay next to a freshly dug grave.

"No one here will care for that wicked woman's half-Japanese girl," the old man said.

David was close enough to hear, and he said, "I'll take her then. I'll bring her with us."

His sudden resolve surprised Yuen. *This is crazy. We can't take care of a baby.* He wondered about leaving David and the child with Lu Gao's men but quickly dismissed this idea. He knew he couldn't return to Yenan without David.

I'll order him to leave her with Lu Gao's group.

But the hard look in David's eyes made him pause.

Yuen glanced at the other soldiers, all of them veterans of many battles with him. *How can I ask one of them to take care of a baby? A commander shouldn't ask something he isn't willing to do himself.* He tried to say it, to give the order, but the words wouldn't come.

"All right," he said at last. "You take care of her."

David, prepared to argue but suddenly mollified, did nothing but stare in astonishment.

Yuen put his pack back on and walked to Lu Gao. He put his hand on Lu Gao's shoulder. "Good fortune to you, old friend."

Lu Gao nodded, saying nothing.

"I know the men do not like the assignment, but I promise we will return for you as soon as we can. If the hiding place is no good, keep moving westward."

Lu Gao nodded again. Yuen started to turn away, then stopped and looked back. His friend looked like he'd aged ten years since the morning.

"I'm sorry about Gu Ying," Yuen said.

Lu Gao's head dipped and he shaded his eyes. Yuen saw the tears and out of consideration turned the other way.

The sun had reached its zenith as Yuen led his men, jogging, out of the village. The Americans' tracks led down the trail toward Fuping, an area known to harbor Communist sympathizers.

What else the path had in store, Yuen could only guess.

TWENTY-SEVEN

Low-lying thicket scratched at David's ankles. They'd jogged the narrow, hilly trail for two hours single file, covering over six miles. David pushed himself hard. He was determined that the child would not slow him down, but the sling he'd made from a long piece of cloth kept slipping, and he feared the baby would fly out of it. He tried holding her in front of him, but this made it hard to run and tired his arms. Bao had kindly lightened David's pack and was carrying his rifle, but David could not help but fall off the pace.

Yuen glanced back and called a halt beside a slow-moving stream. Exhausted, David sat on a large rock. He brought the little girl to his lap, and for the first time, he got a good look at her. Her hair was dark and long—down to her shoulders. Her round eyes seemed outsized compared to her small face. Tiny dimples formed next to her mouth when she smiled.

Can she walk? David stood her up, softening his grip as he tested her legs. The child wobbled unsteadily, eyes darting up to him with a hint of fear. David let go and set her free—she stayed on her feet. With a look of concentration, she toddled forward, barefoot in the dirt by the stream. The men watched, smiling. She took two steps, then another—then another. When it seemed she might go straight into the water, David lurched forward and scooped her up. She giggled and flashed a toothless grin, eyes wide and bright. David smiled back.

"Let me show you something," Jou said, coming up to David. "Take off your shirt." David stood the baby on the ground next to the rock and wriggled out of his shirt. Jou did the same. The bright white skin of David's chest stood out from his tanned arms and neck.

"I once played a mother in an opera," Jou explained. "Some woman showed me how to do this." He tied the two shirts together in a cross and showed David how to fashion this into a baby backpack, with knots secured across his chest and waist. They put the little girl in; she felt light and secure on David's back. He could now move his arms freely.

"That's a lot better, thanks."

"You're welcome," Jou replied. "She's cute."

"Yes, she is."

"I think you did a good thing, saving her."

David nodded.

"What's her name?"

"I have no idea."

"Call her Mei Mei for now," Jou suggested.

David agreed and put Mei Mei on the ground. She walked raggedly toward the stream. Squatting down, she began picking up rocks and tossing them into the water. The little splashes delighted her. A shaft of sunlight broke through the clouds and sparked the stream. David realized how thirsty he was and knelt down to fill his canteen. The water was warm and a little muddy, but he dropped in an iodine tablet and drank it anyway. Then he offered water to Mei Mei. She sipped from the large opening, and then, without warning, she began to cry.

"Oh…great," David said.

She'd wet herself. Her cloth diaper was drenched.

Jou laughed at David's surprise.

"Here," David heard a low voice say, "use this."

It was Yuen, holding out a clean handkerchief. David unpinned the dirty diaper and fashioned a clean one with the handkerchief. Yuen unwrapped a lotus-leaf covered ball of rice, pinched off a bit, and fed it to the little girl. She ate it without fuss.

Yuen eyed David as he knelt by the stream, washing out the wet diaper. He began to regret how stubbornly he'd opposed his decision to save the child. Now that the village was behind them, he saw David's resolve to save one life as more than mere kindness. It was the most selfless thing he'd ever seen a foreigner do.

When the child had eaten the last of the rice ball, Yuen asked, "Would you like me to carry her for a while?"

David gave him a hard look. "No."

Yuen shrugged. Mei Mei seemed to like the movement, for she smiled at him. Yuen shrugged again, which made her laugh. When he held his index finger out to her, she eagerly grasped it with one hand.

"How far ahead do you think they are?" Jou asked.

Yuen looked away from Mei Mei. "I'm not sure," he said. "They have a day's head start, but they must have stayed to the back trails, like us, which would slow them. With only four men carrying a cripple, they could not have gone very far."

A distant, low hum reached their ears.

Yuen was the first to realize what it was.

"Airplane!" he hissed.

The men scattered, scrambling for cover in the underbrush. David clutched Mei Mei and rolled with her underneath a tall azalea bush. He used his hands to keep the branches away from her face and she giggled, thinking it was a game. The engine noise grew louder. David tilted his head back, looking straight up. A small, single engine plane came into view, flying low, inching across the sky.

Not a fighter, David thought. *Fixed landing gear, sputtering engine. Probably reconnaissance.*

The plane slid in a straight line across the sky, giving no indication they'd been spotted. Mei Mei settled down, and for a moment, David almost forgot she was resting on his chest, absolutely still. *She's a good girl*, he thought.

They started out again, walking now, slower than before. David moved much better, and soon Mei Mei fell asleep to the rhythm of his walking. Along the trail there were signs the airmen had preceded them: fresh scuffing of the earth, clusters of overlapping footprints in tight spots where it must have been a struggle to maneuver the sedan chair. The occasional familiar geometric print of U.S. Army issue boots gave David confidence that Yuen was leading them the right way.

"Ehh! Look there!" shouted Jou, pointing to a pile of fallen leaves nestled at the base of an oak tree. Stuffed among the leaves, Jou found a brown leather American bomber jacket with a fur-lined collar that kept flyers warm at high altitudes. Jou held it up, turned it around. A silk map of China and Japan was sewn on the inside lining.

Why did they abandon this? David wondered. *Probably so they won't stick out so much.* He took the jacket from Jou and examined the insignias.

"This group flies B-29s," he said.

The men stared at him with no comprehension.

"The Superfortress!" David stretched both arms out wide. "Huge, silver bombers that can fly higher than anti-aircraft fire can reach, probably even higher than the Zero can reach. They must've finally gotten that airfield at Chengdu ready. This means they are starting to bomb Japan!"

With this news, the men smiled and clapped each other's backs. There was something unthinkable and even romantic about raining bombs on Japan. David shared the feeling.

They pressed on until dusk and their shadows grew long on the trail. David intermittently fed Mei Mei more rice and a little dried fish. She had finished the goat's milk he'd gotten at the village.

Yuen decided they must stop soon. He didn't want to pass the airmen at night, or worse, surprise them and get shot in the dark. He was just beginning to look for a suitable stopping place when a cry rang out in English.

"Hey!"

Thirty yards off the trail, behind an overgrowth of low-lying bushes, a Caucasian face popped up, and man's arm waved to them.

"Hey! American right? Chinese?"

David peered in his direction. The young man was hopping up and down. David raised an arm and shouted back, "Yes, that's right. American with Chinese soldiers!" Speaking English again made his mouth feel strange.

He and the men rushed over. The young man looked to be about eighteen with curly, brown hair and a baby face. An older man lay at his feet next to a sedan chair, rigged with poles. His dark brown hair had streaks of gray. Off to the side, the four young men from the village scrutinized the armed Chinese, wide-eyed but not afraid.

David held out his hand. "I'm David Parker, from General Stilwell's staff. These are Chinese soldiers with me."

The young man grabbed his hand and pumped it. "I'm Billy Johansson. Wow, glad to see you, but what are you doing out here?"

"Looking for you."

"I don't understand."

"We came upon that village you landed near. The Japs were there looking for you. We followed your trail."

Billy grinned. "Thank God. When we heard you comin' we thought you must be Japs, but when I spotted you, I knew you had to be an American." He glanced down. Suddenly embarrassed, he said, "And, sorry, this is the captain."

Grimacing, the wounded captain held up his hand. David took it gently.

"Pleased to meet you. I'm Scott Masket, Army Air Corps." The captain pointed to his right leg. "Broke, I'm afraid. Hurts somethin' fierce." The leg was bent outward at mid-calf, where a piece of tibia was pressing hard against the inflamed skin.

"Well, Captain, we've got to get you some help," David said. "It's been quite a race trying to catch up to you."

"I still don't get what you're doing out here in the middle of nowhere."

"I'm on patrol with these men from the Communist base in Yenan. We stumbled on that village, just before all the people were about to be massacred by the Japs for helping you."

Captain Masket's eyebrows shot up. "What happened?"

"We stopped them, killed all the Japs."

David looked up and saw Yuen talking to the four villagers. He lowered his voice. "But we know they radioed some of their buddies, so we have to assume they're out looking for you. For us."

Captain Masket heaved a sigh. He slumped back and rolled his eyes, the look of a man who couldn't catch a break.

The four villagers emitted a sharp, collective gasp, causing David, Billy, and Captain Masket to look their way. Fear spread across their faces. David tilted his head to listen. Yuen was telling them about the massacre the Japanese had planned and how the villagers had left in search of a hideout.

"Tell me," the Captain asked David, "do you speak Chinese?"

"Yes, I do."

"That's good. We've had a hell of a time talkin' to these fellas." He jutted a thumb at the villagers. "They've helped us, sure, but mostly we get the sense they just want to dump us somewhere."

"Whose baby is that you're carrying?" Billy asked. Mei Mei was asleep on David's back.

"It's a little girl whose mother got killed back in the village."

Seeing Billy point to the girl, Yuen said to David in Mandarin, "The villagers say the girl's name is Su Pei."

David nodded. He looked at the four men. If they felt any disapproval of Su Pei or her mother, they didn't show it.

Billy stared at Su Pei, fascinated.

"What happened to you guys?" David asked, pointing skyward.

Captain Masket sighed, and slowly explained, "We were out of Chengdu, planned to be over Tokyo yesterday morning. After takeoff we realized no oxygen was coming through our masks—there must have been a leak. So going to high altitude was out, and we broke off from the formation to fly lower."

The Captain paused, as if the memory pained him.

"Three hours into it, coming up on Peking, four Zeros attacked us. They must've been on the alert because the main formation passed by ahead of us. We didn't stand a chance all alone against those fighters. They shot off our starboard wing; we went into a spin. I ordered abandon ship, but it was hell trying to get out. I barely managed to find the door myself. I think I was only a few hundred feet up when my chute opened, and I came down really hard—broke my leg, obviously. Lucky for me, Billy landed nearby."

Masket slumped back, finished.

"We sure were lucky these Chinese were so close," Billy added.

"Yes," David said. "And now with all of us helping, we'll be able to move much faster."

Yuen asked David, "Now that we have them, do you think they could start moving now? It will be slow carrying the wounded one in the dark, but we could make progress."

David asked Billy and the captain, who both enthusiastically agreed.

The four villagers were offered the chance to join if they wished, and they did. Yuen didn't tell them what he thought—that sticking with them could be a bad decision. Traveling undetected would be much more difficult amidst an all-out Japanese manhunt, and he was sure that manhunt had already begun.

Twenty-Eight

The dense gray clouds hung low, dimming the moon. David heard but couldn't see the man in front of him. He walked carefully, searching for firm footing on the overgrown, rocky trail. Su Pei's body was warm on his back, a comfort and yet another reason not to stumble and fall. Grunts from the men carrying Captain Masket were interspersed with the piping of crickets. Other than footfalls, the only other sound was the constant noise of night insects. After two hours of punishing slowness, Yuen called for a rest.

Four hours later, they were up and prepared to move again. The men gnawed on hard, stale bread as the sun's glow appeared on the eastern horizon. Both Jou and Yuen offered to carry Su Pei, and this time David acquiesced, secretly pleased when Su Pei clung to him and cried as he passed her to Jou.

With the men taking regular turns at carrying the captain, the group covered seven miles by midday. Su Pei fussed with Jou, so Yuen took her. She seemed to accept the transfer willingly and let Yuen tie a loose rag around her head to keep the sun off her neck.

Small hills, then larger ones, slowed their progress as they moved westward. Yuen stopped the group at the edge of a steep rise, the crest of a hill, many pine trees. The others rested, while Yuen stared at a very different landscape.

It was a long, flat valley. The expanse stretched far to the north and south, lush and green. Across it, a half mile away, the land rose again, a chain of foothills running parallel to the range on which they stood. One straight, lonely road traversed the valley floor.

Yuen hesitated. Straight across would be the fastest, most direct route. *But also too exposed.* Looking left and right, there was no narrowing, no safer crossing. In fact, the valley opened up to a plain farther to the north. As far as he could see, the valley and road were empty.

He decided to go straight across.

The group of sixteen men, including David, the four villagers, Captain Masket, and Billy, descended the hill and emerged onto the soft valley floor. *More than soft*, Yuen thought. *This is from more than just rain—some kind of bog?*

Sunlight had yet to reach the base of the valley. Small groups of cattails grew in patches of shallow standing water. Knee-high sawgrass hid the sticky mud that sucked the soles of Yuen's shoes, slowing him. Three times he lifted his foot completely out of his shoe.

Yuen reached the road. *Halfway across.* The elevated roadbed was hard-packed dirt, the single lane straight and dusty. Yuen glanced up and down its length. *No one in sight.*

He looked back. The sedan chair had fallen behind. *We've got to get moving.* He took another close look at the road and saw fresh tire tracks, several of them.

This road is well traveled.

Suddenly, his eye caught sight of a quick-moving shadow gliding across the ground. Yuen's head jerked upward, a sense of dread in his gut.

He squinted at the sky.

Nothing.

A reddish hawk floated overhead.

Yuen exhaled slowly.

"Come on, let's get across," he called to the men. "Bao, Jou, please give them a hand," he said, pointing to the sedan chair.

Yuen felt something wriggling on his back. He jumped, startled. Now he remembered. Su Pei. He'd taken her from Jou. She made a whining sound.

"Shh," Yuen coaxed over his right shoulder. He bounced at the knees, hoping the movement might settle her, but she was close to crying. Then he realized the sun was shining on her face. He turned around to face the other way and she quieted.

The sedan chair finally reached the road, which they crossed, and the whole entourage descended the short but steeply banked roadside, continuing west. Grasses around them bowed to gusts of wind, which rolled down the long axis of the valley. The rustling sound was pleasant, and it was easy to picture the men wading through a sea of grass. Yuen observed they were halfway between the road and the wooded foothills ahead.

Then, a sudden shout. Jou's voice, high pitched, alarmed.

"Japanese!"

Yuen spun and saw a convoy of two troop trucks and a jeep in the distance, coming from the north. A plume of dust kicked up behind the vehicles. The trucks sped up.

"Run!" Yuen shouted.

They would not reach the tree line in time. The Communists sludged across the muddy ground, stumbling and cursing while trying to crouch low. Behind them, the trucks skidded to a stop. Two dozen soldiers clambered out, bayonets affixed to rifles.

Yuen stopped. The trees ahead were tantalizingly close. Thirty yards, maybe less, and Yuen was closer than anyone.

He looked back. *We're spread all over the place. No cover. Where's the sedan chair? Dammit! Get moving!*

Still forty yards back, the chair was an easy target. Yuen looked past it to the enemy soldiers bobbing through the boggy ground with speed that surprised him.

Have to make a stand. Yuen spread his arms out, barked orders.

"Stop! Stop! Form a line, covering fire!"

The men obeyed, dropping into the grass behind a few small boulders. Steady fire began. Enemy soldiers dove into the grass; some were hit.

"Keep it up!" Yuen shouted. He squeezed off two bursts with his PPS-43. Smoke in the air; the steady sound of the B.A.R off to the side.

"Get down!" a voice bellowed at him—Bao, carrying the sedan chair with the others, straining, running.

Yuen ducked down. Su Pei was screaming.

"You!" Yuen hollered, pointing at the four villagers. "Keep going with the American!"

He knelt down to untie Su Pei from his back.

Zip! Zhap!

Bullets incoming, zinging, cutting grass. Yuen held Su Pei out to Jou.

"No. I'm staying here," Jou said, kneeling, both hands on his rifle.

"Shut up and take her. That's an order. Get those Americans as far from here as you can. I rely on you."

Jou made a face.

"Get out of here! There's no time!"

Jou gathered Su Pei into his arms. He handed his rifle to Yuen and ran after the sedan chair.

Yuen flinched. A bullet hit nearby rock. He peered through the smoke and saw the enemy scrambling forward one by one in isolated spurts.

The young one. Yuen searched for Billy, saw him behind a rock shooting his pistol. Yuen ran to him, crouching low. He pulled Billy's shoulder.

Billy looked up, surprised, fright in his eyes, his pistol barrel smoking. Yuen jerked his thumb to the woods. *Go on, get back.*

Billy ran for the trees.

Yuen scanned the battle line. The Chinese were using the M-1s with accuracy. A soldier beside Yuen was firing steadily: one, two, three, four shots—*clink!*

The clip ejected. Yuen saw two Japanese fall, then another. Somehow they seemed to be moving in slow motion.

Now THEY'RE stuck in the mud! Yuen thought.

The soldier jammed another clip in, took aim, then cursed: "Ma de! Zhong danle!"

He fell back, shot in the arm.

Yuen ducked. *Where's David? I've got to get him out of here too.* He looked, peering through the smoke. *Where is he?*

Finally Yuen saw him, lying prone with the B.A.R. at the other end of the line, his brown hair barely visible above the grasses. *Too far. He's on his own.* Yuen did a quick count. *Three men down.*

He faced front, gasped at the close enemy, their greater numbers. He crouched down, planted Jou's M-1 on a boulder, fired at a darting Japanese soldier and missed.

The soldier dove into the grass. Yuen gripped the rifle hard. A dark green cap popped up to the left. Yuen yanked the rifle over and fired two quick shots. *Damn! Nothing. Calm down!* He tried to slow his breathing. Flashes of fire from the grass. No targets. A comrade yelped next to him, on the right, falling over.

Yuen jerked the rifle right, left, scanning, frustrated. Movement in the corner of his eye, gone before he could react. Then, the soldier from before rising up right in front of him, beginning to run. Yuen took dead aim at the man's chest, leaned forward, lifted the rifle a little to get a clear shot, and squeezed the trigger.

A sudden punch in Yuen's left shoulder. He dropped Jou's rifle, his hand going to the wound. He tried to get up but another punch hit his right thigh. He felt the slug pass through to the other side. Unable to prevent it, he toppled forward into the grass.

He blinked hard and brought the mud into focus. He stared at the blades of grass, dazed. His left ear, planted in the mud, heard the vibrations of stomping feet, the echo of gunfire. The stabbing shoulder pain was intense, worse than the thigh, and it brought him back to the present. Sounds through his right ear grew louder: shots cracking, screams.

Get up. Get up!

Yuen willed himself to move. He reached for the strap of his PPS-43 and slung it over his neck with his right arm. He tried to push up, but a bolt of pain lanced through his shoulder. He dropped down again.

Then hands were tugging at him, rolling him over.

David.

"We've gotta go!" David shouted.

Yuen gritted his teeth. "Leave me."

He saw David's eyes dart up, heard Bao's voice off to the left. "Go! Go! Get him out of here!"

David hoisted Yuen, tried to bring the left arm over his neck. Yuen howled. Switching to the other arm, David began to drag Yuen toward the trees, but he was dead weight.

David stopped. He knelt down and let Yuen fall over his shoulder. Grunting, he then stood, lifting Yuen with a fireman carry, and drove forward, forcing his eyes to see only the tree line thirty yards away.

Twenty yards.

Ten.

Yuen grimaced as David crossed the tree line and went up a short rise, ground drier here. David sat him down quickly and looked back.

Only four Chinese remained. They were outnumbered two to one—the attackers almost on top of them. Now fighting hand to hand. Men wrestling and tumbling to the ground.

Two Chinese were bayoneted.

Another was shot at close range.

One left standing, a big man—Bao! He'd just killed a Japanese soldier with his knife and was now wrestling with another, smashing the man's head against a boulder.

Three soldiers raised their rifles. Bao roared—his only weapon the knife—and charged. The bullets thumped into his chest. He staggered, still driving forward like an enraged animal. The Japanese soldiers scurried back, one fumbled to reload, dropping his clip in the grass. Bao slowed, stumbled, and dropped to his knees, head down, gasping for air.

One soldier lunged forward and bayoneted him in the chest.

David rolled back behind a tree trunk, breathing hard, bracing himself for what would come next. Pine needles on the tree's lower branches brushed the top of his head. He peeked around again.

Six Japanese left, shouting, pointing at him.

"Go on! Get out of here!" Yuen stammered. He slumped against the tree at David's feet.

David shook his head. He reached down and took Yuen's PPS-43 from around his neck. The stock was bent at an angle. He extended it fully and darted to his left, behind another tree, away from Yuen. Bullets whizzed by, peppering the ground. He turned, pressed close against the tree, and opened fire—hitting two soldiers.

Then: *click*.

Click.

What the hell? David lifted the rifle. The clip was empty after only half a dozen rounds. Disgusted, he threw it aside.

Four more Japs, he counted, twenty yards away. He saw one kneel, rifle raised. David dropped behind the tree as the bullet struck bark and sent it flying like shrapnel. He drew his Colt .45, right hand shaking. He pulled his dagger from its sheath with his left hand. Then he held his breath, knowing his aim was worthless at anything but point-blank range.

A quick glance showed the enemy heading straight at him, not spreading out to surround him. When he dared not wait any longer and imagined them only a few feet away, he spun and fired at the closest body.

He aimed for the soldier's chest but hit the man low in the gut. Close behind, he shot another in the shoulder, barely grazing him—but the man yowled and fell over.

A third charged with a bayoneted rifle. David jumped to the side to dodge the thrust, but he stumbled and fell on his back. The attacker lunged again, thrusting his bayonet into the ground inches from David's hip.

David shot him in the face.

Before David could think, he saw a blur to his right and raised his arm in defense.

A terrible pain seared his forearm as the last soldier's bayonet sliced deeply.

David dropped his pistol.

The soldier was on him, knife drawn. He wore round spectacles. Sweat dripped on the inside surface of his lenses, pooling there, magnifying his eyes.

David rolled to his left, just dodging a knife thrust near his right ear. With a hard roll back to the right, he plunged his blade, left-handed, into the man's torso.

He felt the tip hit the thin man's spine.

The soldier's body went rigid. He screamed, anguished, animal-like. David jabbed his blade in again and again, digging to the right, then the left. Then he pulled out and pushed the body away.

The dying man's face looked small, his glasses fallen off.

David got up and stumbled to Yuen.

The wounded Japs—he saw them now, the ones he'd shot, crawling ineffectually. He helped Yuen to his feet and they started to climb the hillside. Only then did David begin to hear the cries, the horrible howls of the eviscerated soldier.

They drove up and on, not looking back, and the sounds grew farther and farther away.

TWENTY-NINE

En route to Yenan, November 7, 1944

The crumpled hills lay below looking like an old cast-off rug.
     A *wasteland*, Katherine thought, as the plane's drone
bore into her skull and gave her the dull throb of a headache.
Even that was less of a discomfort than the strange feeling of
being the only woman on a plane full of military men, none of
whom missed the pretty pink blouse and pleated skirt she was
wearing. Still, she had to smile remembering how easily she'd
been given a pass to join General Hurley's mission to Yenan—his
staff was only too eager to grant her permission to cover the
historic breakthrough Hurley promised to broker.

     Thus far, Hurley had failed the president's primary charge to
improve relations between Chiang and Stilwell, whose

relationship remained as acrimonious as ever. In Katherine's eyes, the job was nearly impossible. The failure seemed to have no effect on Hurley's confidence, however. The general was positively set on tackling the next biggest problem: relations between the Nationalists and Communists.

General Hurley's hell-bent on being the savior of China, Katherine thought as she tried to block out the plane's loud engine noise. *He may not succeed, but one thing's certain, he's sure to make an entertaining go of it.*

Preparing for the trip had helped her stop thinking about An Li, who'd disappeared after their quarrel. At first, Katherine had thought she'd just needed to be alone, like her. After two days, she decided to look for An Li, but she was embarrassed to admit that she had no idea where her friend lived. Finally, she'd gone to the Nationalist liaison, the man who'd originally brought An Li to the British embassy for work as an interpreter. To her dismay, no one seemed to know where she had gone, and Katherine had to conclude that her rejection had driven An Li away, perhaps for good. It was a cold, hard fact she was still coming to terms with.

But now the plane touched down and bumped along the dusty airstrip, an unnaturally flat plain nestled amongst the craggy hills that surrounded it.

Looking out her window, Katherine saw Colonel Barrett and Zhou Enlai at once, but she was surprised there was no one else waiting for the plane to arrive. Barrett and Zhou were conversing like they were barely aware the plane was there. Their faces registered complete surprise when General Hurley disembarked, ramrod straight and squared off in his full dress, medal-blazoned uniform.

To Katherine, it seemed the two men had no idea Hurley was arriving!

Zhou whispered something into Colonel Barrett's ear, and when Barrett whispered back, Zhou's eyes widened. Then, without a word to General Hurley, Zhou walked briskly off the field toward the city.

Katherine and the others deplaned and began to unload, taking time to stop and stare at the unfamiliar landscape and relish the dry air. The lonely sound of the whipping wind befitted the open landscape that seemed to stretch as far as the eye could see.

Soon, an old Chevrolet ambulance pulled up to the plane. Out stepped Mao Zedong, Zhu De, and Zhou, as well as a hastily assembled honor guard of a half-dozen men.

"Yahoo!" General Hurley bellowed.

His outburst, reminiscent of an Indian war cry, stunned both Chinese and Americans alike. An awkward silence followed. Even Zhou was at a loss for words, uncertain if a like response might be expected. Oblivious, Hurley sauntered forth and proceeded to pump Mao's hand up and down.

Mao was quick to recover and offered a warm welcome to the new guests. He suggested some group photographs, and when this was done, Hurley, Barrett, and Mao climbed into the ambulance and bumpily sped back to the city.

Katherine walked with the others into town, guided by the six Communist soldiers who were dressed in homespun, gray cotton shirts and short-billed caps. Rifles previously held at attention were now slung behind their backs.

Don't get your hopes up, Katherine told herself. *He probably isn't even here.* There'd been no letters from David, and so she assumed he'd not returned.

The journalists were shown to their barracks: a long, adobe-style building near a few others the Dixie Mission used for meals and meetings. Around every corner, Katherine checked for any American who might know about David, but there were none.

She hid her disappointment, set her bags in the sparsely furnished room, and asked one of the hosts where the first group of Americans was billeted. An escort pointed to a hill behind the complex. Thanking him by clasping her hands together and giving a short bow, she walked in that direction, skirt billowing in the wind.

She found Jack Service sitting on a porch fronting the row of cave dwellings. He was scribbling in a notebook when she came up to him.

"Hullo Jack," she said.

Jack looked up and almost fell off his stool. "Katherine! What are you doing here?"

"I came in with General Hurley. He's here to meet the Communists. I'm the British press corps, it seems."

"Hurley's here?"

"Indeed he is."

Katherine filled him in on their arrival. When she told him about the surprise on Zhou's face, Jack chuckled.

"Wish I'd been there to see it," he said. "We had no idea he was coming."

Katherine ran her hand over the rough earthen wall behind Jack. Then she stuck her head into the open doorway, peeking inside the small, dim room.

"Fabulous place you've got here, Jack." She gave him a little smirk.

"Hotel Savoy, Yenan style. Actually, they've been awfully nice to us. No complaints."

"That's what I've heard."

Jack grinned. "The people *are* something. You'll see."

"Yes, we shall see."

She took a long breath and leaned against the wall. "David's not here, is he?"

Jack's smile slipped away.

Katherine's heart stopped.

"Katherine, right now all we know is that his group saw action. Heavy action. The Communists got word through their underground network, but even that information was at least a week old. Apparently, they rescued some downed airmen, but they had some casualties after engaging the Japs. They're supposed to be on their way back, but we don't know where they are at the moment."

Katherine's eyes filled with tears. She could not stop them, and she didn't try. The long separation from David, the breakup with An Li, the sordid night with Enfield—all of these had made her want David again. David, the way he was when they first met: shy, a little aloof, sensitive, and much more innocent than she ever could've imagined. She wanted that David. And now he was gone, and she felt her heart sinking into an abyss. Somehow, all this time, she'd held fast to the hope that they'd be together again. She felt herself falling, the light dimming. His absence seemed almost unendurable at that moment.

Jack stood up and touched her shoulder. "I'm sure he's alive, Katherine. You and I know what an amazing guy he is. If anyone's alive, he is."

"I hope you're right about that..." Her voice trailed off. She shuddered. "Why did I know something terrible like this would happen?" She glanced at Jack, who seemed unsure of what to say. "He already feels so...gone."

Jack said nothing, but handed her a handkerchief.

Katherine wiped her tears and forced a brave but false smile. "So go on, Jack, tell me what this place is really like, what you do for fun, and if there are any good-looking girls."

He offered a weak half-smile of his own. "Oh, you may find the women here a bit forward. Why don't I show you around?"

"Please do."

They started walking down the hill.

"Really, I'm sure David will be back," Jack said.

"I'm sure," Katherine replied.

And she wished she really were.

THIRTY

Shaanxi Province, January 1945

The man tou was dry and crumbly, but David devoured the pale, yellow bun just the same. He'd come to the small hut to visit Yuen, and he was glad to be out of the cold night air. Yuen was sleeping, curled in a corner on top of a thin, brown blanket laid on the pounded earth floor. The walls were made of straw and mud bricks. A single candle burned, set on top of a wooden crate in the center of the room.

David swallowed, exhaled. The vapor of his breath hung in front of his mouth: a ghost, insufficiently present. With his arms outstretched to either side, he could almost touch opposite walls of the hut. He sat down next to Yuen and leaned against the wall. Yuen lay on his side, wrapped in two coats. He'd endured the six-week-long trek since the battle. Now, a day's march from Yenan, David tried to remember the city almost four months ago. It seemed like a lifetime away.

A wooden latch connected to the outside went up, lifting a piece of rope off its hook. The door opened slowly. A middle-aged woman with a broad forehead and matted black hair entered, shutting the door behind her. She smiled at David, showing her blackened teeth. In one hand, she held a faded, blue porcelain bowl, the rim chipped in two places. It was full of broth, steaming, but not too hot to hold.

"Ji," she said. *Chicken.*

David raised his eyebrows; his nostrils widened as he inhaled the wonderful aroma. The woman smiled again and knelt before him. Her hand disappeared into the folds of her patchwork overcoat. She drew out something wrapped in brown cloth, handling it with the greatest care.

"Ji dan," she said. *Egg.*

She presented it to David ceremoniously. David felt his heart swell with gratitude for this stranger and her simple act of great sacrifice. He knew what a chicken meant to these peasants, what an egg meant. In the best of times they might butcher one chicken a year. He shook his head, tried to push the gift back, but she held it out to him again and nodded toward Yuen.

David looked at Yuen and hesitated, then he looked at the woman and dipped his head slowly. Pleased, the woman passed David the soup and egg. She rose to her feet. Dirt from the ground clung to her thin pants at the knees.

The woman lifted the latch on the door, but before she walked out, David remembered to ask, "How is Su Pei?"

The woman chuckled. "She is fine. Do not worry."

The woman left. David knew Su Pei was in good hands. Kind women had cared for her in the last three villages. In one of them, a mother of four even offered to adopt her. Yuen had advised against it.

"There is a good orphanage in Yenan," he had told David. "The war's made a lot of orphans, and they're adopted readily. It is considered very patriotic to adopt a child. A couple in Yenan would do better for her than these peasants."

David smiled when he pictured Su Pei charming villagers wherever they went. The soldiers had come to love her too, and she got the best of each man's rations. They'd even made a game of having their names be her first words, but there was still no understanding of the little girl's cheerful babbling.

David listened to Yuen's rhythmic breathing. *I should get some sleep too*, he thought. His mind drifted; he daydreamed of his cot in Yenan, of the tepid bathwater, and the outhouse. He chuckled when he recalled Billy's crestfallen face the other day, when he'd asked about Yenan. *Have we been talking about Yenan like it's Paris? I don't know where the kid got the idea that it's some sort of desert spa. There are no showers, no white sheets.* David chuckled again. Billy had acquitted himself well on the journey by doing more than his share of work and showing special concern for Captain Masket. The captain's leg was in bad shape. The broken bone had partially healed, the large bump under the skin ossifying, becoming hard. Without ever having been set properly, he would probably never walk again without crutches—so a Chinese doctor had told Yuen. David overheard this but didn't say anything to the captain.

Yuen stirred and took an offbeat breath. David held the bowl of soup in his hands, enjoying the warmth. He saved it for Yuen and tried to avoid smelling it, so as not to tempt himself. Cupping the bowl with one hand, David clenched his right fist, testing the muscles of his forearm. He felt the thickened skin stretch tight underneath his jacket. *Thick scar but not painful*, he thought.

He'd been lucky the bayonet gash wasn't as deep as he'd first feared. His meticulous efforts to keep it clean had kept it from getting infected before they'd found a village doctor capable of stitching it up. The same doctor had managed to remove the bullet from Yuen's shoulder.

Yuen coughed. The collar of his coat was turned up, covering the bottoms of his ears. He moved his arms and legs and rolled onto his back, blinking.

"You're awake?" David asked.

Yuen gave a quick nod, sat up, and leaned against the wall of the hut.

"Already dark?" he muttered, gazing mistily through the gap under the door.

"Yes. I've got food for you."

David passed him the bowl. Yuen took it and looked into David's eyes for a moment. The folds of Yuen's forehead and crow's feet seemed etched more deeply in the shadowy candlelight, and his eyes looked tired and a little sunken.

Yuen drank the soup hungrily. Then David handed him the hard-boiled egg and his eyebrows lifted.

"Where did you get this?"

"One of the women gave it to me—gave it to you, I mean."

Yuen stared at the brown egg almost as if he didn't know what it was. Small black dots speckled the shell.

"Please eat it," David urged. "I tried to refuse it; it would be impolite to try again."

Yuen rubbed his jaw with his hand, his fingers running over a thin, patchy beard.

"All right. But you eat half."

Yuen tried to wipe the dirt off his fingertips before cracking the shell and peeling it away. He took one bite, filling his mouth with half the egg, and handed the other half to David.

David took a smaller bite. The yolk crumbled in his mouth; he pasted it to the roof of his mouth with his tongue. He'd never tasted anything so delicious.

"Ready to go home tomorrow?" David mumbled.

Yuen grunted.

Yes, David thought.

He'd learned Yuen's guttural responses to such questions, and yet he asked them anyway. Over a month in close quarters now, and they knew one another quite well. Wounded, Yuen wasn't as commanding as usual; the forced inactivity had mellowed him. With David's arm injured, the other men usually insisted he join Yuen in preferential accommodations like the hut, and the two had passed many nights talking for hours. Yuen spoke about a great many things, and David listened.

He told David of his past. Just two nights ago, he'd spoken of attending the earliest Communist meetings at Peking University. One of his mentors, a librarian named Li Dazhou, invited him to go.

"Perhaps the old man, Li, I mean, saw something in me, though I was only an ill-tempered island boy. He took me, so I went," Yuen recalled. He laughed as he remembered. "Sometimes it was only a half dozen of us—students, teachers— meeting in some dusty classroom to discuss world politics, Marx, Lenin. Little did I know how the seeds planted in those rooms would change everything..." Yuen shook his head as if he still couldn't believe it. "And I certainly had no idea that I might spend most of my life being a soldier."

Without ever saying it, Yuen seemed to trust David. He'd never said anything about the battle in the valley, and if he felt any special gratitude, David never knew it. This didn't bother David. It felt good enough to know he'd done the right thing— the honorable thing—and survived.

David finished the last of the egg and squinted at a spider web in the opposite corner of the hut. Even in the faint light, he could see a trapped fly buzzing as it tried to break free.

"What do you think will happen after we win the war?" David asked.

Yuen brought a fist to his mouth and breathed into it. "You sound certain we will win it." David looked for a smile, a chuckle, the hint of a joke, but Yuen's face was unchanged. "When I was your age, I was optimistic too."

"Where were you then?"

"Let's see, how old are you?"

"Twenty-five."

"Twenty-five…twenty-five…" Yuen scratched his head. "We were already on the run at that time."

"On the run?"

"From the Nationalists. After they betrayed us."

David nodded, as if making clear he was familiar with the history. "You mean you were already fighting back when the two sides were united?"

"Of course!" Yuen laughed. "Don't you know I've been doing this for a very long time? I was one of the first Whampoa cadets."

David whistled. He'd not known Yuen was a graduate of Whampoa, the West Point of China.

"Chiang Kai-shek was the commandant and Zhou Enlai was the political officer. It was a special time. An *optimistic* time. There were young cadets from all over China, all of us wanting to unify the country, foolishly thinking that that goal would override all other differences." He took a long breath. "But it was a mirage. Zhou was popular with the cadets and influenced many toward Communism. Tensions developed. A friend of mine stopped talking to me. He knew I went to the Communist meetings, and *he* had sworn an oath to Chiang. It all eventually led to the betrayal..."

Yuen stopped. He scuffed the heel of his sandal into the soft earth, making a small mound, which he then carefully flattened.

"Would you tell me what happened?" David asked.

Yuen pretended not to hear. He closed his eyes, and what was then became now in his mind. For a moment, he let the memory sweep him along like a river current.

It was 1927, during the struggle for Shanghai—a vital objective of the Northern Expedition and one of Chiang's biggest obstacles in his quest to wrest control of the country from the warlords. Yuen was with Chiang's army outside the city when he learned that Shanghai's Communists had completed their part of the plan—to organize a massive worker's strike and take control of the city—all before the army even arrived.

Yuen was ecstatic—this was one city they could take without a fight. When the army entered Shanghai, the Communist-led union workers laid down their arms...all according to the plan.

Then—the day Yuen would never forget.

He'd gotten separated from his unit after stopping to help a young boy find his parents. They were supposed to regroup at an old textile factory not far from the foreign concession.

When he got there the first floor was deserted.

That's odd, he thought.

Shouts on the second level. Yuen took the stairs three at a time.

Breathing hard, he was about to open the door wide when he heard the first shot. The door was ajar, and through the crack, he saw the body fall. A flurry of flashes, the reverberating sound of a volley. Yuen threw his back against the wall next to the door.

Men of his unit were executing their own soldiers!

Yuen blinked hard, eyes wet, confused. He'd looked carefully at the kneeling victims for a split-second, long enough to recognize the faces and understand.

They're executing the Communists!

Shouts through the doorway, sounds of a struggle, then isolated pistol shots.

Yuen dashed down the stairs, burst out into the open, and ran. He ran out of the city and somehow linked up with other survivors of what, he learned, had been a well-organized purge of Communists and union workers in Shanghai and other cities across China. Thousands were killed. The survivors, including Zhou Enlai, went into hiding. From that day on, Chiang made Communism illegal in all of China.

"Yuen?" David said.

Yuen looked at him strangely.

"I was asking if you'd tell me what happened."

Yuen rubbed his eyes, shook his head. "I don't remember it so well," he said. "I'm sorry."

The door to the hut opened. Jou stepped in, rubbing his hands.

"Shut the door!" Yuen barked.

Jou closed it quickly, but not before the cold air leapt in, almost blowing out the flickering candle. Stooping, Jou ducked low so his head wouldn't hit the roof. Then he hunkered down opposite David and Yuen.

"Are the men all right out there?" Yuen queried.

Jou drew a crooked cigarette out of his pocket. His thin, calloused fingers trembled in the cold as he lit it. He took a long drag and the tip glowed as he inhaled.

"The men are fine," he said. "These villagers said they had a decent grain harvest. Not great, but the best in years. They're grateful to some comrades who helped them bring it in a few months ago." He exhaled. The cloud of smoke—and the smell—filled the room. "So they're inclined to share what they have."

Jou looked at David curiously. "Well, David—was it worth it being on this rough-and-tumble mission with us?"

David leaned against the mud wall next to Yuen. "Worth it? That's a funny way to put it. We survived, didn't we?"

Jou cupped the cigarette in his hands, as if garnering its heat for some future use. He grinned. "So, what will you tell your powerful friends? That we fight well? That we should be armed with the very best weapons?"

Yuen snorted, glanced at Jou. His eyes said the rest: *leave it.*

"I'll tell them what happened," David said.

"All of it?" Jou asked.

"All that I saw with my own eyes. It's not up to me, but I'd sure like to see you get more supplies."

The corners of Jou's mouth flattened. He wanted to say more, but Yuen's face told him not to, and so he clamped his lips shut.

For a while, no one said anything.

Then, Jou asked one more question, but he didn't address it to David and instead spoke philosophically to make it seem like he was merely thinking aloud.

"What is it that Americans have against Communism?"

The question lingered, and David shifted uncomfortably. He felt compelled to give an answer, but he wasn't political. He'd never felt strongly that China should have one type of government over another. He'd only cared about winning the war.

Finally, David said, "I suppose they just think democracy is better. That it's important for people to have choice and to have a say in things. That it's a better system for the people."

"You think Communism isn't 'for the people?'" Jou asked pointedly. "Communism is *of* the people, *by* the people, and *for* the people—like your Lincoln said. The *people* is what Communism is about."

David felt ill-equipped to engage in a debate. He wished Jack or Davies were there to speak for him. Yuen, for his part, listened though he pretended not to.

"Communism in China is different from Communism in Russia," Jou added. "There's no Stalin here, oppressing everyone. It's the old system of rich landlords that oppresses Chinese. You've seen how our people live, how poor and uneducated we are. Our style of Communism is not only the *best* way of uniting this country, it's probably the *only* way."

Jou was leaning forward, only a few feet from David in the small room. Vapor from their breaths intermingled and rose before mixing with the cigarette smoke above. His eyes darted to different parts of David's face, searching for further understanding. When David shrugged, Jou looked at Yuen, who was smiling, eyes closed.

"Well, you've seen how we fight. You need to tell your countrymen," Jou stated.

"What makes you think he won't?" Yuen commented with his eyes shut.

Jou, unsmiling, got up. "I suppose I better go get some rest before we move out in the morning."

He unlatched the door and left. The cold, unwanted and insistent, took his place.

David sighed. "I don't think Jou's happy with me."

"I don't think you really know him," Yuen said. "Don't worry about it. He respects you. Otherwise he wouldn't be talking that openly."

With a hint of sarcasm, Yuen added, "He wants you to believe Communism is perfect."

"And you don't think it is?"

"Of course not."

Of course not?

David wanted to ask Yuen more, but before he could speak, Yuen had already rolled toward the wall, saying, "Put out the light. We have another long walk before we're home."

Another time, David thought. He blew out the candle and lay down on the dirt floor next to Yuen. He pulled the short collar of his overcoat close around his neck and brought his knees up to his body. In the darkness, he heard Yuen's deep breathing and envied his ability to sleep so easily.

Something else I must learn, David said to himself.

And so saying felt himself already drifting off.

PART THREE

War's Ending—War's Beginning

January 1945 – September 1945

THIRTY-ONE

Yenan, January 1945

The low rays of sunset cast haloes of glowing light around the dark, squat buildings at Yenan's outskirts. Above, the doors of cave dwellings were closed, silent. Two small boys, bundled up, the only people in sight, kicked a ball against a crumbling wall.

They saw Yuen's men. One raised a hand—a shout, recognition—and the boys ran off to spread the word.

David rubbed his right shoulder, the thin leather strap cutting into it. Su Pei seemed to have grown heavier—or was it just the long journey? An old couple appeared up ahead, in the road, between the buildings; then a woman, two young girls. By the time the soldiers reached the center of town, a small crowd of twenty had gathered. A woman bumped David as she ran by—not stopping to apologize—a wife, no hat, coat unbuttoned. She sought her husband and flew into his arms. Men moved quickly away with their families, toward home and food, out of the cold. Medical staff arrived to examine Yuen and Captain Masket.

David saw a tall man running toward him, drawing closer, waving his arms over his head.

David smiled; it was Jack. He waved back. Then, as Jack drew near, someone else behind him, running, a wool hat pulled down over her ears—Katherine!

She burst past Jack and ran into David's embrace. Her slender body felt light. David's tired mind spun with questions, but for a long moment, he just held her close and pressed his cheek into the soft top of her hat. Katherine felt welcome relief at David's greeting. She didn't need words to know he felt the same way she did, that the past was behind them, and that they were, for the moment, in the clear, away from danger, and together.

"What is that?" Katherine said as she broke her embrace and glanced at the movement on David's shoulder—his knapsack straps were rising and falling, as if…

"What's doing that?"

Then she heard the babbling of a child, and a small face rose above David's right shoulder.

"Whose baby is this?"

"Well…mine I guess," David said, half-smiling.

Katherine gazed at Su Pei, who was chewing the end of the leather strap.

"It's a long story." David knelt down and began to unbundle Su Pei. "The short version—her mother was killed. I brought her back here."

David gave Su Pei a squeeze. She was heavily bundled against the cold, and he could barely feel her body under the oversized coat she wore. Su Pei touched the stubble under his chin and made a delighted noise. David held her out to Katherine, and the child reached out to touch Katherine's lips.

"Oh my," Katherine said. "She's a dear."

"David!"

It was Yuen; a nurse was pushing him away in a wheelchair. Another nurse walked alongside.

"This nurse will take Su Pei to the orphanage," Yuen said. "They will take good care of her, and you can visit her there."

"I guess that's the way it's going to have to be," David said. He hugged Su Pei again and handed her over to the nurse. Su Pei held her arms out to him as she was carried away, but there were no tears.

Katherine shook her head in amazement. "How long did you have her?"

"About six weeks."

"I would have guessed a lot longer."

David pulled her close with another hug. "I can't believe you're here," he whispered.

Jack patted his shoulder. "Why don't I catch up with you two later?" he said.

"Thanks, Jack, great to see you."

"You were right, Jack," Katherine said, eyes glistening.

Jack smiled. "I know. I told you he'd be perfectly fine."

Katherine put both of her hands on David's shoulders. "So I surprised you?"

"How did you get here?"

"Sometimes a girl has to take matters in hand."

His hands found hers. "Really? How?"

"I came with General Hurley."

"General...who?"

Katherine smiled playfully. "I'll tell you all about it. Meantime, why don't we get you cleaned up?"

They walked to the barracks holding hands. Katherine told him about General Hurley, who'd left Yenan more than a month ago. "He only stayed a few days. The man's a character out of a comic strip."

David looked at her quizzically.

"Larger than life is what I mean," she said. "No disrespect, but I've never seen anyone so deluded. What's more—so ignorant of Chinese customs and manners. He actually pronounced Mao Zedong's name as 'moose dung!'" Katherine chuckled. "Back in Chungking, I heard him once call Chiang 'Mr. Shek.'"

David grinned but said, "It'd be really funny if it weren't so sad."

"You're right about that. So far, he's been a fantastic disappointment. The Communists told him they'd be happy to be part of a coalition government with the Nationalists, as long as they had fair representation. Hurley made them feel like he was completely on their side. Of course, Chiang would have none of it—so, no agreement, and we're no better off than before. The whole charade was merely a chance for Hurley to learn how complicated things are."

"Sounds like a diplomatic disaster."

"It is that, indeed. But I mustn't fuss and fume; it was my ticket here. Nobody minded me staying on, and now that *you're* here"—she squeezed his arm—"I'm so glad I did."

They paused to watch a girl prodding an ox harnessed to a millstone. The stone turned slowly in the gathering dusk, and there was something beautiful about this simple, ancient action—the grating sound, the trickle of crushed grains dropping out of the bottom, the wheel's gravitational rotation and the ox patiently circling.

"You must be starving!" Katherine said. "Should we get some food right away? Why don't you bathe while I find something for you to eat."

David tugged her close to him. "Stay with me a while longer," he said softly.

Katherine looked at him in the fading light, at his dirt-darkened face and the crusty hair sticking up on the left side of his head. There were a couple of new scars but she looked past them into his brown eyes. She wanted to say something, and her mouth opened to say it, but all that came out was, "Of course, dear," as she drifted back into another embrace.

When they arrived at his quarters, Jack wasn't there. David dropped his gear on the floor and walked the length of the room cautiously, like an animal unaccustomed to being indoors. He retraced his steps a few times, then went to the bathhouse while Katherine disappeared to find some food.

She managed to get a hot bowl of noodles from the cook, who she'd found cleaning up in the Americans' mess hall. David returned to the room, his hair damp, face and neck shaved and clean but blemished by a few scabs and scratches.

He sat on a stool at a small table, drawn to the steaming bowl of soup. He burned his tongue with the first taste, then blew on the next spoonful and sipped it carefully. Katherine watched him as he savored each chew and swallow.

When he finished he moved next to Katherine on the bed. He leaned in close to her, so close she could feel his soft, warm breath on her skin. She rested back on her elbows and a shiver ran through her.

"You smell a lot better now," she said.

"Shh," David whispered.

His hand caught the solid warmth of her shoulders as his fingertips ran the length of her collarbone, underneath her thick cotton blouse, and under the thin strap of her black silk camisole.

Her body lowered, and he traced the outline of her hip, letting his hand wander along her side, under her blouse, until he felt the rise of her breast. Gently but firmly, he reached behind her back and raised her body upward, so he could kiss her on the mouth. Her lips were soft and moist, and as he kissed her, he inhaled the sweetness of her breath. Then he captured her dreamy gaze and held it with his own. She was wonderful; she was whole; she was...his.

She tugged at his shirt buttons, pausing to let him pull her blouse up over her head. Katherine murmured deep in her throat. She responded to the pleasure of David's touch. He slid down her pants, and his hand rested again upon her hip, the beauty of it, the hardness of bone and flesh. He worshiped her hip with his hand, caressing it and then moving to the other side and caressing that. Finally, he let his hand flow between her thighs and heard her sigh and felt her body arch.

There was a slight tremor as she let her fingernails go into the hot skin of his back. They were enraptured with touch—not doing more than touching. Just feeling one another's body and relishing the thrill of human contact—close, warm, serene, and safe.

There was a soft knock at the door.

"Hello?" David called, awake but lying in bed, unwilling to move until now. He saw Jack sleeping and wondered how late he'd come in.

The door opened; sunlight burst in.

"Davies!" David said.

John Davies grinned as he set down a tray of scrambled eggs, bacon, and toast on the table. Then he pumped David's hand.

"Great to see you! Thought you might be hungry—for American grub, I mean."

"You bet, thanks." David sat up, the cold air a surprise after the thick blanket. He put his feet into slippers and sat at the table still dressed in a cotton pajama shirt and long johns.

"When did you get here?" David asked between mouthfuls.

Davies watched him eat, amused. He sat on a stool opposite him. "I actually came once before, in late October, but you'd already left by then."

Jack was awake. He stretched his arms up over his head and said, "Good morning. Room service again, Davies? I told you I wouldn't tell your wife about what goes on here."

Davies smiled. "Can it, buddy. You're just lucky you room with this guy."

"You fellas eat like this regularly?" David asked.

Davies nodded. "They keep sending up ration crates. In case we don't like the Communist food, I guess. Not much variety, though."

"I love it. Four months without anything remotely like it."

"Those months probably went by a lot faster for you than they did for us," Jack said.

"I missed Christmas, didn't I? You guys do anything special?"

"We had a little celebration," Jack said. "Despite the religious overtones, the Communists were very curious about it all."

"Did you have a tree?"

Davies laughed. "Are you kidding? See any pine trees in these parts?"

"You mean the generalissimo didn't spring to have one shipped up here?" David quipped.

"Because he's such a fan of the mission, right?" Jack said.

"Right."

Davies leaned forward. "So tell us what happened to you."

David recounted the highlights for his friends: the blockhouse, the battle at the village, Su Pei, and finding Billy and Captain Masket.

"You make it sound like a walk in the park," Davies said admiringly.

"It wasn't that. Have you ever gone four months without bathing?" All three friends laughed.

Jack shook his head as he lay on his side in bed. "I can't believe you carried that baby all the way back."

"It was really all of us helping out."

"It's amazing that no one else would take care of her."

"Maybe so." David paused to swallow. "But I learned a lot about the Chinese. They've been through hell; they're still going through hell. Things that we would consider unbelievable, like letting this girl die, are happening out there. People are just trying to survive."

A few somber seconds passed. David tasted the coffee, raised the mug in a salute to Davies, and took a long drink. "Where's Ray?" he asked.

Jack replied, "You didn't know! Ludden got a mission of his own. He was so envious of you that he went off with the guerillas to Fuping, where some big shot communist named Jin Cha Ji is based."

"Fuping? In Hebei? That's near where we were, too."

"That's right," Davies said. "They left about a month after you did. I told him he was crazy to go with winter so close, but he was determined."

David glanced at the foot of the door, where wind was whistling through the narrow gap. "It's cold out there. I hope he's all right," he said. His friends murmured their agreement.

"So now, what's the situation with supplying the Communists? Is it going to happen?"

Davies groaned, while Jack exhaled and let his head fall back against his pillow.

"That bad?" David said.

Jack answered, "We've written reports in favor of it. Even General Stilwell was in favor of supplying them to some extent. But the Nationalists and plenty of people back home are totally against the idea. Bottom line—no one wants to spend the political capital needed to push Chiang to accept it."

"Why does Chiang matter? Why not just go ahead and do it?"

Jack shook his head. "We know he'd put up such a stink it could further diminish our ability to get him to get off his ass and do some fighting."

"So, same old story," David said. "We're chicken."

Davies added quietly, "And now the Old Man is gone."

"What? Stilwell?"

Davies nodded. "The generalissimo got him recalled; he's already on his way back home. FDR tried to back him, but he couldn't do it anymore without embarrassing Chiang—who's still the head of a sovereign nation, after all. Now Wedemeyer's in charge."

David whistled. Despite his frequent absences and rough-hewn manner, Stilwell was well-liked and respected by his men.

"What's more, Hurley's replaced Gauss as ambassador."

"Hurley? I'd never heard of him 'til Katherine told me last night."

Davies lit a cigarette, took a drag, then held it between his fingers. "Jack and I aren't on the best footing with the new ambassador."

"Just say it; he hates us," Jack said.

"All right, he hates us."

"Why?"

"He doesn't like the—what did he say?—the *tone* of our reports?"

"That's ridiculous."

Davies shrugged. "Anyway, I won't be surprised if he asks for me to be reassigned. I'm expecting it."

"No way. Who else knows more about what's going on here?"

Jack sat up and said, "Let's not dwell on this stuff—too depressing. It would be much more fun to talk about your blissful reunion last night."

David grinned.

"Sorry guys, not telling. Anyway, thanks for giving us the time alone, Jack."

Jack smirked. "Well, you're not welcome until we get some details."

David threw a piece of toast at Jack like a boomerang, hitting him on the forehead.

Jack smiled and wiped the crumbs out of his hair. "And this is the thanks I get." He picked the toast off his bed and stuffed it in his mouth.

～

The hospital's fortress-like façade displayed wide vertical columns that jutted out of the cliffside like the buttresses of a cathedral. Large arched gates filled the spaces between the columns. David steered Katherine toward a pair of thick wooden outer doors.

Katherine liked holding David's arm. For the first time in months, she felt content and truly safe now that she was with him. The last twenty-four hours had been emotionally intense. David had admitted he'd used opium, and he told her how he'd thrown the opium ball away and left it in the dust forever. She believed him when he said it was over. Though she'd resolved not to tell David about Enfield's attack, she did tell him about her ardent friendship with An Li. He listened without interrupting or judging. He'd put it in the past, where it belonged, and afterwards, she'd felt closer to David than ever before.

"I'm looking forward to meeting this man," she said as they entered a dark, windowless lobby. "The way you talk, you're quite fond of him."

"He's a good man. He saved my life out there."

"What?"

"Shh," David chided. An orderly motioned them to follow.

"You didn't tell me about that," Katherine whispered.

"I will."

They entered a long, narrow room with an antiseptic smell and a dozen wooden beds lining each side. Most of the beds were empty, but David saw Yuen lying in one on the far left, a Chinese doctor by his side. Captain Masket slept in a bed nearby.

David walked over and asked, "How's he doing, Doctor?"

The doctor was middle-aged, thin, and bald. He looked over the rims of his reading glasses at David. "He's weak, but he'll heal. Are you the one who brought him back here?"

"Me and some others."

"An amazing feat. You saved his life."

"Well, he's a strong one."

"What he needs now is rest."

David nodded. "Thank you for taking care of him."

The doctor left. Yuen looked tired. Though his wounds had healed over during the journey home, there were fresh, heavy bandages around his shoulder and thigh.

A young girl sat on a wooden chair at Yuen's bedside; David hadn't noticed her at first. Her feet dangled above the floor. She looked about nine years old, with long and tightly braided hair.

"Hello," David addressed the girl in Mandarin, "my name is David Parker, and this is my friend Katherine."

The girl looked at them with narrowed eyes, a penetrating gaze that belied her child-like appearance.

"Mei Mei, these are Ba Ba's friends," Yuen said. "This is *Shu Shu* David." *Uncle David.*

Mei Fong's face softened, but she did not speak.

Yuen said to David, "This is my daughter, Mei Fong. And who is this woman?"

"Her name is Katherine. She's the woman I told you about. I didn't know she'd be here."

"Ah, fortune smiles on you at last," Yuen said, smiling weakly. "I see why, to you, she is like spring's first blossom."

"What are you talking about?" whispered Katherine.

"Just introducing you. Katherine, this is Yuen and his daughter, Mei Fong."

"Pleased to meet you both," she said. David translated.

"Please, sit," Yuen said, gesturing to nearby stools with his good arm. David and Katherine brought them over and sat.

"How are you feeling?" David asked.

"I am fine. They are giving me fluids." Yuen pointed to the glass bottle hanging from a pole next to his bed. "They say I am lucky I did not get an infection."

David touched the faded, brown blanket at the foot of Yuen's bed. "Well, now you've got to rest."

Yuen frowned. "We need to go back for Yang Lu Gao and the villagers," he said, his voice firm.

David had almost forgotten about the other group. "Surely there are others who can go."

"Perhaps, but I am worried no one will because of the winter."

Yuen's head tilted back against his pillow. He stared at the thick beams running across the ceiling. "The Party leaders may not allow anyone to go," he said.

David didn't know what to say. It made sense; the winter could be brutal. Why risk soldiers on a guesswork mission to rescue civilians they might not even be able to find?

Yuen sighed and said, "I will speak to the leadership." He looked directly at David. "I made a promise to Lu Gao."

THIRTY-TWO

Jiang Hong hated the Yenan winter. She'd grown weary of wearing all the clothes she owned day after day—four layers of thin cotton shirts under one beat-up jacket. She particularly hated the jacket, the thrice-mended elbow patches, the mud stains on one arm that wouldn't wash out. She sighed heavily and watched her breath as it drifted toward the wood stove.

The month has been warm in other ways, she thought, trying to cheer up. Zhen Guo's attention had blossomed into a passionate affair. They were careful—getting caught would bring serious consequences, the least of which would be the ruin of Zhen Guo's career. Still, fueled by a passion Jiang Hong had never experienced before, the two lovers managed a morning rendezvous at least a few times each week. With limited time, they'd stopped having long conversations. Sometimes, he rushed or finished too soon, and he'd stopped making thoughtful, chivalrous gestures. The changes irritated her—*but there is nothing perfect under heaven*, she told herself.

She thought of Yuen, the sunken eyes, the bandaged wounds. He looked terrible. She'd only stayed at his bedside for a few minutes that morning. Mei Fong wanted to stay longer so she let her. On the way home, Jiang Hong realized she pitied him, but not because of his wounds. It was because he made such large sacrifices for so little reward. *Any common soldier can bleed and die. Great men lead and decide the fate of others. Yuen's a soldier, nothing more.*

She bundled up the food she'd prepared to bring to him: rice with preserved turnip and spicy red peppers. She wrapped a single warm potato in cloth and placed it in the small pail with the rest. She'd taken a nap—almost dinnertime now.

She heard the door open without a knock and looked up. Zhen Guo appeared, shutting the door quickly behind him.

How handsome he was! Much more so than Yuen. Jiang Hong smiled at him, expecting him to rush her and take her in his arms as he usually did. Instead, he stood there, staring at her, brow furrowed.

"What's wrong?" she asked.

Zhen Guo took a step closer and sat down on a wooden stool. He kept his heavy woolen military coat on but took off his cap and scratched his head.

"How did Yuen look?" he asked.

Yuen? It felt strange to hear him say her husband's name.

"Tired and wounded," Jiang Hong said.

"Yes, I know. Comrade Peng met with him and said he left some men behind to hide civilians from the Japanese. They are hiding out near Hunyuan, and Yuen wants a rescue party to be sent."

"Hunyuan? That's hundreds of miles away! Might as well go to Peking! And in this freezing weather? Anyone who goes is begging to die."

Zhen Guo nodded.

"Yes, that's why Comrade Peng told him he'd not assign another group to go. Then, Yuen insisted he go himself. When Peng refused, Yuen called it a matter of personal honor, because he promised to go back for them. He wants to take a handful of volunteers with him. There's no talking him out of it. In the end, Peng threw up his hands and left the decision up to"—Zhen Guo searched Jiang Hong's face—"me."

"He wants to go even though he can barely walk? That's absurd."

She knew Yuen, but even this surprised her. He was more stubborn than a water buffalo.

Zhen Guo stared silently at the floor.

Jiang Hong turned her back to Zhen Guo and busied herself packing Yuen's meal.

"Would it be very dangerous?" she asked.

"Yes," he said softly. Then, more loudly, "Very dangerous."

A moment of silence passed.

"Would you like me to—"

"Let him go," Jiang Hong interrupted.

"Really?"

She moved to him and started to unbutton his coat.

"Yes, let him go. If he wants to get himself killed, let him. He'll be a martyr, and we'll be free to do as we please."

Zhen Guo's mouth widened into a smile. He kissed her, picked her up, and carried her to the bed mat in the back room.

Yuen's dinner could wait.

—

Yuen was discharged after three days in the hospital. He'd begun to gain weight and strength, but he was under orders to remain at home. Jiang Hong dunked the bowls from lunch into a bucket of murky water, rubbing off the grease with her fingers. Yuen rested on his bed mat in the back room, playing Chinese chess with Mei Fong.

Mei Fong moved one of her round wooden pieces on the paper game board.

"Ba Ba, why did that American man and woman come to see you?"

Yuen studied the board, then made his move. "The man is an American. My friend. And the woman is British. She is his *nu peng you*."

"Girlfriend? Does that mean they are arranged to be married?"

"No, no," he said, chuckling. "They like each other and are trying to decide if they like each other enough to get married."

Mei Fong looked up, confused. "They look too old to *not* be married, or at least arranged to be married."

"Westerners do not have arranged marriages."

She nodded. "I don't ever want an arranged marriage. I don't want to get married at all. I hate cooking and cleaning."

Yuen smiled and suppressed a laugh. He stole a look at Jiang Hong in the front room, who didn't appear to be listening.

"Yes, Mei Mei. You should only marry if the right man comes along and wants to marry you. But I would be sad if you did not marry. How else would you ever know the joy of having a daughter like I have?"

Mei Fong smirked and made her next move on the game board.

The following afternoon, Yuen woke from a nap and stared at the wall, its fine grains like hard-packed sand. He worked his joints.

Am I that old already? Everything's sore.

He tested his shoulder by shrugging it. It ached, but no pain.

Mei Fong will be home soon. I'll get up then.

Clacking sounds from the front room meant that Jiang Hong was knitting. They'd not spoken to each other all day.

His formal request for a ten-man squad to retrieve Lu Gao and the others was under review. He thought about what another mission might be like, then he thought about weeks of staying warm indoors and playing with Mei Fong.

Was it a mistake? Should I stay?

Stop that. There is no choice; there is no one else to do it.

Suddenly, Mei Fong burst through the door panting, grinning.

The wind chilled the room, and Jiang Hong shouted, "Ai ya! Shut the door! Shut the door!"

She closed the door.

"Ma Ma, Ba Ba! They chose me to lead the Youth Guard at school!"

Jiang Hong's knitting needle froze in midair. Her hands dropped to her lap. "Really? That's wonderful!"

Jiang Hong looked at Yuen through the narrow opening to the back room and said, "They're organizing the school into groups to study the Chairman's teachings. It's very important."

"What does this mean she'll do?" Yuen questioned.

"They'll learn the Chairman's words by heart, of course. Also study the Revolution, organize group marching drills. It's quite an honor!"

His face hardened. *Both of them are so excited about this? It's hard to believe Jiang Hong doesn't see this for what it is.*

"What's wrong, Ba Ba?"

"Mei Mei, are you sure you want to do this? Marching around town? Shouting slogans? All performance and—"

"How can you say that?" Jiang Hong broke in. "It's a great opportunity! She'll be leading the students when they march before the Chairman, and there's no greater honor than that!"

Yuen shook his head.

"It's all propaganda. Brainwashing our children."

Jiang Hong turned red.

"Just because you no longer care about the Party, you shouldn't deny your child a chance to rise in it!"

He looked at her coldly. "Are you so blind that—"

He turned to Mei Fong and spoke sternly. "Go outside so your mother and I can talk. Now."

Mei Fong looked on the verge of tears, but she turned and obeyed.

Yuen sighed. *I should just let things be,* he said to himself. He wanted to say something kind to Mei Fong, but she'd already gone.

"What's wrong with you?" Jiang Hong shouted, hands on hips.

What's wrong? What's wrong with Mao's methods of strengthening his hold on people? It's a sham, but how can I reason with her?

"She should be enjoying her childhood, playing with other children, not burdened with responsibilities such as these," Yuen said.

"You're a fool. You've lived your life, had your chance. Why can't you just be happy for her? You go off for months on end. She misses you so desperately; she only wants you to be proud of her. When I married you I never thought you'd be like this. You were the one who convinced me to adopt Communism, remember? That man is gone. You've lost sight of who you are, and you're hurting your daughter."

The words stung, his wife's unfiltered judgment of his life. A long, tense moment followed, a staring contest. Then, a rap at the door. Jiang Hong froze. Yuen wondered if their words could be heard outside.

Jiang Hong opened the door. It was Zhen Guo.

"Good evening, Comrade," he said to Jiang Hong, bowing formally.

Jiang Hong blushed, but her back was to Yuen.

"Good evening. Please, come in."

Zhen Guo entered and stood there rubbing his hands together. Jiang Hong shut the door behind him and went to the stove.

"Yuen, it's good to see you. Feeling better?"

"Yes, Comrade," Yuen said, putting on a welcoming face. "Please, be comfortable." He gestured to the stool in front of the stove. "Have you eaten?"

Zhen Guo's eyes darted to Jiang Hong then back at Yuen.

"Yes, I have, thank you. I can't stay, and I don't want to disturb your precious family time. I only stop to tell you that I'm approving your patrol to Hunyuan."

Yuen sat up straighter. "Thank you, Comrade."

"I was against it at first," Zhen Guo said. "The risks are serious, and I would hate to lose you, but I understand your promise to your men. I respect that."

He paused, then his lips parted in a smile. "Without honor, we wouldn't be comrades, would we? So I wish you luck, old friend."

"Thank you, Comrade."

Zhen Guo turned and reached for the door handle. Then he looked at Yuen once more.

"There is one more thing. Choose the men you want, but I'd like to assign someone to your team, a man named Huang Su. He's served with other patrols and is due for reassignment. He's quiet, but you'll find him capable. I hope you don't mind having him along."

"Of course not."

With a short bow to Yuen and another to Jiang Hong, Zhen Guo departed.

Yuen lay back down on the mat. *So I'm going again.* He let out a long, slow breath. Then he remembered the fight they were having and looked at Jiang Hong. His wife was knitting again, her face full of concentration.

Suddenly, it came to him—*she's upset because I'm leaving. How can I be so stupid?*

And how am I going to tell Mei Fong?

THIRTY-THREE

A group of four boys shot past David and Katherine in the hallway. They were spinning about as they moved—a game—and giggling, almost knocking Katherine's canvas bag off her shoulder.

"Man dian!" *Slow down!* an older woman scolded. She hustled after them, hand outstretched and clutching, as if that might reel them in.

"Boys, you know, so much spirit," their host said. He was a thin, small man on crude wooden crutches. His left leg was gone at the knee. "I hope you don't mind, their spirit keeps this place happy, I think."

David nodded, smiling politely. He and Katherine walked along slowly to avoid outpacing their host. The orphanage, a square, free-standing building, was one of the few brick structures in the city. The floors were tiled, black interspersed with white. They passed several doors, sounds of laughter, babies crying, flashes of moving children seen through windows of frosted glass.

"How many children live here?" David asked.

"One hundred and fifty this week." The thin man swung his leg forward with a thrust of his hip. "The number is always changing, of course. Ah, here we are. Please, after you."

They passed through a doorway, above which a square of white paper displayed two characters: "Yi sui." *One-year-olds.*

The room was large, square, and windowless. Two dozen children populated the tile floor, some standing, many crawling, others stretched out on their backs. Three women wearing plain blue jackets stood around the room's perimeter, watching the children. A young couple knelt in one corner, playing with a little girl.

"There she is," David said. He pointed to the toddler playing with the couple. Su Pei, thumb in mouth, giggled as the young man tickled her.

I've seen them somewhere, David thought.

Su Pei brightened when she saw David approach. She got up and toddled toward him.

"Lieutenant?" the young man said in English.

David looked up as he hugged Su Pei and lifted her into his arms.

"Do you remember us?" the young man continued. "We met on the day you first arrived."

Of course! It was Sun Fong and his wife Wai Ling, the couple who had practiced English with him and Jack.

"I remember," David said, nodding and shaking hands. "This is my friend, Katherine."

"Lieutenant," Wai Ling said, "when they told us an American had brought a girl all the way back from the east, I imagined it was you. What a wonderful thing you have done."

"Well, she's worth it. Look how healthy she is." David set her down, and the four of them watched as Su Pei played with a wooden giraffe.

"We are going to adopt her," Sun Fong announced.

"Really? That's wonderful," Katherine said. "Don't you think, David?"

David beamed. "Fantastic!"

"We've been unable to have a child of our own," Wai Ling said, "but now I think fate is smiling on us at last." She squeezed her husband's hand. "Yesterday, when we visited for the first time, they told us of a girl who had just endured a terrible ordeal but was also the happiest child here. It was Su Pei. When we met her, we both knew right away—she was meant to be with us."

"You'll make a beautiful family," David said.

The four of them played with Su Pei for almost an hour. Near the end, Katherine gave David's arm a little squeeze and said, "You did a good thing. She's wonderful."

"I know."

When it was time to leave, David gave Su Pei a long hug. Then he stood up and turned toward the door.

"Zai jian," Su Pei said. She shook a small fist at David—a wave.

David laughed. "So you're saying goodbye now? Zai jian, little one."

~

Katherine's long brown hair flowed over the pillow. David watched her quiet breathing, her perfect repose, and thought of how lucky he was. They'd spent three evenings together in his room and each moment was heavenly.

Should I tell her now? he wondered.

"Katherine?" he whispered.

"Mmm?" she murmured sleepily. On the wall, her shadow quivered in the candlelight.

"I've something important to tell you."

Her eyes opened slowly.

"What is it?" Her voice was drowsy and soft.

David took a deep breath. "I've talked to Yuen. He's going out again to rescue the people we left behind."

Katherine turned her head and focused on his face.

"They're letting him go?"

"Yes."

"When?"

"Couple of days, I guess." His voice trailed off as he said, "I believe I'll go with him."

Katherine sat up. "Why, David?"

"I want to help him. He's a good man. I know he'd do it for me and—"

"You don't have anything left to prove or give. You've done so much already."

He ran his fingers through his hair. "You don't understand. We left men behind. I need to do this."

Katherine touched his shoulder, and for a moment, they looked into each other's eyes. "Are you asking my permission?"

"More like…your blessing."

Risk his life, leave me alone, and all for a Chinese man and a few soldiers off in the mountains?

She saw the pained look in his eyes.

Would he stay if I asked him to?

How could I do that?

"You're sweet," she said at last. "I'm frightened. I don't want you to go, but you don't need my permission. And I don't want you worrying about me either."

"Thank you, sweetheart. You always say the right thing."

David kissed her forehead, held her close, and hoped he was making the right decision.

—

The moon shone bright, casting the city's rooftops in a luminescent glow. David sat at the edge of the porch, more awake than when he'd walked Katherine back to her room. He was not bothered by the cold. His mind wandered from Katherine to the mission.

He felt apprehension, but then he thought of Yuen, the man's dedication.

He remembered the hut and the look on Yuen's face when he'd said that Communism wasn't perfect.

David wondered what he'd meant by that.

An owl called from a nearby tree. Footsteps on the path. David looked up and saw Jack.

"Coast clear?" Jack said.

"Yeah, I walked her home. Thanks for keeping busy."

"No problem. We were just trying to get some war news on the radio." Jack tightened his coat around his body. "Aren't you cold? Let's go inside."

David got up and followed Jack through the doorway.

Inside, Jack bent down to unlace his shoes. "We also listened to Communist records. They've got some really patriotic songs." He smiled. "Loud, but patriotic. They sure have plenty of spirit."

"Yeah, maybe they do," David said, moving to his bed.

Jack looked up. "What's that mean?"

David sat down and leaned against the wall. "It's just…I know you really think they're amazing, and I do too—"

"Just say what's on your mind."

David removed his boots. He looked across the room at Jack, past the glow on the table, the candlestick almost burned down all the way. "Sometimes I wonder how realistic this place is. Yenan, I mean."

"We said before it can't be a sham."

"Oh, no, I don't think it's being staged, and I agree they're impressive. But out *there*, I thought the Chinese were the same as Chinese anywhere—they just want to survive. They wouldn't care if the Communists or Nationalists were in charge, so long as whoever it was provided stability and let them eat the food they grow."

Jack sat at the small wooden table. He stared at the smoke trailing from the candle. "Has your opinion about them changed? What about how great you said they were at fighting?"

"I meant that. They were top notch—but we fought for each other. I mean, we didn't want to let each other down. That's where the loyalty comes from. I don't think everyone thinks Mao's the greatest."

Jack scratched his chin. "Do you think our reports have been overly…enthusiastic?"

David shook his head. "I don't know. You've called it as you've seen it. This isn't earth-shattering; I just think Yenan is unique. The peasants out there don't study Marx and Lenin by firelight. They aren't debating the finer points of land redistribution or grain taxes. They keep their heads low and hope the violence passes them by."

Jack slipped off his trousers and pulled on a pair of long johns. "Well, I don't know what to say. I've tried to analyze them objectively. But you've been out in the field—"

David interrupted, "Listen, that's not what I'm saying. The people here would follow Mao to hell if he asked them. Just realize you're a pilgrim in Mecca. Here, the people who stick out are the ones who *aren't* falling over themselves to prove they're zealots."

THIRTY-FOUR

Yenan, January 1945

The ten soldiers set out on a rare rainy day, the road a dark swath on the earth. David kept his head down, felt the soft drops patter on the short brim of his rumpled cloth cap, red star sewn on front—a gift from a Red Army official.

He kept a Russian-style hat—fur-lined with earflaps—stuffed in the center of his pack, the one spot he knew would stay dry. His body was warm, three layers under a heavy overcoat, but his toes felt cold and his socks were already damp from rain permeating his boots.

No one complained when Yuen ordered to move out in bad weather, but David wondered if the chance to show he was fit, at full strength, had something to do with the decision. He looked up front, the lines of rain forcing him to squint. Yuen led the way, but from the way he shuffled—a slight catch in his stride—David knew he wasn't in top form.

The new man, Huang Su, walked in front of David. He was thin and clean-shaven, with round wire spectacles that gave him an intellectual air. He looked about Yuen's age. At first, David thought he might be a veteran, but then there was something uneven about the way he carried himself, swaying under the weight of his pack, gripping his rifle with two hands in front of him—he looked uncomfortable.

David came up beside him.

"It might feel better if you cinch it up higher, it'll swing less," he said, touching the strap of his pack to show how far he'd pulled it.

Huang Su raised his head and looked at him silently. Raindrops zigzagged across his lenses. He looked miserable.

"Just a suggestion," David said, pointing to the man in front of them, as if to say: *See, he's got it my way too.*

Huang Su looked down, not taking the advice.

David made another try at conversation. "Have you been on many other missions?"

"Several," Su replied, an edge in his voice.

Taking the hint, David was about to drop back behind him again, when Su added, "I am a veteran of the Long March."

"Really? So was Yuen. Did you know him?"

"I did not know him."

They walked along in silence for another hundred yards, then David did drop back.

By the time the rain stopped, they'd made twelve miles. At night, the bitter wind stung their faces. The men huddled close together, wrapped in their quilted bedrolls, shielded by a cluster of rocks. David had never felt so cold.

In the morning, a thin film of frost coated the brown, flat earth. David couldn't feel his toes, and he started to unlace one boot to check them but then thought better of it. *Better to just start walking. I might not get the boots back on.*

A week into the journey, a soldier became ill. The cough he'd had for a few days grew worse. He spat dark yellow sputum, blood-tinged. Soon the stricken man was unable to walk, then unable to stand, and his comrades made a stretcher to carry him. He was slowing them down, and Yuen knew he had to find a village or town that would take him in. He was grateful to still be in Communist territory.

They waded through the shallow but frigid Yellow River and drew near a small village near Xingxian. Yuen led the men up the dirt road toward the settlement. The ground was snow-dusted, and a dozen huts lined the street, surrounded on three sides by bald, windswept hills.

Passing the first huts, Yuen glimpsed a large home on a hill to the north. It was an estate, a large red-tiled house surrounded by six outbuildings. The entire property was enclosed by a high wall.

Closer now, Yuen saw patches of vegetation growing on the roof where tiles were missing. Laundry hung on lines strung between trees in the yard. There was no one in sight.

Sounds of a commotion up ahead, where the road opened up to a wide patch of ground—the village center. Yuen and his men went that way and saw a crowd gathered—about forty—cheering, focused on something in the middle.

It looked like some sort of celebration. People were laughing, their breaths smoking in the cold air. Yuen maneuvered through the gathering. Villagers noticed him and his men, and they began to part, clearing a path. In the center of the crowd, Yuen saw a man kneeling on the ground, stripped to his underwear and shivering, hands bound behind his back. Tufts of gray-flecked hair showed beneath the rim of a tall paper hat—a cone.

The man lifted his head, the dunce cap almost falling off. He looked at Yuen with one desperate eye. The other eyelid was purple, swollen shut. Dried rivulets of blood, from the nose and scalp, ran across the creases of his face.

Two young men stood behind the kneeling man, dressed warmer than the others, in drab brown jackets and fur-lined hats with the Communist red star sewn on front. One was almost as tall as David. He kept his arms crossed tightly over his chest. The other was short and chubby and wore spectacles. Both men eyed Yuen suspiciously.

He went directly to them. "Who are you?"

"Who are *you*?" the tall one asked back.

Yuen stepped up close to the two men and whispered something David couldn't hear. Suddenly, the men stood at attention. David moved closer.

"We are jun wei," the tall one said. *Political officers.*

"What is this man's crime?" Yuen demanded.

"He is fu nong," the spectacled one said.

Rich peasant? David thought. *What's that supposed to mean?*

"Yes," the tall one added. "He owns a half acre of land, two donkeys, and five chickens. *And* he hires two workers each year to harvest his field."

A woman's shrill voice wailed, "He hires workers because we have no sons, and he works beside them!" She was on her knees, off to the side, crying. *The wife*, David concluded.

"This is his only crime?" Yuen asked.

The tall political officer hesitated. Then he said, "Yes. His land must be redistributed. He must be—" the man stiffened and rattled off the familiar slogan: "—cured of his evil bourgeois ways."

"Does he live up there?"

The officer followed Yuen's finger to the hillside estate. "Oh no, that landlord was punished and executed months ago. This man—"

"Executed?" Yuen said, and spat. The tall officer glanced nervously at his partner, who stared at Yuen with a hint of defiance.

"Yes...as an example to others. We have permission to punish this man severely as well. Execution is authorized."

Yuen glared at the taller officer, who averted his eyes. Then Yuen walked behind the kneeling man, unsheathed his knife, and cut his hands free. Muted gasps came from the crowd. Yuen knocked away the dunce cap, which flipped end over end, blown away by the wind. He took off his jacket and put it on the man. Then he moved to the wife and spoke into her ear. She stood, went to her husband, helped him up, and began to lead him down the street.

Yuen turned to face the political officers and the silent villagers. Speaking very carefully, he said, "I am a comrade from Yenan on a mission to rescue civilians behind Japanese lines. I am saddened by what I see here and can tell you that this is not what Chairman Mao and the Party leaders would find correct."

The shorter Communist officer cleared his throat, as if to say something, but Yuen ignored him and went on. "I've been a member of the Party for over twenty years. I survived the Long March. I tell you that you should not persecute this man. Some of you may not like him. He may have treated you poorly or unfairly in the past. But whatever his faults, being a *rich peasant* is not a crime. Bloodshed only brings more bloodshed, and one of you may be next."

Most of the villagers looked down at their feet. David saw that many were without shoes, with feet that were wrapped in bundles of cloth, tied up with string. Slowly, the villagers began to disperse.

Suddenly, the short political officer accosted Yuen and blurted, "We were given explicit orders on these matters!" His fat, round face flushed red. "Liu Shaoqi himself lectured us on how to treat these swine!"

Yuen shook his head. "Use your common sense, man. You can't win loyalty by fear and persecution. Or didn't they teach you that already?"

The man clenched his fists but held his tongue.

Yuen looked him in the eye. "By my authority I order you to let that man leave with his family. Redistributing his property, taking all he has, will already be too much, but I can see that you consider granting him his life an act of generosity."

Neither officer spoke.

Yuen added, "I am leaving a sick man here under your care. You will help him recover and send him back to Yenan. When I return, he will confirm that you have carried out my orders."

The rich peasant and his wife returned. They were warmly dressed, each carrying a small basket of belongings. The husband's hands trembled as he gave Yuen his coat back. Then the beaten man bowed low and grasped Yuen's hand in preparation of kissing it. Yuen drew his hand away and pointed down the road leading east, toward Japanese-held territory. The couple slowly shuffled backwards, bowing repeatedly. Finally, they turned and left.

Yuen glanced at David, who stood expressionless.

Standing behind David, Huang Su's face was set in an angry scowl.

THIRTY-FIVE

David tried to wiggle his fingertips, which were numb inside his gray wool gloves. He knelt down to scratch at sharp rocks lodged in the hard ground, clearing the space between two raised roots of a thick oak tree. The wind whistled, and a flurry of dead leaves and loose dirt pelted his bedroll as he unrolled it in the prepared space. A spasm of pain in his stomach made him pause. He thought of eating the crust of hard, dry bread in his pocket, all that was left of his only meal that day. Still more cold than hungry, he forced the thought of food from his mind and folded himself between the layers of the thick quilt. All around him, men were doing the same, and like them David bedded down, boots on, heels facing the fire.

There was a moment when, lying on his back and staring past the bare branches of winter-stripped trees, he felt his body warming a little, and his eyes met the thousand stars glittering in the sky. As he stared into the infinite, there came a steady breathing all around him, and David realized the others were already asleep. His eyes, however, stayed open, and the array of stars morphed back to the images he couldn't shake: the old man, the dunce cap, the jeering crowd. This reel of human cruelty wound and re-wound in his tired brain and kept him awake so that an hour later he was still open-eyed. The sound of a snapping twig turned his head, and he saw Yuen sitting alone on a felled log next to the fire.

David unwrapped himself and, careful not to bump the men on either side of him, catwalked to Yuen.

Shivering in the frosty air, David sat down on a flat rock very near the flames. A trail of smoke blew to the west, got tangled in the forest, and spread into the darkness beyond. A small stream, partially unfrozen, murmured over cold stones a few feet behind them.

Yuen looked at him but didn't speak.

"Colder tonight," David said.

Yuen replied with a grunt. He wore a heavy wool coat, collar upturned. His hand, seeking something inside the coat, emerged with a corncob pipe. From an outer pocket, he withdrew a small pouch and extracted a pinch of tobacco from it.

"Didn't know you smoked," David said as Yuen cupped his hands and lit the pipe.

Yuen took a long pull on it, then exhaled and held the pipe out to him. Arm stiff, David reached for it. The last time he'd smoked it had been opium. He examined the bowl in the firelight and ran his gloved fingers over the dried-out corncob. Just holding the pipe, he felt a twinge of the old craving in his chest.

Yuen cleared his throat. David looked at him, then brought the pipe to his lips. A bitter taste filled his mouth, his throat—he coughed.

A corner of Yuen's mouth went up, the smallest hint of a smile. "I don't bring it out too often," he said.

David handed the pipe back. "I can see why. Did you make it yourself?"

"I didn't." Yuen drew on the stem. "An old friend gave it to me. He made it long ago. Said it meant a lot to him."

"War buddy?"

Yuen shook his head. "No. A writer. He gave it to me the last day I saw him."

The howl of a wolf tore at the night air. It sounded close by, a primal sound that gave David an involuntary shiver. Yuen smiled.

"He sounds as hungry as we are."

"Your friend—what happened to him?"

"I am not sure."

"Meaning what?"

"He was…taken away."

"By who?"

Yuen rubbed his chin, didn't answer. For a while, he just stared into the flames. Far off, another wolf howled and was answered on a distant hilltop.

Yuen chuckled. "Somewhere, they have a camp just like ours," he said. "And a sentry just like me." Then his grin faded. "Some things we're told not to question. Sometimes it's better to forget. I smoke to remember my friend…and better times."

"Are you able to forget what happened at the village today?" David questioned.

Yuen sighed, resigned. He held the pipe in front of him, stared at it. "The Party leaders would not have wanted you to see that."

He dropped the hand holding the pipe and poked at the logs with a stick in his other hand. Bits of ember climbed skyward into the night air. "And they would not want me to discuss it with you."

"I saw what happened. No one can tell me different—I know what I saw."

Yuen studied the dark lines of David's firelit face. *He's fought with us, bled with us. Yet there's so much he doesn't know.*

Knocking out a knot of burnt tobacco on a stone, Yuen refilled his pipe. He spoke as he tamped a fresh brown pinch into the hollow bowl. "What we saw should not have happened. It is not supposed to be happening."

"You're talking about what exactly?"

"The persecution. I'd hoped these mistakes would not return."

"Mistakes? But I thought—"

"Let me explain." Yuen lit and drew on his pipe. A sweet, pungent smell of smoke came out of his mouth.

"I will tell you. Years ago, before the Long March, we were in Jiangxi Province, in the south. That is where we learned to fight as guerillas against the Nationalists. Mao was in charge. He experimented with land and wealth redistribution, and he was aggressive. To him, the feudal system was a curse on China. He said the whole system was based on landlord greed. For society to change, the landlords had to be smashed."

Yuen puffed on his pipe, looked through the firelight into the darkness. He clenched, then unclenched his jaw, and pulled his coat in tight around him. David sat quietly.

"It seemed reasonable at first. Organize the peasants, confiscate the land, and redistribute an equal share to each person—that's man, woman, *and* child—so larger families had more land to grow food on. But then, two things began to happen. First, landlords were beaten and humiliated, just like today. Second, in practice, land redistribution is complicated—not every plot of land is the same—"

A man stirred on the ground, and Yuen froze. The soldier rolled on his side, grunted in his sleep, then lay still. Yuen waited several seconds. A small owl made a tremolo sound over the babble of the little stream.

Yuen shifted closer to David and spoke very softly, "We made many rules about land differences: land with buildings, ponds, and hills, land with and without crops. And there was another problem—what is a landlord? The definition changed often. Was a landlord anyone who owned land and rented some of it to others, no matter how meager? Was a rich peasant anyone who'd ever 'exploited others' by hiring them to help harvest his crop? Should a middle peasant who owned a cow or a few chickens be disciplined as well?

"Poor peasants were afraid of advancing to middle status—these definitions became a matter of life and death! The poor suddenly had the power. They used the rules to settle scores. They figured out quick—the more people they classified as rich, the more land there would be to share amongst themselves."

Yuen moved his arm in a small circle, the familiar soreness in his shoulder.

"What I am about to tell you I have never told anyone," he said in an even lower voice. He then stared at his boots, as if about to talk to them and not to David.

"One day, three of us were sent to visit a landlord: a young soldier, me, and a big shot political officer, one with a reputation for cruelty. He ordered me to rough up the landlord, so I did. His family and the villagers watched. I beat him as hard as I could. I broke his nose. Maybe I thought if I satisfied the big shot he wouldn't hurt the wife and son, so I exhausted myself. The crowd loved it. They were cheering."

Yuen balled his hands into fists. Then he laid his palms flat on his knees, and slowly turned them over.

"I can still see his blood on my hands and the faces of his wife and son. It went on until I couldn't throw another punch. Then, with everyone watching, the big shot handed me a pistol and said, 'Do it.'"

Yuen held his head with both hands. His shoulders sagged.

"And then...I did it. I'm so ashamed...I pointed the gun and fired."

He pointed an index finger toward the fire. "Then the big shot said, 'Them too.'"

Yuen's face had a haunted look. "I would not do it. The crowd was shouting. The wife and son were sobbing over the dead body. The big shot screamed at me. I dropped the pistol. He ordered the other soldier to do it, but that one was just a boy, and he froze. Then the political officer picked up the pistol and shot the two of them in the face, the young boy first. The woman did not even resist. She just stared at the barrel, ready to die."

Yuen swallowed slowly. "I got reprimanded for not obeying orders. I was forced to write my own self-criticism. I went on being a good soldier, but...from then on I vowed to stop climbing the Party ladder. I was disgusted by what was happening."

David's eyes searched Yuen's face. The hint of a tear glistened in the corner of his eye, but then it seemed to harden and freeze.

"But you stayed with them—"

"Of course," Yuen said quickly. "I wanted to save our country, bring the masses out of poverty, kick out the foreign imperialists—those feelings were still present. The Cause was my whole life; I couldn't abandon it. For some time, I told myself what had happened might only be temporary, that perhaps Mao might loosen up after he solidified his hold on power. But then..." Yuen stared into the flames. "I didn't realize things could get worse."

"Worse?"

"The purges."

Yuen stretched, looked at the stars. "In the early thirties, Mao campaigned to eliminate what he called 'counter-revolutionaries.' It was his way of eliminating his enemies. Thousands were murdered."

"Thousands? How?"

"People had incentive to accuse as many suspects as possible, almost like a competition to show who was most loyal to Mao. Those accused—guilty or not—were tortured until they confessed. Anyone who refused was executed. Those who confessed had to give the names of other traitors. So names were named. People would say anything just to stop the pain."

"Were *you* ever accused?"

"No. I was lucky. But I'll never forget the fear. You never knew when you might be taken"—Yuen held up the pipe—"like my friend."

"But wasn't this a long time ago? In the thirties? Isn't it different now?" David asked.

Yuen shook his head. "My friend was taken *two years ago.* Mao invited everyone to criticize the Party. He said we should work together and improve things, but it was all a trick to get the critics to expose themselves."

"So it's still going on."

"We saw it today. It's not spoken of in Yenan, you'll never see it there, but..."

Yuen threw up his hands.

"Oh, it may be a big illusion," he said. "No one knows, for sure, what is or what isn't. Suppose today was a fluke. That could be. Or maybe it is happening in villages all over north China. That could be as well. Who knows?"

David's mind reeled as he wrestled with the sheer madness of it all.

The two men sat in silence until Yuen finally spoke once more.

"You asked me once what I thought would happen when the war ended. For you it *will* end. But for us, there will be a new war. A civil war. Winning, one way or another, will not solve the problem. The mistakes of the past have a way of creeping into the woodwork of the present building. No wooden edifice is safe from the termites of the past. The sounds of the dead are not entirely gone—not ever."

THIRTY-SIX

Northern Shanxi Province, February 1945

The bald, rolling hills, sparsely dotted with stunted pine, showed no signs of life. The sky—a cloudless sheet of icy blue. Yuen felt a pang of desperation in his gut. He had no idea where the tunnels were. Hunyuan was close; the scouts had confirmed it. The villager who'd known about the tunnels said they were south of town, far from the roads, and that the entrance was well hidden, deep in a canyon.

Canyon? Yuen thought. *The hills are rounded and far apart. I don't see anything like that.*

The sun hung just over the treetops in the west. Yuen stamped his feet, waiting at the agreed upon point beneath a copse of trees surrounded by boulders and sheltered from the wind. He'd tramped over a dozen hills and not seen another soul nor any trace of a canyon. Seven soldiers sat near him, smoking, trying to keep warm. Like Yuen, they'd found nothing in their day-long searches. Yuen had hoped at least one of them might pick up a lead, perhaps meet a friendly farmer or child who knew about the hiding place, but none had.

Lu Gao, where are you?

Yuen reached for his canteen, forgetting it was empty. He tapped it, the tinny sound made him thirstier, and he thought of the campsite near the stream and the cold, clear water of two weeks ago. They'd not seen another stream like it, and lately, the men had resorted to collecting water from muddy, half-frozen creeks and dirty snowmelt.

Yuen looked at them, searching for any sign of discontent, but he found none except for David, who sat staring at a rock. *Bored or mad? Maybe mad at me. Someone needed to stay behind and guard the supplies. Couldn't risk him wandering around by himself. He knows that.*

"Look!" one of the men shouted, pointing west. It was Jou, running toward them. His coat was open, unbuttoned. He wore a beige hunting cap, pulled low to cover the tops of his ears.

"I found them!" Jou reported, gasping for breath.

"Where?" Yuen asked.

"They're about three miles that way. I wandered around for hours. Caught sight of a man, but when he saw me he ran. I caught up to him, and he realized I was Chinese, not Japanese. He was one of the villagers, but I didn't recognize him—he looked starved. He said he was scouting the area for Lu Gao. He took me to a tunnel entrance. It's very well hidden. Thirty people there. We should go."

The men gathered their gear and started off. Yuen walked beside Jou. Voice low, he said, "How did they look?"

Jou slowed his pace, allowing several men to pass him. "Not good. They ran out of supplies a week ago. I think there were some dead people in their cave...the older ones."

"What about Lu Gao?"

"He's starved, like the rest of them. I didn't even recognize him at first. He said he'd sent two men to Hunyuan to find food but neither returned. He thinks they might have been picked up by the Japanese."

"If so, they'd torture them and end up finding out about the tunnels."

Jou nodded. "That's what he's thinking. I don't think he has slept in days."

They walked for thirty minutes. The scrubby, desolate landscape frustrated Yuen. Every direction he looked was the same, and he began to wonder if he'd walked right past the tunnels, or if he'd walked this way at all.

Jou led them through a deep ravine. A small stream flowed through it, and the men stopped to drink. Yuen studied the close-set hills and saw how the little valley narrowed to a point. They went farther, dead-ending at a solid wall of rock. Yuen could actually touch both sides of the yellow-colored slot canyon by holding out his arms. He ran his fingers against the walls; sandy particles crumbled down.

Jou called out, "Hello?"

After a few moments, Lu Gao appeared in front of them as though out of thin air. His gaunt eyes scanned their faces, roving like a nocturnal animal. His mouth was barely visible behind his dirt-flecked beard, the fullness of it disproportionate to the thinness of his face. He grunted and pointed at Yuen. Yuen went to him.

"Comrade," Yuen said. "It is our good fortune to see you again."

Dazed, Lu Gao stumbled a bit. Yuen caught him, embracing him at the same time.

"Thank you for coming," Lu Gao rasped.

A moment later, Yuen and the others followed Lu Gao through a narrow gap between two tall boulders, revealing the entrance to a tunnel that was almost completely hidden from view. They squeezed through the gap one at a time, then crouched down to enter a four-foot-high tunnel. After thirty feet, it opened up into a larger space, and Yuen took a deep breath. The cave smelled of stale bodies and rotten flesh.

He blinked, eyes adjusting to the darkness, and scanned the cave. It was forty feet across. Two kerosene lamps smoked and offered a feeble light on the sandy floor. Two dozen people lay on the ground. There was another tunnel in the back, leading farther into the hillside. Without this extra outlet, the smell of foulness might have been unbearable. The top of Yuen's head almost touched the cave ceiling, and he noticed David stooping like an old man.

"They found us!" Lu Gao croaked.

Some villagers lifted their heads; a few smiled weakly. The soldiers who'd stayed behind with Lu Gao greeted their comrades joyfully. Three or four of them scratched their heads and bodies incessantly. *Lice*, Yuen suspected.

Yuen's men went to each of the villagers sharing rations and water, while Yuen walked the length of the cave. He shivered from the cold damp that seemed to come off the walls. Three dead bodies lay side by side at the back of the cavern: a man and two women. They'd not yet begun to decompose, but the smell was like sour fruit about to turn.

Yuen sat beside Lu Gao, who was gnawing on a piece of hard bread.

"Sorry it took so long, my friend."

Lu Gao chewed slowly, savoring every swallow. "You came when you could."

"Have you thought about how to get out of here?"

Lu Gao nodded. "I didn't dare bring these people out without knowing the land. I sent out scouts, but I never saw them again. It's going to be difficult, Yuen."

"It is good we did not see Japanese in the area, but weather will be the larger problem—and food. Perhaps..." Yuen paused.

"What?"

"Perhaps we should stay here, try to bring supplies in. Just for a while."

Lu Gao shook his head, coughed, spat. He stared with watery eyes. "We must get out of this cave," he said. "This place is a tomb. These people are willing to risk their lives to leave it."

Yuen looked at the villagers. Some were old and feeble. A few could hardly walk. There were kids and at least one baby.

"What about splitting up into smaller groups and trying to mix into some nearby villages?" Lu Gao suggested.

Yuen shook his head. "That may work for two or three people, but there aren't many villages nearby, and there is no one on the roads these days. Arrive with a group of starving people and you will raise a lot of questions."

Yuen touched Lu Gao on the shoulder. "Do not be anxious. We will go together. We will make it home."

A few minutes after this, Yuen told everyone they were breaking camp at dawn. Then he put the soldiers to work cutting up aspen saplings that were growing by the stream. These would be made into stretchers to carry the elderly.

The night passed slowly. Yuen lay awake for hours, hearing every movement, every cough echoing in the pitch-black chamber. The foul odor of human decay made it unpleasant to breathe.

Later, he awoke, not sure if he'd slept for four minutes or four hours. He got up and peeked down the entrance tunnel, a faint glow shone through the narrow crack at the opening. The others were still sleeping, and out of curiosity, Yuen took one of the lamps and went into the tunnel at the back of the cave. He crouched in the narrow space and tried to avoid rubbing up against the damp rock walls. After ten yards, it branched into three different tunnels. He chose one, then looked back, noting a bird-shaped rock to remember the way.

As he moved forward the air became thicker, harder to breathe. His foot landed on wood, and he looked down. With the lamp, he saw the wood planks covering a pit. He couldn't see the bottom. *Booby trap.*

One step at a time.

There were other caves, larger spaces. Near one entrance the tunnel zigzagged at ninety-degree angles. He slipped into recesses cut into the walls and peered through several rifle slits. *Engineered for defense*, he thought, picturing intruders entering the dark tunnels, advancing blind, a few cut down at every turn. Yuen spent an hour exploring the tunnels. Their size and complexity impressed him, and he realized they could easily hide hundreds of people.

When he returned to the group the villagers and soldiers were preparing to leave. Despite their fatigue, the civilians moved with new purpose. He tried to help a few of them, adjusting their packs and pointing out what should be left behind. There were a few familiar faces: the man who'd known about the tunnels; the petite woman he'd seen clutching her baby just before the Japanese were about to open fire.

Yuen approached this mother and offered to carry some of her things. When she smiled at him gratefully, he was surprised at how pretty she was. Her name was Wen Ping. Her baby, a boy named Jingwei, was now just learning to sit, and he amused the nearby grownups by pushing himself up with his arms, then drifting to one side and toppling over.

Yuen was the last one out of the cave. No one looked back. They headed west—an exodus of old and young—their shadows pointing the way home.

THIRTY-SEVEN

"He's dead," Jou said.

Yuen knelt beside the old man whose toothless mouth was gaping, his lifeless eyes glazed. Yuen leaned down, listening and feeling for a breath. Then he tried for a pulse.

"Nothing. He's gone."

Yuen glanced at the villagers stirring in the wrappers of ground-hugging mist that clung to their bodies.

"Two nights of this cold damp and these people are beginning to fade one at a time," Yuen remarked with a shake of the head.

Jou, weary from night watch, rubbed his eyes. "What choice do we have?"

Yuen released the dead man's hand, but the arm joint, already stiffening in the cold, resisted, and the hand ghoulishly remained suspended a few inches off the ground.

"See if you can get this body settled somewhere before the others notice. I don't want anyone wailing over it right now."

Jou kicked at the crusted, frozen earth. "We won't be able to bury him…"

"Take him behind those trees over there," Yuen said. "Lay a few stones around him. Take off his coat and most of these clothes—give them to someone who can use them. And the shoes…" Yuen looked down; the man wore thin cloth slippers. "Never mind. Just do what you can."

Yuen forced himself to stare at the rising sun. Closing his eyes, he reached out for the sun's rays with his mind, feeling for any warmth, but there was none, only the bitter wind whipping his cheeks. *It's going to be another bad day*, he thought.

The motley group continued west—a thin, snaking line on the barren landscape, which was flatter now, more open, with fewer trees. Yuen liked being able to see a long way in each direction. But, as he always did, he scanned around, making mental note of the best place to run and hide in case of trouble. Here there was nowhere to go.

The soldiers took turns with the three stretchers, carrying short, hump-backed elders who weighed little but slowed them greatly. Yuen looked at one of them: a man with closed eyes and bony fingers clutched around his neck. Yuen tried to suppress his annoyance but couldn't help the feeling. Secretly, he was relieved that one old person had died in the night. *What kind of life would he have had, anyway? More hardship and hunger. It is a mercy to die.*

Their rations—stale bread, nothing more—were almost out and Yuen knew he had no choice. He'd have to find a village and risk asking for help. He stared at the horizon and at the small hills breaking the line.

At least four days before we're out of enemy territory.

Yuen looked again at the stretchers and then at the people. They shuffled slowly, silently, like the walking dead.

We'll never make it unless we stop and find food.

He sent two scouts to the main road to look for nearby villages.

Jou returned mid-afternoon.

"There's a small village north of here," he reported. "Only about ten huts. They don't have much, but they seem willing to help us. They said the Japanese drive through about once every other week. They always steal from the village, so they hate the enemy as much as we do."

Yuen felt many eyes on him—half-frozen civilians, bundled and stamping their feet, following his every movement.

They're probably wondering why they followed me.

We've got to try it.

"Let's go," he said.

From above, the road snaked between two hills, curving lazily. The valley was cloaked in shadow—the lowering sun blocked by the steep hill to the west. The village was no more than a group of mud-brick huts clustered in the valley, straddling the road. Snow-dusted pine trees dotted the hillsides.

As they trudged toward the village, an old man tottered toward them, leaning heavily on a cane. The wind twisted his wispy gray hair into his face. The man brushed it aside and waved to them.

"Welcome, welcome," he called out. "You must be exhausted. And, oh my"—he looked at Wen Ping, who carried Jingwei in her arms—"you have a little one. Please. Come inside, out of the cold."

The man led them into the village. "Thank you for helping us," Yuen said. "My name's Lin Yuen, and these people are refugees fleeing the Japanese."

The old man nodded. "I'm Liang. We're happy to help. It's our bad luck the Japanese use this road sometimes, but we're only a group of old men and women, and they can't do too much to us anymore." He flashed a toothless grin. "We don't have much, but we'll share it with you."

Most of Yuen's group crowded into the largest hut—one with wood flooring and a fire burning in a stone fireplace. The village residents, about nine or ten families, congregated outside the structure, curious to see the newcomers. Some large bowls of cabbage soup were offered, and Yuen's people passed them around, taking turns drinking from them.

"I'm sorry, we haven't had meat for many months," Liang said to Yuen.

"Please, you are too polite."

"You must stay here tonight."

Yuen glanced at the room's one small window, covered with greased paper. It was already getting dark outside. "But you are already taking a risk—"

Liang held up his hand. His finger joints were swollen, knobby. "I insist. You have elderly here. Children too."

Yuen looked at the civilians, crowded together on the floor, drinking the soup in quiet, intent desperation. Wen Ping struggled to nurse Jingwei by the fire. She was half-starved, like the rest of them, and her small breasts, limp and empty, couldn't satisfy the wailing boy.

Yuen nodded to Liang. They all needed a rest. Then he sank down to a seated position. Feeling the warmth of the flames, he lowered his eyelids.

Yuen opened his eyes and stared at the rough hand-hewn pine beams that supported the ceiling. Light leaked in through the window. *What hour?*

He tried to get up, but he was wedged between two other people. Gently, he worked himself to a stand. Then he tiptoed between the tightly packed bodies, making his way to the door. Lifting the wooden latch, he pushed the door open and stepped outside.

There was less wind now; the air was warmer. The sun peeked over the top of the eastern hill. On the other side of the road a gray-haired woman stirred a large black pot hanging over a fire.

Yuen walked across the road.

"What are you preparing?" he asked.

The woman looked at him, a kind face. "Cabbage soup again. I'm afraid it's all we have."

Yuen bent down close to the top of the pot. Flakes of brown-green cabbage floated on top.

"We are grateful."

"Good morning!" a voice called out. Yuen turned. It was Liang. "Sleep well?" he asked.

"Very well. The warmest night these people have had in three months. We cannot thank you enough."

"I've been talking it over with the others," Liang said. "We want you to leave the oldest ones here with us."

Yuen looked at him but said nothing.

"You'll have a better chance of saving the others. Perhaps you could come back for them in the spring when the weather improves." Liang put his hand on Yuen's shoulder. "It's all right, son. You carry a heavy load on your shoulders, and your face has too many lines for someone so young. Let us take them."

Yuen's head dipped, a nod.

"Very good!" Liang said.

"What about the Japanese—"

"We'll say they're our relatives. It's no risk. The Japanese never bother to look at our faces."

When word spread about the villagers' offer, everyone thought it was a good idea, especially the three eldest.

After their cabbage soup breakfast, the group prepared to depart. The air was crisp and dry. Laughter near the door of a hut reminded Yuen he hadn't heard any in a long while. The baby, Jingwei, was walking his hands up the mud wall.

Yuen watched as some villagers handed baskets to his soldiers. *Food. We were lucky to find this village and these good people.* He'd almost forgotten about the lookout he'd stationed atop the east-facing hill, a point from which the road could be viewed in both directions for at least a mile, so he was startled by the shout—loud and unintelligible—followed by the sounds of a man clambering down the hillside.

"A truck! A truck is coming!" the lookout yelled.

Yuen felt an icy shock in his belly. *A truck. Japanese. Has to be.* An old woman wailed. A man's voice shouted the names of his children. Yuen looked to the hills. *No time. Too many of us. Do we make a stand?*

He searched for his soldiers, bunched up with the civilians. *All these villagers might get killed. Got to hide,* he thought, just as Liang shouted, "Quick! Into my home. There's a cellar that can hold almost all of you. Any others—hide in the other huts. Hurry!"

The soldiers looked to Yuen, questioning.

Yuen shouted, "Yes! Get out of sight!"

Yuen followed the large group of people heading into Liang's hut, the same hut he'd slept in. Cane in hand, Liang hobbled across the plank floor into the far left corner of the room. He dropped the cane and laid his hands on top of a table.

"Help me!" he said to the two closest men. They shoved the table and three chairs aside. Beneath it, a small rug and...a trapdoor! Liang lifted the door up.

"Hurry! Get in!"

A scuffle of crouched forms, and, in what seemed like seconds, all had disappeared under the floor. Yuen imagined the door dropped, the rug returned, the table in its former place— perfect. He listened to the muffled gabbling and stamped once to indicate his wish for them to be silent. Then he strained his ears and heard the distant whine of an engine.

"Get in!" Liang hissed. Almost reluctantly, Yuen ducked down and eased himself into the darkness. Instantly, Liang dropped the door over his head. There was a scraping sound as another villager helped him drag the table over the floor.

The crawl space was only four or five feet high. The ground was soft, a little muddy. Straight lines of light from gaps in the floorboards ran over the frozen faces staring up. Yuen counted twenty people in the cellar. Short people were sitting; taller people were curled in fetal crouch around crates and barrels.

David was here, lying on his side, up on one elbow. So was Wen Ping, stroking Jingwei's forehead, trying to coax him into falling asleep.

The engine's far off whine had now turned to a nearby groan of gears. *Please pass by!* Yuen pleaded. He heard the truck pass the hut; the wall rumbled.

Then the engine stopped.

Yuen held his breath. There were footsteps, shouting in Japanese, and Liang's voice saying, "We have plenty of water. Please help yourself."

There came the voice of a young person, a man who spoke Mandarin poorly. "Have you seen any fugitives come this way? Two days ago a man was caught stealing food. He came from a village that harbored enemy pilots. He showed us a cave near Hunyuan where a lot of people had been hiding. Now they could be heading this way."

As Yuen listened, he heard the rise and fall of many Chinese voices wash over the young Japanese soldier.

"You are sure you have not seen anyone?" the soldier asked.

A scraping sound in the corner. Yuen's head snapped. David, shifting, had un-holstered his pistol.

No! Yuen wanted to shout. *We can't shoot our way out of this. No idea how many are out there.*

"We haven't seen anyone," Liang said.

There was a long period of silence.

Footsteps thudded past the hut—up the road, down the road. Minutes dragged by seeming like hours. Finally, the Japanese voice spoke again.

"If you are hiding anyone, you will be shot."

"We would never do that!" Liang said in an offended tone.

Out in the road, the truck ignition stuttered, caught, began to run.

Yuen exhaled slowly.

Suddenly, a loud wail ripped the silence. It echoed in the crawl space for a second then was abruptly cut off. Yuen's gaze darted to Wen Ping—her eyes wide with fear, her hand clamped tightly over Jingwei's mouth. The muted boy began to buck and kick like a berserk marionette.

The truck engine droned, roared, died.

331

"What was that?" the same Japanese soldier shouted.

Yuen froze, muscles tight.

Liang's voice, rising: "I don't know. I didn't hear anything."

There came more scuffling sounds, boots thudding in unison.

A loud, meaty thump, followed by gasps.

"Stupid old man. Do you think we are fools?"

A tangle of Japanese words, phrases. Heavy feet running toward their hut. The front door creaked open. Loud, heavy footsteps above them. Skeins of road dust filtered down through the cracks, settling on heads and faces.

Yuen felt his heart pounding. His eyes darted up through the floorboards. He blinked. His eyes itched, but he dared not touch them.

"There is nothing here," Liang sang out in a high, nasal voice.

"Shut up," someone said in Japanese.

Yuen moved his head slowly, his fingers closing around his rifle. Using his knee as a post, he sighted the trapdoor. Despite the cold and damp, sweat runneled down into the corners of his eyes.

For several seconds, the crashing sound of furniture being upturned above them. Then, a Japanese soldier cursed. Heavy feet thundered out of the hut. The truck engine started stuttering again. The ignition didn't catch. The driver tried again, and this time the engine leapt into action. Yuen smelled wreaths of exhaust enter the hut's open door and waft under the floor.

The truck cranked sluggishly forward.

Yuen took a deep, sweet breath and relaxed his locked hands and knee, lowering the rifle. *Too close*, he thought. *Much too close.* He stretched his legs where the tense muscles had knotted up and rubbed them with his hands.

A sharp, piercing wail slashed the collective relief. Yuen cringed, peered through the shafts of dusty light, and saw Wen Ping on the floor, red-faced, wild-eyed. He thought she was having a seizure: her body quaked, her head and legs flung violently side to side. Those around her leaned away, ducking to avoid her.

Then Yuen saw the bundle in her arms.

He felt an awful twist in his gut.

It was Jingwei's body: limp, motionless...dead.

THIRTY-EIGHT

As the fifth son of a farmer, Huang Su's parents never paid him much attention. They didn't call him by his real name; he went by Number Five Son. He wasn't strong like some of his brothers, who were a big help in their father's fields. He wasn't smart like another brother, the one for whom his father scrimped and saved to send him to a university. Su was just Number Five, only slightly more important than his three sisters.

He was fifteen when his father told him to leave to seek his fortune. By then, his oldest brother had married and inherited the farm. There were no tears when Su left, just a goodbye from mother and a nod from father. He'd not seen them since.

He traveled to the city of Tsunyi, where he was robbed the day after he arrived. His small pouch of coins was taken by three bandits who beat him—and worse—broke his only pair of glasses. He could laugh now, picturing himself crying in the alleyway, feeling for his cracked glasses in the rain. He'd almost gone back home. But that seemed so long ago, before he'd found his new family: the *Party*.

To those who did not know him, Su often lied about being a veteran of the Long March. It was a useful fib, one that commanded instant credibility. He *had* seen them, after all, when they'd passed through his city. Watching them through the window of the paper factory where he'd found work, he remembered their faces—dirty and serious, but not unfriendly. They marched past in tight formation, surprising discipline with the Nationalist Army on their heels, he thought. Though Su liked what he'd heard about the Communists, he saw no point in joining a hopeless cause.

But then, against all odds, the Communists survived, and Su decided to journey to Yenan. What a wonderful place it was! No one cared that he was poor and uneducated. In fact, these were considered virtues.

Su eagerly learned all he could about the Party. The best way to make a name for himself, he realized, was to be completely loyal, to follow the Chairman's wishes without question, to always ask himself, *"What would the Chairman do?"*

He suffered through the military training—required of all Party men—and landed a job as a political officer. It was the job he was born for. He ferreted out counter-revolutionaries with unmatched dedication. More than once, he turned in men who thought they were his friends. He wasn't surprised when his superior recommended him to comrade Chen Zhen Guo, commander of guerilla forces, when someone was needed for a special assignment.

The first time he saw Chen Zhen Guo, Su knew he would do anything to please him. Zhen Guo was strong, with a commanding presence. He was very handsome. Sometimes Su found himself admiring Zhen Guo's lips as they moved or imagining how his chest looked under his shirt. He had never acted on his attraction to other men, but if he ever did screw up the courage, Zhen Guo would be the kind of man worth taking the risk for. For now, Su held his tongue and hoped he'd impressed Zhen Guo with his eagerness to carry out the mission.

"There is a man named Lin Yuen," Zhen Guo had told him, "a strong leader, beloved by his men. Despite his long history with the Party and his excellent war record, we have reason to believe that he is now a counter-revolutionary. This has become important because he appears to have befriended one of the Americans, whose impression of the Party could hurt our prospects for American aid. I want you to accompany them on their next mission and observe what you can. You should never confront Yuen, just report back to us. Pay close attention to what he and the American discuss."

That had all been well and good, something Su could do easily, but the mission had been much more than he'd bargained for—tramping day after day through the freezing countryside behind Japanese lines. Several times, Su thought he'd collapse from fatigue or die from the cold. Only the thought of advancement and winning Zhen Guo's approval kept him going.

And now it had all been worth it. What a report he would give! No doubt, Lin Yuen was an enemy of the Party. Su had heard it all, at the fireside, as Yuen told the American things that had made Su want to jump up and put a bullet through his heart. It took all the self-control Su could muster to pretend he was asleep.

It would be very gratifying to watch Yuen be disciplined. Perhaps he could be rehabilitated, but Su doubted it.

THIRTY-NINE

Yenan, April 1945

The black, leather dress shoes felt alien to David's calloused feet. His legs were sore, but he felt almost weightless without his pack and rifle. Yenan's moonlit streets were empty, resembling an eerie ghost town, but the strains of a dance tune wafted over from the Saturday evening dance, where David felt sure he'd find Katherine.

The Reception House came into view—its double doors wide open with a dozen people spilling out onto the front steps. Two Americans wearing olive green uniforms sat to the left of the stairs, on a wide, square stoop. David didn't recognize them. One had a voice that carried—a square-jawed, big-boned sergeant who said, "It's only a matter of time now before we're in

Berlin. I'd like to see what they end up doing to Hitler when they catch 'im."

The other G.I. lit a cigarette with a flick of his lighter. "I heard the Russians might get there first."

"Don't matter. Actually, scratch that. 'Course it matters. Russians ain't gonna take 'im prisoner. Can't say I disagree. It'd save everyone a lot of trouble." Both men chuckled.

David was on the steps now. They eyed him curiously, but David didn't look at them.

At the door, David hesitated. The bright, electric lights made him blink, and there was a wall of people, more than a hundred crammed into the room. He searched for Katherine and spotted at least five Americans he didn't know. Thick, blue cigarette smoke rose over their heads, propelled this way and that by three small ceiling fans. He scanned the crowd some more: dancers in the center, many more people milling about along the perimeter, chatting in groups of two or three.

David waded into the room. He heard his name called out above the ambient chatter, but he pretended not to hear it. Then—for a split second—he saw her, before the bodies shifted, and she disappeared amidst the partying swirl of garments and smoke. He tacked in that direction and nearly knocked over a short-haired Chinese girl carrying two small teacups.

"Dui bu qi," *Sorry*, David said. The young girl stepped back, checked her cups, and smiled. No harm done.

He found Katherine's head again, her brown hair resting gently on her shoulders. It looked like she was waiting in line at the punch table, behind a tall American officer and two Chinese girls. David took a shortcut across a corner of the dance floor and dodged a spinning couple. He came up behind Katherine and touched her arm. She turned.

"Oh! Darling! You're here." Her lips parted in a smile.

"Hi, baby," he said, grinning, and he folded Katherine into his arms.

"Lieutenant!"

David glanced at the officer standing next to the punch bowl. It was Robert Enfield.

"Major," David replied, trying to hide his surprise. He released Katherine from his embrace, but felt her grasp his left arm and shuffle a little bit behind him.

Enfield slapped him hard on the shoulder. His other hand held a small teacup, filled with yellow liquid. "How was it, man?"

David coughed. "Fine, sir," he said thickly. "It went fine."

"Kill any Japs?"

"No sir."

"Not this time, eh?"

"No sir. Didn't run into any this time."

It was impossible to miss the strong smell of alcohol on the major's breath, and it seemed to David that he was making a special effort to ignore Katherine.

"That's probably good. Still, I bet you figure you deserve a promotion, eh?" Enfield said.

"What, sir?"

"You don't want to be a looey all your life, do you? Can't figure any other reason why you'd stick your neck out—with these Commies, no less. I've been here two weeks, and I don't see what all the fuss is about. These people, they're barely civilized. At least in Chungking we had a proper roof over our heads. Far as I'm concerned, there's no solving the problems these Chinks have got with each other, and it probably doesn't matter anyhow so long as we win the war. I say let's whip Japan and get the hell out of here."

David and Katherine stared at Enfield, who raised his teacup. "Here's to your safe return, Lieutenant."

Enfield tossed his head back and drank. Then he emitted a small belch and said, "I'll let you two have your little reunion now."

Before David or Katherine could respond, Enfield turned and pushed off into the crowd like the prow of a ship.

"You told him about us?" David asked, reaching for Katherine's hands.

"Yes, he knows."

"What's he doing here?"

"I don't know. A lot of you Yanks have come up here recently. He just showed up on the plane one day. Darling—"

"Your hands are trembling."

"They are?" She looked up at David, embarrassed. "They are, aren't they?"

She started to pull them away but he held on tight.

"Let's get out of here," he said.

"Sounds marvelous."

Leading her by the hand, David waded through the crowd. He kept toward the outer wall, hoping to go unnoticed. Once they were outside and down the front steps, David paused and took a deep breath, letting the fresh air fill his lungs. Katherine clung to his arm. Her body, soft and inviting, caused him to shiver slightly.

"Where are we going?" she asked.

"First—there."

David pointed at a one-story brick building across the road. He led her behind a corner of the building, where the darkness was almost complete. Now out of sight, he held her close. Slowly, he lowered his head and kissed her. She closed her eyes, and for long, precious seconds they were lost to the world around them.

David felt Katherine's lips curl in a smile. She giggled, and he loosened his hold on her.

"What's so funny?"

"Sorry, my dear," she said, chuckling. She ran her fingertips over his lips and chin. "You're rather tickly. You could use a shave."

David felt under his chin.

"Didn't have time to shave. I bathed, didn't I?"

Katherine wrinkled her nose. "You did? I wasn't certain."

Together they laughed quietly, and she pressed the side of her face against his chest.

"It's splendid to have you back. My goodness, you're so much thinner, worse than the first time, I think." She tilted her head up. "Was it *really* all right?"

David ran his fingers through her hair. For a moment, he remembered the bone-chilling cold, the burning numbness in his toes. He saw the faces of the dead villagers, and the baby boy.

"It was rough," he said, "but we made it."

They began to stroll toward the Dixie Mission compound, holding hands, and the music from the dance yielded to the sound of ratcheting crickets.

"This may sound strange," David said, "but all these buildings, all these people...it feels like a dream to me."

"Do I seem real?"

David squeezed her hand. "It's sinking in."

"I *will* say it's been dreadfully boring without you."

"So I didn't miss much? By the way, where's Jack? Didn't see any of his things in the room."

"Jack? Oh, he left a month ago. Davies too, I'm afraid. You were gone three months, you know. They were right about Ambassador Hurley having it in for them. Jack was ordered back to Washington. Davies was transferred to Moscow."

"Moscow?" He tried to picture Davies in front of the Kremlin.

"Yes. He tried to be upbeat about the change, but I could tell he was devastated." Katherine exhaled slowly. "I'm afraid your colonel is gone, too."

"Barrett?"

Katherine nodded.

"Where is he?"

"They sent him to Kunming."

"Why?"

Katherine shrugged. "I gather Hurley didn't like him either. I think he's intended to help train Chinese soldiers there."

"That's a load of crap. There's nothing going on in Kunming." David shook his head. *They just pushed them all aside,* he thought. *Our best China experts.* "So who's in command now?"

"Colonel Depass replaced Colonel Barrett, but he's gone, too. Now Peterkin's in charge."

"Major Peterkin? Just a major?"

"They promoted him lieutenant colonel." Katherine sighed. "At least they didn't choose Robert."

They walked in silence for a while. A drifting cloud obscured the moon, and David strained his eyes to see the street, looking for familiar storefronts on either side. He followed the line of telephone poles on one side of the road and thought he saw the patch of open ground where he'd watched children play soccer in the summer.

"I'm sorry your friends were sent away," Katherine said.

"Me too. Tell me what else I've missed."

"Well, the war's going well in Europe. We're closing in on Berlin. You have a General Patton who seems determined to beat the Russians there, like it's a race or something."

"Finally. It won't be much longer."

"The Japanese are holding out on some island called Okinawa. It's the same as every other island. Terrible carnage. Japanese soldiers refusing to surrender. Civilians, too."

"That figures," David said, with irritation that made Katherine glance up. They made the turn into the American complex through an opening in the low wall.

"Are you sure you're all right, dear?"

David sighed. "Just tired, I guess."

"Of course. Why don't we go straight home? You've got the room to yourself now."

They wound past the familiar buildings. In the dimness, David spied a few plants sprouting along the wall of the largest. Then the smell of new paint made him look up, and he read a large sign mounted over the doorway. He stopped.

"Why does that say 'Whittlesey Hall?'"

Katherine gasped, and her hand shot up to her mouth. "Darling...but of course, you wouldn't know. It's bad news, I'm afraid. You remember that Ray went on a mission with the guerillas?"

David nodded.

"And Henry Whittlesey. You remember that American chap?"

"Of course."

David liked Henry, a bespectacled first lieutenant with a witty sense of humor who often talked about his wife and daughter back home. His job in Yenan was to facilitate the rescue of American pilots shot down in Communist territory.

"Henry went too. On their way back, he and his Communist interpreter entered a village they thought was safe—but they ran into the Japanese and were captured. Then...they were executed. I'm so sorry, darling."

David's gaze fell to the ground.

"The Chinese lost twenty men trying to rescue them, but they couldn't get there in time."

"So they named this building after him?"

"That's right, dear."

"What about Ray?"

"He made it back, though the journey was very difficult. He was sent back to Washington too, while you were away."

David closed his eyes and rubbed his forehead. A coyote's howl carried from one mountainside across the plain. *Maybe he's lost friends too*, David thought.

He and Katherine trudged the rest of the way to his room in silence.

—

Huang Su sniffed the dank, stagnant air of the windowless room and felt himself starting to sweat. It was a room he'd never seen before, some place Zhen Guo had led him to in the darkness after Su had shown up at his door. He balanced on the wobbly, wooden chair at the center of the room. A single electric light bulb hung from the ceiling; it buzzed.

Zhen Guo stood under the light and pared his nail with a razor-sharp, bone-handled penknife. Su watched, momentarily mesmerized, as Zhen Guo expertly rounded off the quarter-moon white of the nail.

Zhen Guo lowered the knife, and Su's bloodshot eyes tracked him as he circled the chair.

"Are you sure he does not suspect you?"

"He does not suspect."

"But are you *sure*?"

Su swallowed. "Yes."

"And did you do anything that might have indicated you were less of a…soldier…than the others?"

Su looked at Zhen Guo, a flash of resentment. "What do you—"

"You showed up at my door and couldn't stop complaining. You made it sound like hell. Maybe you're right, or maybe you're soft. I need to know."

"I did my best to fit in, Comrade. The rest of them were already friends; they've known each other for years. I did everything they asked of me."

"Hmm," Zhen Guo murmured. "And the incident with the political officers at the village...you say that Yuen *ordered* them to let the landlord go?"

"Yes!" Su leaned forward and lifted off the chair. "That's right. He stopped that landlord's rehabilitation, and he criticized the political officers in front of the peasants. Those officers should have held their ground. As the Chairman says, 'He who—'"

Zhen Guo cut him off with a dismissive wave of his hand. "Save your slogans for your boss." He pulled a handful of cigarettes out of his breast pocket, picked them over and selected one, then returned the others to his pocket without offering one to Su. He struck a match and lit the cigarette.

"And everything you said about him talking to the American is true?"

"Of course."

Zhen Guo took a drag and exhaled the smoke over Su's head.

"No exaggerations? Because it's going to be your word against his."

Huang Su straightened his back. "I know what I heard. I can personally make sure—"

Zhen Guo put a hand on his shoulder. Su's heart beat faster. He felt Zhen Guo's strong hand give him a little squeeze.

"Relax. I believe you." He chuckled. "Yuen may have a lot of friends, but he won't put up a fight. He's too honorable, always follows orders. I just hope he's smart enough to admit to it."

He lifted his hand, and Huang Su took a long breath.

"Go wash up," Zhen Guo said. "I'm surprised you came and found me before you even went home. That shows excellent dedication."

"Thank you, sir. I'm glad you feel I did my duty."

Zhen Guo ignored him and moved to the door. He turned and said, "Let us hope the American doesn't ruin our chances of getting weapons. Tomorrow, file a report for Liu Shaoqi. Include everything you've told me."

As Zhen Guo left the room, Su heard him say to himself, "Then we will deal with Yuen."

FORTY

Bao'an, June 1945

The dripping water drove Yuen crazy. It was inside the wall, each drop like an explosion inside his skull. He tried to curl up again, in the corner, his head against the damp, concrete wall.

The cell was a windowless vault: four paces deep and two paces wide. There was a square opening to the outside corridor at floor level. When Yuen stood up, his hair grazed the ceiling, and the square opening came up to just above his knees. It was barely large enough for a man to crawl through, and it was covered by an iron door that slid up and down. A rectangular cutout in the door—like a mail slot—let in the only daylight Yuen ever saw. Sometimes, it was bright enough to see the scratches he'd made on the wall with a loose rock to count the days. There were sixty marks.

Three times a day, he saw a set of boots march by. Once a day, a saucer came through the slit in the door. If Yuen wasn't there to catch it, the guard would drop it, and half of the thin rice porridge would splatter out as it hit the floor. Once a week, the door slid up, and the guard shouted, "Give out your bucket! Hurry up!" And Yuen would push the full bucket—his week's worth of excrement—though the opening. Then the guard would curse Yuen as he emptied it and tossed it back in.

Yuen knew where he was: Bao'an. It was a smaller city about forty miles northwest of Yenan. He knew it well—the Long March survivors had settled here for a time before moving to Yenan more permanently. Bao'an was once a frontier garrison during the Tang Dynasty, and as they'd marched him past the high stone wall of the inner city, he knew escape would be impossible. He guessed this was a secret prison for political prisoners, but he decided it was mostly empty. One night, he'd heard another voice, distant and garbled. Then he realized it was a song—"The East is Red"—and he'd called out in response. No answer. The next night the voice was gone, and it never returned.

Yuen shivered in the pitch black and tried in vain to shut out the dripping. He felt the tear in his sleeve and remembered the night the four soldiers had come. It was only two nights after he'd returned from the winter rescue mission. He hadn't resisted, but one of the louts felt the need to hurt him, hence the tear. He'd been glad that Jiang Hong and Mei Fong were not home to see him taken.

At the time, he'd expected a reprimand for some small offense—maybe something that could be kept private. How naïve he'd been! *And now my family has no idea what happened to me.*

For days, Yuen sifted through his memories.

What am I accused of? What have I done?

No one told him.

Sometimes, sifting, he tried to recall a single incident when he might have offended some Party member, or when he could have been on the wrong side an issue, so that the Chairman now wanted to make an example of him.

Maybe Mao doesn't even know I am here. Maybe it is all a mistake! And if it is? Have they forgotten me?

He tried to block out the memories of others he'd seen spirited away—men who'd never returned.

It was a week before he got any answers. He remembered it was night…

The door slid up. He'd hoped for daylight, but it was dark.

In the single bulb corridor, he saw two pairs of boots.

"Get out," said a voice.

Yuen crawled out.

He blinked in the bulb glare and stared up at the two guards. They wore dark green uniforms and red-starred caps.

"Go," one commanded, shoving Yuen's shoulder with the sole of his boot. Yuen got up—sore joints aching—and stumbled down the narrow passage. He passed a dozen soundless cells like his.

"Why am I here?" he asked the guards. His voice was dry and cracked from disuse. The guards ignored him. They shoved him down a tight passageway that dead-ended at a thick, wooden door. One guard opened it; the other pushed Yuen through. The door closed—*click*—behind him. There was a finality about that click.

The windowless room was twenty by ten. There was a table, a chair, a high ceiling. Yuen sat down on the chair, savoring the feeling of sitting and surprised at how weak his legs had become.

Two smoking kerosene lamps cast flickering light against the far wall.

The door opened and a thin, young man entered. His clothes were too big, frumpy—the style of a political officer. In his hands he held a small stack of paper. He looked Yuen up and down, frowning and pursing his lips.

"You are Lin Yuen?" he said.

"Yes."

"I expected...more."

For a moment, the two locked eyes, then the officer looked down at the papers and without looking up said, "What have you to say for yourself?"

Yuen coughed. "Why am I a prisoner?" He stood up shakily; the chair screeched behind him.

The officer continued to peruse the papers in his hand. He didn't move a muscle.

"What am I accused of?" Yuen rasped.

"You must think I'm a fool," the political officer replied. "Everyone pretends not to know anything."

"This is insane. I have no idea why I'm here!"

"Sit down and shut up!"

The two guards standing by the door, armed with truncheons, scuffed forward. Yuen heard their unison breathing by his shoulder. The political officer added, "No wonder you're here—such insolence!"

Yuen forced himself to sit back down. The officer walked to the other side of the table.

"I suppose it must be official," he said. He flipped one paper, then another. The pages were crowded with characters: dark, rapid brushstrokes.

The officer read aloud, "Lin Yuen is accused of the following crimes against the Party: interference with political officers in the field; spreading lies to discredit the Party to foreigners; conspiring to inspire loyalty from his men toward himself and not to our great Chairman; errors in judgment where he endangered the lives of innocent civilians so that he himself could escape."

The officer looked up.

"Ridiculous!" Yuen blurted. He felt his empty stomach knotting.

"You all say the same—"

"There are many others who will confirm that I—"

"Did you not listen to what I just read? Your friends are suspect, too. Their loyalty is also being tested. *And* we have sworn testimony against you!"

Yuen sat back, stunned. *Who would speak against me?* It hit him. *The new man. Huang Su.*

Yuen clenched his jaw. "Comrade, I have sacrificed much for the Party. I—"

"Silence, dog!" the younger man seethed. "The past is no matter. Even old heroes can be corrupted by power and greed. Did it make you feel important to have the ear of an American officer? They said you always insisted on picking your own men. Why? Because they idolized you? Because they'd obey without question, even when your actions undermined the Party? There is only one hope for you now, and you're lucky you've been given this chance. Write a long self-criticism and admit your crimes. You know the policy: clemency for those who come clean, severity for those who refuse to confess. Perhaps the Party leaders will find you worthy of rehabilitation. Or, perhaps not—"

Yuen exploded. He vaulted over the table and plowed into the slender man, crushing him against the opposite wall. The papers fluttered like butterflies to the floor. Yuen pounded the man's face, breaking his nose, knocking out a tooth, before the guards descended on him. They smashed their billy clubs into his back; Yuen dropped to the floor. They struck him again and again—in the ribs, in the head. He lay on the cold stone floor, absorbing the blows.

Before he blacked out, Yuen noticed most of the papers were blank.

He awoke in his cell; it was dark. He didn't move for a long time. It hurt to breathe, and when he reached up to feel his side—a stabbing pain in his chest. When a little light began to show through the door cutout, he couldn't see out of his left eye. It was swollen shut.

An hour later, the door slid up, and a pencil and ten sheets of blank paper were slid under. With his better eye, Yuen saw a new set of boots—shiny, black leather.

"For when you decide to confess," a soft voice said. The door slid down. Footsteps echoed. Silence.

Yuen left the papers where they were.

For days after this, the same small voice spoke to him through the door.

"Why don't you just confess?" it asked in a soothing tone. "You know it will go much easier on you."

"When you confess, I can arrange for you to have more food. Better food. However, if you insist on refusal, I shall have to curtail your food altogether. Do you understand what I am saying?"

Yuen said nothing.

"If you do not confess, you will die in here. Your family will never know what became of you. Do you not want to see them again?"

Eventually, the requests stopped. Three times, they took him out to beat him in the corridor. The same cruel guards who'd broken his ribs. They liked to kick him in the belly and stomp on his legs. They chuckled when Yuen spat blood. They liked to see him bleed. As he drifted in and out of consciousness, the guards talked about their prowess, their skill at softening people up. When they finally tired, they shoved Yuen back into his cell.

No matter what pain they subjected him to, Yuen withstood it. He refused to confess, and he marked the wall with the days. He kept his mind clear with this one act.

One night, a new voice came from behind the door.

"Lin Yuen?" The voice was almost inaudible. "Lin Yuen? I know you can hear me. I'm your friend. I know you don't want to confess, but they told me to ask you if you still love your daughter. I'm sorry to have to ask you this."

Slowly, weakly, Yuen lifted his head off the floor.

The voice continued in a gentle singsong.

"Your daughter. She's already been disgraced at her school, stripped of her leadership position, ostracized by her teachers and the other students. Your wife is the subject of ridicule and gossip. Everyone believes your long absence has resulted from traitorous acts."

"That's what I am to confess?" Yuen rasped. "To being a traitor?"

"You could just say you made mistakes. Maybe you were influenced by the Americans."

"I won't say that. Confessing isn't going to help my family, and you know it."

The man's voice changed, became almost effeminate. "Oh, that is so unfortunate. I must ask again. Do you really love your daughter?"

Yuen sucked air into his lungs. The tiny cell smelled of urine and dung. The air was awful, almost unbreathable.

The eerie voice continued, "No one would question it if your daughter was taken into custody. No one would care, in the community at large, if she met with…an unfortunate accident. Such things happen. They do. And I know this is what will happen if you do not write self-criticism."

Yuen summoned what was left of his voice. He shouted hoarsely, "Leave my daughter out of this, you coward!" But even as he said this, he heard the boots tapping away in the infinite silence of his confinement.

"Wouldn't it be easier to simply confess?" the man called from afar. In the silence, his voice seemed close, but it was not. Then Yuen heard laughing. "Perhaps all could still be well!"

The next morning, at first light, Yuen put pencil to paper and confessed his crimes, everything he thought they wanted to hear. He felt his honor die a thousand times with each scratch of the pencil. When he finished the confession, he felt ancient.

In the afternoon, a set of eyes appeared in the cutout—a man on his hands and knees. It was the same sweet, prying, patient voice.

"There! I see you have done it. Was that so difficult?"

The door slid up—a chubby hand with fat fingers gathered up the papers—the door slammed down.

Yuen closed his eyes, exhaled slowly. The piss didn't smell so bad at that moment.

An hour later, the voice was back.

"This is not adequate!" the voice reprimanded. One at a time, the crumpled papers came scrunching through the narrow slot. "There's nothing here about the conspiracy to turn the Americans against the Party! We know what you told him. We know you have long harbored counter-revolutionary feelings."

The door slid up, and a new stack of blank paper appeared. "Do it again!"

This went on for three days. Each day, Yuen added to his confession. Each day, he was compelled to *improve* it. After the third revision, nothing happened.

And the drip in the wall had started again—annoying him, infuriating him. Yuen spent hours lying on his back, trying to ignore the pangs in his stomach and his sore ribs. He felt his beard, grown to the point he could grab a fistful of hair. His thirst prompted dreams of rivers, streams, waterfalls, thunderstorms—anything to do with water. At night, he listened for the mice scurrying in the walls or in the corridor.

He tried his best not to think about Jiang Hong and Mei Fong. Thinking of them, wanting to see them, would drive him mad. There was no telling how long he would be imprisoned. It could certainly be years. If he was going to survive, he needed to stay detached and keep his mind clear.

And yet, each morning, Yuen wondered if this would be the day he would be taken out and shot. He'd been in the Party long enough to know the odds of this were better than good, it was only a matter of when.

Three days after his last revision, the door slid open.

"Please come out," the guard's voice said.

Yuen crawled out, blinded by sunlight in the corridor. There was only one guard, and Yuen thought he looked strange, before he realized this was because the guard was not scowling at him. His face was serene and was not unpleasant.

"Please follow me," the guard said.

Yuen followed him down the tunnel of dimness. They turned right, then left. Yuen blinked—there were windows that looked out on the world. It was a sunny day. He saw rooftops, the huge wall of the inner city, a pagoda-like tower in the distance.

They stopped at an open door. It was a cell, but one with a window. He went to the window and leaned his face against the bars. Staring at the blue sky, he breathed deeply. There was a narrow iron bed. He sat on it, feeling the prickle of straw poking through the mattress cover. He looked up and saw a sink. Turning the faucet, he could hardly believe it when water came out. He bent down and drank and drank until his stomach was full of water. The guard studied him from the doorway.

"Is there anything you want?" he asked.

Yuen looked at him in disbelief.

"We're bringing you some food, some new clothes. Is there anything else you would like?"

Yuen felt his chin and squinted at his reflection in the metal spigot. "I could use a razor." After saying this, he half-expected the guard to come at him with a stick. The man merely said, "I'll bring one."

Then he closed the door and left, but Yuen didn't hear him lock it.

He eased himself onto the bed. *What does this mean? I thought they were going to execute me. All I wanted was for Mei Fong to believe I was a good man and to one day know the truth about what happened to me.*

The guard returned with the razor and a small mirror. Yuen couldn't help gasping when he saw his reflection. The sunken cheeks and hollow eyes, the matted hair and beard, it all seemed to belong to a stranger. The guard watched him as he shaved, and when Yuen finished, he held out his hand for the razor and mirror. Yuen handed them over and the guard left. A few minutes later the door opened again, and Yuen was surprised to see the first face he recognized since being imprisoned.

It was Chen Zhen Guo.

"Hello, Yuen," he said.

Yuen stared at him.

"When I found out where they'd taken you, I came right away." Zhen Guo stood just inside the doorway. "We've all been wondering what happened to you."

"What did happen to me?"

"They haven't told you? I've only just found out myself. One of your men filed a report, called you a counter-revolutionary. Liu Shaoqi said he had no choice but to interrogate you. But I had no idea they would treat you as harshly as this."

"Zhen Guo—that so-called mole was the very man you asked me to bring along."

"It was? How can you be sure?" Zhen Guo's expression softened. "If it's true, I'm sorry. You know, it *was* Comrade Liu who asked me to put him in your group. I'm sorry, Yuen."

Zhen Guo shifted his gaze, out the barred window. "Yuen, many friends have been asking about you, including myself. They finally told us you had been taken to a retreat to contemplate your deeds and write self-criticism. We did not ask questions, but as time went on, others did. Particularly your American friend, Lieutenant Parker. It sounds like he has been demanding to see you."

"Only him?"

"Jiang Hong and Mei Fong were afraid to ask about you— you understand. I have tried to keep watch over them..."

Yuen stared at Zhen Guo, not saying anything.

Zhen Guo cleared his throat.

"The Party leadership has considered and approved the self-criticism you wrote. They consider you rehabilitated now. They agree to release you. You can go home and see your wife and daughter again. They summoned me to tell you this."

"Why you?"

Zhen Guo scratched his head. "I asked the same thing. They wanted me to tell you there is one condition. You will inevitably have the chance to see Lieutenant Parker again. They think it would be better for all concerned—and this *includes* your wife and daughter—if you do not tell the Americans about the conditions of your…internment."

The two men stared at each other. Zhen Guo added, "I'm sorry, my friend. Is this acceptable to you?"

Yuen's gaze drifted to the floor. "Yes."

FORTY-ONE

Yuen settled into a corner of the horse cart. The right wheel's flattened rim made the ride very bumpy, and he winced with every jolt. He closed his eyes and felt the wind on his face. When he opened them, he squinted at the cloudless blue sky, the wide-open land, forbidding and desolate but altogether wonderful to him. If the flat-nosed, dark-skinned driver wondered what his shuffling, black-eyed passenger was guilty of, he didn't ask. He kept his eyes on the road and on his beast: a thick-hoofed, raw-boned gray mule. Yuen's new clothes were made of brown burlap material—stiff and irritating—yet the scratchiness was one more reminder that he was alive and out of the hellhole that had almost killed him.

No one recognized Yuen as the cart came to a stop at the small ramp leading up to his home. He slid out of the cart and gently set his feet on hard ground. After a nod to the driver, he faced home, his focus narrowing. *One foot in front of the other. Steady.* He glanced up the incline, which was steeper than he'd remembered. An old, persistent thought haunted him—*What am I going to tell Jiang Hong and Mei Fong? What will they think?*

He made the climb slowly, but without stopping. Their small garden had been trampled, torn green leaves scattered beside boot prints in the dirt. He stopped at the front door and listened. The sound of the wind. Then he opened the door.

Jiang Hong was at the stove transferring a pan of noodles to a plate. She spun around and shrieked. The contents of the pan tilted, and noodles fell to the floor.

Gripped tightly in her hands, the pan came up to her right shoulder—a weapon.

"Jiang Hong, it's me," Yuen said softly. Her hair was disheveled, with new gray streaks. Her face had dark half-moons under the eyes. She looked at least ten years older.

"What do you want?" she cried.

He held his hands out, open. "It's me, Yuen."

She stared blankly at him. Then she emitted a high-pitched squeak. The pan clattered to the floor.

"Yuen? Is it you?"

He went to her. She fell into his arms and began to cry.

"I'm sorry...so sorry," he whispered.

"Why? Why?" she murmured. She was trembling all over.

Yuen gently cupped her face in his hands. "What have they done to you? Did they hurt you? And where is Mei Fong?"

"Nobody hurt me." Jiang Hong sniffed, wiping her eyes dry with the back of her sleeve. "Mei Fong is at school. Where *were* you?" For the first time, she looked closely at his swollen eyelid, the newly healed cuts, and older scars on his face.

She shrunk back a little. "What happened to you?"

"They took me to a prison in Bao'an. I am accused of being a counter-revolutionary. For a long time, I refused to write self-criticism, but in the end...I did."

"Oh!" she said, drawing a deep breath.

Yuen gazed into her frightened eyes. "Are you and Mei Fong all right?"

"So everything they've accused us of—accused *you* of—is true?" Her brows narrowed. "Are you a traitor?"

"Of course not. I would never have confessed to lies, but they threatened to kill you and Mei Fong if I did not cooperate."

She stared hard at Yuen for a long moment. The sound of the wind whined through a crack in the door. She bit her lower lip.

Yuen wondered if she believed what he said.

For a long time, it seemed to him she stayed like that—somewhere between belief and disbelief.

Then she moaned deep in her throat and threw her arms around his neck.

"It has been terrible! There were rumors about you, bad things. No one wants anything to do with us. Our friends are afraid to come near. People say things whenever I go out. They throw our clean clothes off the line and trample them in the dirt. They uproot the garden like pigs. Poor Mei Fong—"

"Did someone hurt her?"

Jiang Hong shook her head. "I don't think so, but she comes home crying. She's humiliated each day." She scowled. "Those rotten teachers give her the worst time, and they teach the other kids to be cruel to her. I think she's almost given up hope."

"Hope of what?"

Jiang Hong's brow furrowed. "That her Ba Ba isn't a traitor. That you aren't what everyone says you are."

Yuen's hands curled into fists. "Let's go get her right now."

"From school? Now?"

He looked down. A roach peeked out of a crack in the floor. It emerged slowly, toddling toward the pile of noodles.

Yuen stomped on it.

"Yes," he said. "We go now."

They walked hand in hand. A few people stared at them, but no one said anything. The sun was high and bright. Jiang Hong shuffled close to Yuen, keeping a little behind him. Yuen took fuller strides, pulling himself forward with a renewed force of will. The simple movement of walking reassured him that his old strength was still there.

Yuen spotted Mei Fong in the schoolyard. She sat alone, legs crossed, at a corner of the one-room schoolhouse. Her teacher stood a few steps in front of her, blocking her view of the yard where the other children played. Yuen angled to the side and watched her. Her back was rigid, up against the wall, but her head slumped as if she wished to bury it in her lap.

She looked up. She'd been crying. First she saw her mother, then Yuen. She stared hard. Yuen was kneeling at the edge of the school yard. He held out his arms and nodded. Mei Fong sprang up and ran toward him, lips parting in a smile, even as tears glistened on her cheeks.

"Stop!" the teacher shouted. She glared at Yuen, but that didn't stop Mei Fong from running to him.

She stumbled into Yuen's embrace. She clung to his arm, sobbing into the crook of his elbow. Yuen wept openly. Then he stood up, and the three of them walked home without speaking a word.

There was a knock at the door. Yuen's eyes opened. He froze, staring at the dark ceiling. His eyes darted to Jiang Hong, who'd sat up abruptly from her bed mat. She looked at him, the whites of her eyes barely visible in the dimness. He turned to peek into the front room and saw Mei Fong sleeping by the stove.

Another knock, softer. Yuen got up, already dressed in street clothes, and tiptoed to the door, grabbing the fire poker on the way. Without opening the door, he said, "Who's there?"

"Yuen? Is that you? It's David."

Yuen opened the door.

"Yuen!"

David ducked through the doorway and surprised Yuen by embracing him. Yuen cringed and coughed—his hand shot to his side. David stepped back. "You all right?"

Yuen grimaced and raised his index finger to his lips, then pointed outside.

They stepped outdoors and sat next to each other on the curb of the slanted street. Across the valley the full moon lingered directly over Yenan's hilltop pagoda, as if balanced on its sharp tip.

"What happened?" David asked.

The pain in Yuen's ribs burned. He took short stabs of breath.

"Nothing."

"What do you mean, nothing? I can see you've been beaten. Where have you been?"

Yuen stared ahead. There was a crooked pine in the line of his vision and he fixed his eye on it. A large raven flew up, flapping.

"What can I do to help?" David asked.

Yuen continued to stare after the bird that was soon lost in the clouds.

"Nothing," he said. "It's over."

"What's over? Yuen, you were gone for two months! What did they do to you?"

A strong gust of wind blew dust in their faces. Yuen shielded his eyes. David lowered his head. The wind spun, making a small dust devil that died. Bits of bark and paper fell to the ground.

David looked at Yuen and said, "You can't expect me to believe that nothing happened, friend."

"I am sorry. I cannot speak of it."

"Why?"

"It would put my family in danger."

"Just tell me one thing—what were you accused of?"

Yuen shrugged. "It does not matter. I am home now."

David bristled. "At least tell me if you did something wrong."

Yuen shook his head. "I did not."

"Of course you didn't," David whispered to himself.

"I know your intentions are good, but—"

"So this is how the Party treats its veteran fighters? Kidnaps them, no trial, no family, nothing but a beating and starvation. Okay, I see how it is. You don't need to tell me, I can see with my own eyes. Colonel Peterkin's going to hear of this—"

"No!" Yuen hissed. He turned and grabbed David's shoulder. "You cannot speak of this. If you do they will think I told you. And I cannot tell you anything. I'm sorry." His eyes pleaded with David. "Promise to be silent...for my family's sake."

David stared at him. "How can you ask me this? If this sort of thing is going on it's important my government knows about it. We've been here a year! You want American help? You want us to believe you're the saviors of China?" He shook his head. "You say you're different from Stalin, but—"

"Please!" Yuen took a deep and pained breath. "Whatever you report, I *know* they will discover it and think that I spoke. This is certain."

David looked at the ground.

"Please, promise me," Yuen begged.

David shifted uncomfortably. He examined Yuen's worried face, and in his mind, old images flashed—there was Yuen in the blockhouse, the fight in the valley. David turned away. The moon had a hint of orange.

He nodded slowly.

"Thank you," Yuen whispered.

Eventually people will forget about all this, Yuen thought. *I'll fade away, and then perhaps my family can live anonymously.*

In a way, he felt good. This was a weight off his shoulders, and for the first time in a long time, he took a calm, deep breath. He was without fear.

Do not be concerned with things outside your door. From now on, I will live for myself and my family alone.

—

Weeks passed and David's days became routine: attending meetings, interviewing Communist officers, observing troops in training. He didn't see Yuen, at Yuen's request. He racked his brain for a way to reveal the Communists' dark side without endangering his friend. *I'm sure I will, eventually*, he told himself. *But for now, I have to believe what Yuen said.*

As weeks turned to months, David's alarm over what happened to Yuen diminished. *They treated him harshly, yes, but he wasn't killed. They let him go.*

The summer wore on, and all attention in Yenan became fixated on the impending invasion of Japan. There'd been a modest celebration in May when news of V-E Day reached the city. In Asia, the Japanese were falling back on all fronts, but no one expected the war to end soon. An invasion of Japan would take months, perhaps more than a year, to succeed. Every American dreaded the bloodbath to come.

Then, to the complete surprise of all, the name of a city no one had ever heard of was on everyone's lips: Hiroshima. What kind of super bomb was it? The idea that one bomb could destroy an entire city was inconceivable to David and everyone else. Time seemed to speed up. The Russians invaded Manchuria, a move that fulfilled their promise to enter the war against Japan but looked like a last-minute land grab. Rumors spread of large-scale, suicidal banzai charges by the Japanese. Word of Nagasaki came three days after Hiroshima's bombing. And finally, David and his countrymen found themselves huddled around a radio, straining to hear Emperor Hirohito's tinny voice through the static.

After the surrender broadcast, all of Yenan's inhabitants streamed out of their homes, and a joyous celebration, unlike any David had ever seen, erupted in the streets.

FORTY-TWO

Yenan, August 1945

The spicy aroma of frying hot peppers drew David to the open window of a small, clay-walled building. Inside, wreaths of steam wrapped around the heads of four cooks—three middle-aged women and an old man. The women hunched over their woks, tossing in peppers and other vegetables that David couldn't identify. The old man tended three steamers, reaching down into the huge pots with long tongs to remove bamboo segments filled with rice, chives, and cabbage. Smoke curled to the ceiling, wafted toward the window, and was sucked out over David's head.

He walked a few steps farther and looked into the adjacent courtyard enclosed by a low stone wall. People were eating—at least two dozen—spread over four long wooden tables. For a moment, David listened to the hum of conversation, the clinking bowls and cups. A small boy, no older than four, was expertly using his chopsticks, transferring small mounds of rice and cabbage to his mouth. Beside him, his mother scolded an older boy who was crawling in the dust under the table.

"Lieutenant!"

David turned. It was Major Enfield.

"You get a kick out of watching people eat?"

David stiffened, saluted.

Enfield brought his right hand up sloppily in an annoyed wave. "Let's get to the meeting, Lieutenant." He brushed past David.

"Yes, sir."

David took a last glance at the chopstick boy, who was now looking at him curiously, chopsticks cradled between his fingers at an odd angle. David smiled and trotted to catch up to Enfield.

"This gathering's for horse crap," Enfield muttered. "Expect the Commies to whine our ears off about this surrender fiasco. I don't want them hoarding Jap weapons any more than Chiang does. Already bad enough the Russians are gettin' their hands on so much of it."

David nodded. Chiang Kai-shek had announced that only Nationalist troops, representing the one "true" government of China, were authorized to accept Japanese surrenders. There were no Nationalist troops in northern China, so Chiang's claim was as impractical as it was arrogant. But so far, the Americans appeared to condone Chiang's claim by not opposing it.

David remarked, "I've heard the Air Corps is planning to fly Nationalist troops to the northeastern cities so they can accept surrenders. Is that true?"

"Hell yes, it's true—and a damn good idea, if you ask me. I even heard there's still some Japs fighting it out, refusing to surrender to the Commies." Enfield chuckled. "Chiang will *love* that—Japs fighting for the chance to surrender to the Nationalists!"

"But you mentioned the Russians too, sir. Maybe they'll get to a lot of them first."

Enfield made a sour face. "Yeah, another bunch of ninnies I hate to see get extra weapons. We've gotta stand up to these Commie sons of bitches today. They're gonna be rounding up all the Japs they can find, and they're gonna try to get us to take their side, but what do we do? Nothing."

He looked piercingly at David. "You get the picture, don't you, Lieutenant?"

"I do, sir."

On their right, they passed a barber shop. The weather was warm but not humid, and a pleasant breeze blew down the street. The barber was set up outside, with a customer sitting on a wooden stool next to the road. The barber bent down to clean out the man's right ear with a long curette. Enfield spat, disgusted.

"I'd grow it down to my toes before I let one of those barbarians poke me in the ear. People back home'll never believe me if I tell 'em the barbers over here cut nose and ear hair." He shot a glance at David. "Ten to one they're selling it for pillow stuffing."

He roared at his own foolish joke, while David maintained an uncomfortable silence.

Then David said, "Can I ask you a question, Major?"

Enfield's smile withered. "What?"

"I'm not enamored with the Communists, but you really seem to hate them. So I was just wondering…"

"Out with it, Lieutenant."

"I'm just wondering why you're here."

The corners of Enfield's mouth turned up in a grin. "You know what they say about keeping your enemies close, don't you?"

There was something in Enfield's eyes, a devious and cunning look, that told David there was more that the major wasn't telling him.

"Now let me ask *you* a question, Parker. What do you think we should be doing in China now that the war's over?"

David chose his words carefully.

"We're between a rock and a hard place, sir. We've stuck with Chiang, but unless he transforms himself and his government, I don't see how he can keep this country together."

"Go on," Enfield prodded.

"Well, we can try to make these two sides negotiate, but the blood between them is so bad, I think it would take a miracle for them to avoid a civil war."

Enfield clapped an open palm on David's back.

"You're right, Parker, we oughta pull entirely out of this country and let 'em kill each other. Then we can chop up and mop up whatever's left at the end. No better way, as I see it."

—

Mao had called for the meeting to take place at the Communists' Central Committee headquarters, a three-kilometer walk northwest of Yenan—in a place called Yangjialing Village. Many of the Party offices were here, and Mao, Zhou, and other Party leaders lived in caves on a nearby hill to the north. David and Enfield entered a small auditorium with a vaulted ceiling. A dozen American officers were already present, sitting on folding chairs arranged in a semicircle and facing an identical semicircle of seated Chinese.

Only two men spoke during the hour-long meeting: Mao and Zhou. First, Mao delivered an impassioned speech on the sacrifices made by the Chinese Communists; next, Zhou gave a well-reasoned argument explaining why the Communists should accept surrender from as many Japanese as possible. David had to admit, Zhou made a lot of sense. But, following orders, he and the other Americans just listened and agreed to nothing.

It embarrassed David that a few American officers had been nodding off during the meeting. *Everyone's hung over*, he decided, *only some hide it better than others.*

Since the Japanese surrender, Army discipline had become more relaxed. The last three days felt like a continuous celebration, and Americans and Chinese alike were looking forward to a new play debuting that night, which promised to commemorate the glorious Allied victory in comedic fashion. Unlike some others, David had managed to stay sober, but he'd had several drinks around noontime and spent the last half of the meeting desperately needing to relieve himself.

"Coming, Lieutenant?" Major Enfield said as he and the other Americans filed out of the room.

"Yes, sir. I'll be along. Need to find a john first."

"It won't be any cleaner here, if that's what you're hoping."

David exited at the back of the auditorium and went down a flight of stone steps into a dusty courtyard. He spotted the outhouse and hurried to it.

When he was finished, he walked back across the courtyard, which was enclosed by a tall brick wall contiguous with the rear wall of the auditorium. There was an arched moon gate to one side, which David headed for, as it was the most direct path to the street. Then, low voices on the other side of the wall stopped him in his tracks.

He recognized the voices.

"...but what is different now, Shaoqi?" said Zhou Enlai. His voice was soft but not quite a whisper.

"Now the question of whether we will receive arms is irrelevant," Liu Shaoqi said. "The Japanese are defeated. Why would the Americans choose to arm us?"

Mao's voice came next, the rustic Hunanese dialect. "You are correct. The question now is: what else is there to gain from the Americans?"

David pressed himself against the wall on his side of the gate and felt his heart begin to beat faster.

Mao answered his own question. "We must convince them to keep out of a civil war. The drama will play out. They will pressure Chiang to come to terms with us and form a coalition government. We'll play along, to buy time."

"More waiting?" Liu said with a hiss.

Zhou's voice. "We are not prepared for the war that's to come. This is reality."

"They have asked me to go to Chungking to negotiate with Chiang," Mao said. "General Hurley is flying here to escort me and guarantee my safety." He chuckled mockingly. "The negotiations will fail, but we must make it look good. Everything rests on the Americans leaving China. We have to appear reasonable and moderate."

Someone sighed, annoyed.

"What's the matter?" Mao asked.

Liu's voice again. "Nothing, you are correct, of course. It's only that we have struggled for so long; we have overcome so much. Sometimes I wonder if our revolution has yet begun and even whether it will occur in my lifetime..."

"Patience, Comrade," Mao said. "There will be a time for revolution. It will be the birth pangs of a new China. But the only thing that can prevent ultimate victory is continued

American support of Chiang. It irritates me as much as you to pander to these Americans. Lucky for us, Chiang is so inept that they are easily impressed. We must continue to bide our time. There will be a time for upheaval. We will see it with our own eyes."

David heard the trio move away down the street. Adrenaline surged through him. *They're screwing with us?* His mind flashed back to earlier times: the welcome reception, the grand pretense of friendliness, happy, dancing Communists, reading Jack's enthusiastic reports. *And now what? We'll spend months trying to negotiate a peace neither side wants. What if Washington decides to send more American soldiers here to fight for Chiang?* He thought of Davies in Moscow. *What if the Russians send in troops to support the Communists? It could start a whole new war...*

David shook his head, rattling the questions away. His body was still stuck against the wall.

I have to report this, he thought.

He moved slowly toward the gate, peeked out, and didn't see anyone. He made an effort at walking out casually. No one noticed him; he breathed a sigh of relief.

There was but one thought in his head.

I need to see Yuen.

—

"Can I come in?" David asked. Behind him, the late afternoon sun cast soft light over the city.

Yuen stared, surprised to see him. He stuck his head out the door, and his eyes darted up and down the street. With a quick hand motion, he beckoned David inside.

"Sorry to show up with no warning," David said, "but we need to talk."

Yuen shut the door and glanced behind him at Jiang Hong, who sat up from her stool and retreated into the back room. Yuen pointed to the stool but David remained standing.

"Yuen, I just overheard Mao, Zhou, and Liu talking about a huge deception. They're going to drag out the talks with Chiang to prepare for civil war. Mao's going to Chungking, but he's just buying time. They're pretending to be moderate, hoping to keep America from supporting Chiang."

"How did you hear this?"

David told him.

"I've got to report this, Yuen. It's my duty. There's too much at stake."

Yuen gazed at the floor and rubbed his chin.

"The last thing I want to do is put you in danger, but—"

"Do what you feel you must," Yuen said.

David exhaled slowly. "I'll keep it secret. I'm going to type it up and go to Chungking. I'll hand-deliver it to General Hurley. That way, people here will never know."

Yuen looked at David. His eyes were dark and quiet. "Thank you. If the Americans change their behavior toward us, it would be better if you are gone. When does the plane depart?"

"Tomorrow morning."

"Will you come back?"

"I don't know. It'll depend on how my report is received. I can try."

"It would be better if you did not return."

David nodded softly.

Yuen reached for his friend's hand. He pulled David toward him in a light, brief embrace.

"You are an honorable man," Yuen said. "I am privileged to know you."

David replied thickly, "I'll find you when this is all over."

Yuen smiled. "I would like that."
Then David left.

—

Jiang Hong trembled as she leaned into the dark shadows of the small rear room. Thoughts raced through her head. *Yuen did not stop him? The American is going to report to—who was it? Hurley? That's the important American general! Everything they said about Yuen is true. He is a traitor.*

She bit her lower lip and peeked through the opening. Yuen was still standing, motionless, by the stove.

I must tell someone. I'll go to Zhen Guo. This is my duty. This is exactly what we are taught to guard against! She recited the tenet in her head: "*Husbands, wives, sons, and daughters can all be corrupted. The only true certainty is the Party and Chairman Mao who leads it.*"

FORTY-THREE

Zhen Guo's feet pounded the sand-packed road. He sprinted past a thin line of spruce trees—just a green, roadside blur. The setting sun flamed the sky with orange streaks. His heart raced, but not from the running. He desperately needed to find Chairman Mao.

The chairman had to be at the theater. He saw it now: Red Congress Hall. The large stone building had originally been built as a Catholic church. He took the front steps three at a time. Inside, sounds of laughter and music. He pulled the door open.

The room was packed. A rolling wave of laughter washed over Zhen Guo; his ears filled with the sound. On stage, actors portraying Stalin, Churchill, and Truman were humiliating others dressed as Hirohito and the Japanese war cabinet. Zhen Guo leaned against the doorjamb and tried to slow his breathing. The door slammed shut behind him and a few back row Chinese turned with annoyed faces.

Fools, he thought. *These people think their troubles are over, but there are enemies all around us.* The Hirohito character was down on all fours, groveling to the Allied leaders. Churchill gave him a hard kick in the pants, and Hirohito did a slapstick face-plant. Another wave of laughter and cheers. Zhen Guo shook his head. *They don't understand.*

He saw the chairman in the front row, flanked on one side by other Party leaders and on the other side by two American officers. He felt a queasy rush of uncertainty. *Do I really want to do this now? What if I upset him?*

The performers finished the sketch and Zhen Guo lost sight of Mao as the audience rose for a standing ovation. He moved to the center aisle for a better view. *I've got to tell him. Time is short; minutes count.*

He started down the aisle in the midst of applause and cheers. Liu Shaoqi was seated on the aisle, third row from the front. Zhen Guo saw him and had a quick thought. *Better for the message to come from him.* He tapped Liu on the shoulder, then bent down and whispered into his ear. The applause subsided and those around him regained their seats as Zhen Guo finished what he had to say.

Liu's permanent weasel-like smile evaporated. "You're absolutely certain of this?" he whispered.

Zhen Guo nodded.

"Stay here."

The lights dimmed; new actors appeared. A Japanese soldier was carrying a bouquet of flowers to a Chinese boy dressed up as a girl.

Zhen Guo watched as Liu scurried, hunched over, to Mao. Mao leaned forward—the two heads bent close together.

On stage, the boy smashed the flowers on the Japanese soldier's head and kicked him in the groin. The crowd came apart with laughter.

Mao stood and strode ceremoniously up the aisle, following Liu, who walked briskly ahead of him.

Zhen Guo met them outside the door.

"What is it?" Mao demanded.

"I'm sorry, Chairman. We can't talk here," Zhen Guo said. He pointed across the street to where some small buildings were clustered. "Over there, please."

The trio walked across the street and entered the shadow of an alley.

"Now, tell me what's so important."

Zhen Guo took a deep breath. "Chairman, tonight I have some alarming news. You know Yuen, the guerilla leader who gave self-criticism—"

"Yes, of course. I know the man and his case file."

"Tonight, his wife informed me that Lieutenant David Parker came to their home and told Yuen he'd overheard a conversation today between both of you and Comrade Zhou. She said Parker plans to report to General Hurley that we've been deceiving the Americans. He's going to tell them we're not interested in peace, and that we're playing everyone for fools."

Mao remained stony-eyed, but it was obvious he'd been struck to the quick.

"Where is the American now? In there?" Mao pointed to the theater.

"I don't think so," Zhen Guo replied. "He may be typing this up as a report. He plans to leave on the airplane tomorrow and deliver it to Ambassador Hurley himself."

Mao shook his head gravely and then spoke in a low monotone. "Before telling secrets on the road, look in the bushes. This is, no doubt, a very serious thing." He looked Zhen Guo in the eye. "The American cannot be allowed to make this report."

"He is only a lieutenant," Liu said. "Perhaps they will not believe him."

Mao bristled with sudden annoyance. "We have to assume they will. He is a good soldier, this Parker, and he performed well in battle." He nodded as much to himself as to the others. "You can be sure they will believe him."

Liu and Zhen Guo stood still, awaiting Mao's next utterance.

"Hurley is just a pawn, but he's sided with the Nationalists now. He will seize on any evidence to demonize us. Therefore, we must do whatever is necessary to reassure the Americans that things are just as they seem to be—unchanged."

"Excuse me, Chairman," Zhen Guo cautiously offered, "I wonder how much difference this could make. Now their war is over."

"You don't understand them, Comrade. Americans are arrogant and impractical. In this way they are very predictable. They try to fit everything into what they think is right and wrong. If they learn to hate us and group us with the Russians, they might go on supporting Chiang for that alone.

"And if America stays..." Mao grimaced. "That would be the greatest threat to our final victory."

He raised a fist and planted it into his open palm. "One mouse dropping may ruin the whole pot of porridge. The American must be stopped."

"But how can we do this?" Liu asked. "How do we stop Parker from going to Chungking?"

The three men stood pensively in the gathering shadows. Far off, the buzz of an airplane engine reminded them that time was of the essence.

Zhen Guo was lost in thought. *What can we possibly do? Anticipate how to control the damage? Prepare to refute what the American will say?*

Mao gazed briefly toward the sound of the distant plane and said, "What if we took him?"

"What?" Liu said.

"What if we eliminated Lieutenant Parker?" Mao spoke softly, as if he were talking about not attending a function.

Liu whispered, "How would we accomplish such a thing?"

Mao ignored him. He stared off into space, lost to his surroundings.

Shaoqi thinks the chairman's mad, Zhen Guo thought.

Mao, looking at neither man, said to the sky, "Yes. I see it now. Parker will disappear and we will know nothing of it. All the Americans have been drinking and celebrating. Their lack of discipline has weakened their eyesight. It may be a day or two before anyone notices he's missing. We'll take him to Bao'an, then we'll decide what to do with him. If necessary, we'll find his body in some ravine, or perhaps we will never see him again at all."

Mao looked at Zhen Guo and said through lips that hardly moved, "This must be done in secret. No one else can know. It is up to you. Abduct him and take him to Bao'an. Can you do this without detection?"

Zhen Guo hesitated. *Why not just kill the American here? Why do I have to single-handedly take him to Bao'an? Does Mao think I'm expendable? If something goes wrong he could claim I'm crazy and was acting alone.*

Zhen Guo searched Mao's face. The chairman's expression was firm and expectant. His eyes were calm, fatherly, and Zhen

Guo's doubts embarrassed him. He felt a twinge of flattery. *Why, this is an opportunity! Pleasing the chairman would be very advantageous. There could be many rewards.*

"Yes, I can do it," Zhen Guo answered firmly.

"Good," Mao said.

"But Chairman, the American is a well-trained soldier. It would be better if I had another man with me."

Mao looked at Liu, who stared at his shoes.

"Choose a man you trust and seize the lieutenant. Comrade Liu will arrange for a select group of Bao'an officers to meet you on the road there."

Placing a hand on Zhen Guo's shoulder, Mao said, "We depend on you." Then, almost as an afterthought, he added, "You must succeed."

Mao turned and walked back to the theater. Without a word, Liu went off in another direction.

Zhen Guo leaned heavily against the sand-surfaced wall of the nearest building. *How will I do this? I must move quickly.* He glanced at the theater. *All the foreigners are in there. Now is the best time.*

He started to walk away and then remembered—*who should I choose to help me?* All the best men that came to mind were men of honor. No doubt all of them would follow a direct order, but each would hesitate and Zhen Guo would waste precious minutes explaining and justifying the action.

No, better to choose someone who will obey without question.

He thought immediately of Huang Su.

He's not much of a man, but all I need is another person to hold a gun on the American…just in case.

Within fifteen minutes, he'd found Su and told him what was needed. Su agreed immediately. There was no need to convince him that the American was a danger to the Party.

The two men sprinted to the American barracks. Slipping quietly between shadows and buildings, they approached the row of caves. Zhen Guo scanned the street and nearby buildings. No one in sight.

The lieutenant's room was the last in the row, five doors down—the only chamber with light in the window. The clacking sound of a typewriter caused the two Communists to look at each other and nod. Pistols drawn, they headed for the door.

—

David stretched and sat back in his chair. *The last time I wrote a report was when? Before Yenan.* He tried to choose his words carefully, knew this would be a bombshell. It wouldn't be as eloquent as one of Jack's memos, but it was the substance that mattered. *Just the facts.* Unexpectedly, he felt a surge of loneliness, regret that his best friends had been ordered out of Yenan long ago. Katherine was sure to be at the play wondering where he was. *It's more important to get this right,* he told himself. He glanced at the thin stack of white paper next to the typewriter. *Five sheets. Enough to re-type at least once, but that's it.*

He re-read what he'd written so far. The words filled two-thirds of one page.

Personal Observations of the Yenan Communists

> *As a U.S. Army officer in China for the last three years, and as one who speaks Mandarin fluently, I write this report in haste as the matter can be considered urgent to policymakers deciding how the U.S. should be involved in upcoming negotiations between the Nationalists and the Communists, and perhaps in a future civil war.*

I have spent the last year with the Communists. Most of this time, I have fought with their guerillas in the field. Many reports have no doubt been filed praising the Communists' organization, determination, willingness to fight, and hopes to reform China. I can personally attest to their excellent fighting ability.

This report addresses observations I have made that indicate the Communists may be presenting themselves as falsely moderate, hiding their true, more radical policies.

I also have reason to believe the Communists do not plan to negotiate with the Nationalists in good faith.

David positioned his fingers over the keys, readying to type again. He heard steps on the porch outside; the unlocked door opened. David turned around in his chair.

Two Chinese men came into his room.

"Get up," Zhen Guo ordered, as Su closed the door behind them.

David stared at Zhen Guo's pistol barrel, four feet away, pointed at his chest.

"Is this a joke?" He looked from Zhen Guo to Su, whom he now recognized. Su also had a pistol aimed at him; his cold stare was not comforting.

"You must come with us now," Zhen Guo demanded.

"Or else—what?"

Zhen Guo took a step closer to David. "Or else I will shoot you dead."

Laughing nervously, David said, "And what would you tell my friends who are due in any minute? You'll never get away with this."

Zhen Guo's eyes narrowed. "Don't underestimate me, Lieutenant. I *will* shoot you. Personally, I would prefer it. We'd make it look like you got into something way over your head, which is perhaps the truth. Any number of loyal Communists will testify that you and your friend Lin Yuen have been planning to assassinate Chairman Mao for some time now. The story won't matter. We are good at creating stories."

Are we betrayed? Are the others being taken hostage at the theater right now? I could bluff these two. They wouldn't kill an American.

Zhen Guo took another step forward.

David moved back, away from the desk. Zhen Guo reached for the paper in the typewriter. He snapped up the page, crumpled it into a ball, and shoved it into his coat pocket.

"No one will ever see this," he said with a snide smile.

How did he know about that?

"Move!"

David looked around the room. A huge moth was circling the burning candles on the table. He stared down the barrels of both pistols. He noticed Su's trigger finger twitching, the hatred in his eyes, and now David didn't doubt he might shoot.

Zhen Guo pointed at the door and jabbed his gun still closer to David's face. There was no time to think. David walked to the door, which Su opened for him. Outside, David searched for the presence of someone, anyone, who might help him—but there was no one.

They escorted him toward the main street, and passed a group of three Chinese ambling slowly, enjoying the cool night air. Zhen Guo and Su concealed their weapons in their pockets, but Zhen Guo kept a tight hand on David's left arm, directing him across the street, toward the town's outskirts and the dark, open area beyond.

At the city's edge, the pistols came out again. David felt Zhen Guo's grip loosen as they passed the last of the small buildings and entered the larger realm of shadow. He felt a hollowness in his gut. *I've got no options.* He glanced swiftly from side to side and realized there was no one in sight.

"Keep moving!" Zhen Guo hissed.

Then, out of a corner of his eye, David saw a darting figure. He looked left.

He didn't see anyone—only quiet buildings and vacant streets.

Ahead lay the dark and level plain, vast and empty and pierced by starlight. David thought of Katherine, and of Yuen. He thought of his report crushed into a ball in Zhen Guo's pocket. He thought of starlight and the sound a pistol makes at close range in the open air.

FORTY-FOUR

David's hands were bound behind his back. He couldn't say how long they'd been walking—it seemed like a long time. *An hour? Maybe more?* The dirt road was dimly lit by pale moonlight. Clouds passed over so that every few minutes the night came close and shrouded them in darkness. At times, David lost the road underfoot, and he would slow to a shuffle. More than once, his captors stopped and spoke to each other in little whispers he couldn't hear. From their indecision, he wondered if they were just lost, and he cursed himself for giving up so easily. *I should have yelled my head off in the streets. Then there would've been some witnesses.*

"Where are you taking me?" he asked, and asked again at intervals.

But neither man said anything. There was only the fateful sound of footfalls on the road—crunching, stumbling footfalls. Once, a small owl called from a nearby tree, and David wished he had the night vision of the bird.

A cold wind parted Zhen Guo's hair, yet he felt himself sweating from every pore. He looked out uneasily into the inky, cloud-hidden night. His thoughts raced ahead of him. *Where are the Bao'an officers? Where's the truck or horses? This endless walking was a stupid idea, and it's getting us nowhere! We don't even know where we are.*

He stared at the back of David's head. *I should shoot you now and get it over with. In the dark, I won't even see your brain splashing on the road.*

Zhen Guo sucked the cold air into his lungs. His fingers clenched his pistol grip; then he forced his hand to relax. *Everything's fine*, he told himself. *The American is cooperating.* He glanced behind. *Su's doing his part, keeping his gun up, staying alert and ready.*

Suddenly, Zhen Guo stumbled on a loose stone. For a moment, he lost his balance and started to fall, but quickly righted himself.

He exhaled slowly. *Stay sharp and don't do anything stupid*, he thought.

The night pressed close—the moon still clouded over.

Zhen Guo heard Su's heavy feet shuffling behind him.

Then, nothing.

Zhen Guo turned around.

Huang Su was gone.

In front of him, David came to a halt.

Zhen Guo crouched in the darkness. He couldn't see or hear anything.

David stood, waiting.

There came a low groan. Zhen Guo squinted and made out something darker than the night itself. It was in the road: a dead, windblown bush, a rock, something. Then it shifted, became two separate things. One of them dropped to the ground with a thud. The moon—at that moment—came free of clouds and filled the road with a milky light.

Now Zhen Guo saw a bright flash in the air.

He aimed at it and fired.

The flash—a blade raised—and the dark shape, charged him.

Zhen Guo fired twice more. One bullet chuffed into the attacker at close range. He staggered, then fell and rolled over, gasping for breath.

David saw who it was—*Lu Gao!*

Incensed, David threw his body at Zhen Guo headfirst, ramming him low in the kidneys.

Stunned, Zhen Guo cried out in startled pain.

David dove into the roadside brush where Lu Gao had fallen, searching for the knife with his hands still bound behind him. Lu Gao lay on his back, choking on short, wheezy breaths.

"Come out, foreign devil!" Zhen Guo snarled. He was on all fours in the moonlit road, but he still had a grip on his gun. He got up, hobbling, and limped over to where David was crouched.

David could see that Zhen Guo couldn't quite straighten himself up. He was hurt, but he had the pistol. David heard him cock it and eyed the dark round barrel pointed at his face.

There wasn't time to do anything but close his eyes.

A shadow came out of nowhere and slammed Zhen Guo in the ribs. Zhen Guo squealed like a stuck pig, his shot went wide, and the pistol rattled off on some loose gravel.

David peered into the hazy ground-level mist and saw the assailant. No mistaking who it was—*Yuen!*

The two men collided.

Zhen Guo, his face a contorted grimace, bent under Yuen's weight. David saw the back of Zhen Guo's shirt stained dark and realized Yuen had stabbed him.

The two men came apart briefly.

Then Zhen Guo dropped, grabbed the gun, and squeezed off two quick shots.

David couldn't tell if Yuen was hit.

Now Yuen had Zhen Guo's pistol hand and was shaking it hard. Again, the pistol spun and hit the dirt. David kicked it away, just in time to see Yuen's knife gleam in the moon. Zhen Guo backed up, out of breath, legs unsteady. Yuen leapt forward, swinging his knife wildly toward Zhen Guo's face. The sudden strike caught Zhen Guo by surprise, and the blade speared him in the left eye socket.

Yuen felt the dagger's tip ram against bone, buried deep.

Zhen Guo screamed.

Yuen drew back, then plunged the knife into Zhen Guo's neck. A jet of blood spurted two feet over Yuen's right shoulder.

Zhen Guo crumpled in a heap. In the white dust of the road, the blood darkened and pooled and turned to dark mud.

Yuen's chest rose and fell as he sucked air into his lungs. Then he staggered over to David and cut his hands free.

David rubbed his wrists to get the circulation back. He picked up Zhen Guo's pistol and tucked it in his pants. "How did you find me?"

"Lu Gao came to me...I—"

Yuen turned his head. To David's surprise, Lu Gao was standing up. His face was contorted with pain, but there was also the glimmer of a grin.

David and Yuen rushed to him.

"Are you all right?" Yuen asked.

Lu Gao grimaced. "Hit me in the shoulder," he murmured.

"You saw me? You saw me and went for Yuen?" David asked.

Lu Gao nodded.

"Thank God," David said, grasping Lu Gao's good arm to help support him.

Lu Gao labored to speak. "Wait, there's more—"

A shot rang out close behind them.

David jumped, startled.

Lu Gao's body flew forward; his arm slid out of David's grip. The body fell face down, and a dark stain blossomed on the back of Lu Gao's shirt.

David and Yuen spun around. Not ten feet away, there was a tall, shadowy figure lowering a pistol.

The figure moved toward them. David and Yuen stepped back. It knelt next to Lu Gao's body and turned him face up.

The figure spoke, a voice David knew at once.

"Dead," the man said with satisfaction. "Got off at least one good shot during this war. Wasn't a Jap, but a Commie's not bad."

"Major!" David shouted. "What are you doing here?"

Robert Enfield straightened up. "I should ask you the same thing."

"I was kidnapped."

"What?"

"Those two men"—David pointed them out—"came to my room. Somehow they knew I was writing a report saying that Mao is putting on a show for us, that he's just going to use the negotiations with Chiang to buy more time. I overheard Mao, Zhou, and Liu saying it today."

Enfield took a moment to digest David's story. Yuen stood still. He couldn't understand the English being spoken, but he kept a close eye on Enfield and the gun in his right hand.

Enfield scowled. There was a wild look in his eyes as he said, "Those sons of bitches. I told you, Parker. You can't trust 'em."

"Why are you here?" David repeated. He pointed at Lu Gao's body. "Why'd you shoot him?"

Enfield said smugly, "Not sure I can tell you that."

"You'd better! He was my friend, God damn you!"

Enfield looked sharply at David. He raised his pistol halfway, and for a moment, David thought Enfield might shoot him—but then he surprised David by laughing. "What's gotten into you? You're a commie-lover, too? Like your friends who all got fired? You want to know what I'm doing? What the hell, I'll tell you. Unlike the rest of you, I'm not here just to *observe*. I've got a job. A secret mission. My orders are to watch these Commies, and to watch our guys, too."

"But why'd you kill him?"

Enfield didn't answer.

"He was my friend!" David bellowed, as if that alone would bring Lu Gao back to life.

"Your friend? He's a Chink. And he *saw* me."

"What are you talking about?"

"He saw me in Mao's office."

"What?"

"Mao's cave, the one he goes to every night. I'd already broken in when that guy came by and surprised me. It was during the play—no one should've been around. I think the damn Chink followed me!"

"What were you doing in Mao's office?"

Enfield spoke in a low but arrogant voice: "I've got orders to kill him."

David's jaw dropped. "Kill Mao? Why?"

"Why not?" Enfield laughed. "None of them matter. They're heathens. We're on the Nationalists' side, so Mao's the enemy. Cut off the head and the snake dies. It's simple. Strangle him, get away, and be on the morning plane before anyone even knows."

"You're insane! Who ordered you to do it? I can't believe General Stilwell would—"

This time, Enfield raised his pistol fully and pointed it right at David's chest.

David stiffened.

"You little prick. You can't talk to me like that." Enfield jabbed the gun forward and David slid back.

"I don't take orders from anyone! Certainly not from anyone in an army that's ignored me for six years and sent me out to this damn country to rot!"

Enfield emitted a sinister chuckle. "So I got my own deal…and it's worth a lot of money."

The thought came to David's mind, and he blurted it out. "It's Chiang, isn't it?"

Enfield chuckled again. "So you aren't stupid. Not Chiang himself, of course. His *secret police*. They trust me. They know I could save them a lot of trouble."

You psychopath, David thought. His mind spun, trying to register all that Enfield was saying.

Enfield looked from David to Lu Gao's body.

"And it's not too late. There's still time to get back tonight and take care of Mao. I just had to eliminate *him* before he told anyone. But he ran like the devil all over town. I thought the jig was up, because I couldn't shoot him with people all around. So I trailed him. He thought he'd lost me. And then he picked up this one"—now Enfield pointed the gun at Yuen—"and they did me the favor of running out to the middle of nowhere. Had a helluva time catching up to them, but now it's for the best: way out here, no one's the wiser."

Enfield extended his arm and set his feet—the pistol barrel was two feet from Yuen's forehead. "Once I take care of this one, we can go back."

Yuen drew a short breath but stood his ground.

David stepped into the narrow space between Yuen and the gun.

"You're not doing anything," he said. "It's over."

Enfield glared at him. "Move aside, Parker. He's seen me; he knows. I'm gonna kill him."

"Major, he's my friend. I've fought with him—"

"Boy, do you have a lot of friends," Enfield grumbled. "Now move! That's a direct order."

David stood frozen for five seconds. His eyes darted from the pistol to Enfield's furious face, and back again.

"I *will* shoot you, Lieutenant! Move, dammit!"

David slowly stepped aside.

The major brought his left hand up, using both hands to steady his grip. He aimed at Yuen's face and squeezed the trigger.

An explosive shot rang Yuen's ears.

Enfield dropped to his knees, a bloody tangle of flesh, hair, and bone where his left ear had been. His body fell forward and to the right. As he hit the ground, his left arm fell across Yuen's feet.

Yuen looked at David, who lowered Zhen Guo's smoking pistol.

"He was going to kill you," David said in Mandarin.

Yuen kicked away Enfield's arm. "Yes, I could see that."

"He told me he was going to assassinate Mao for the Nationalists."

"I see," Yuen said without emotion.

"But Lu Gao saw him, and—"

"Shh!" Yuen hissed. He spied a flicker of light in the distance, to the north.

They both watched it silently for a few seconds. The beam of light steadied and separated into two. Then, the faint sound of a motor.

"Trouble," David said.

Yuen nodded. "A truck. Mao's men. We must go. Now."

Yuen grabbed Enfield's gun and they ran off the road into the low scrub. After fifteen minutes of hard running, the two men climbed a steep hillside and collapsed behind a tumble of giant boulders. In the valley below, a mile distant, David saw the stopped trucks surrounded by the golden glow of lanterns held by many men.

"What now?" David asked between breaths. Yuen did not speak. Their heavy breathing was the only sound in the vast, dark expanse of empty country.

"How did those men take you?"

"They came to my room. They knew all about the report I was typing."

Yuen turned and sagged against one of the boulders. In the moonlight, David watched him furrow his brow the way he always did when thinking hard.

Finally, he said, "We must run. If we are caught, we die."

"Why don't we just go back to Yenan? I'll find my friends. I'll be safe there. We'll explain everything—"

Yuen shook his head. "Soon there will be hundreds of comrades all around Yenan searching for you. You will never reach your friends. We have no choice but to head south—"

"What do you mean *we*? You don't need to come. You don't have to be a part of this, Yuen. Go back. There's still time."

The whites of Yuen's eyes flicked away from David. He spoke slowly, staring into the night. "You will not reach safety without me. The Nationalist lines are south; that is where you must go. I know the way. Alone, you are an easy target."

Below, in the valley, a line of lights began to snake in their direction.

"We must go," Yuen said. Reading David's mind, he added, "With good fortune, they will not know I am helping you. I will be all right."

David wanted to say something, but the words wouldn't come. He looked at Yuen, who was already on his feet and moving away.

David stood up and followed him into the darkness.

FORTY-FIVE

David awoke with a start. His face was pressed on the loess earth that smelled of minerals and tiny, ground-hugging plants. He tasted the dust on his dry tongue and coughed, feeling the agonizing thirst rise in his parched throat.

Yuen was next to him, sleeping with his shoulders drawn in, hunched and small. Rays of dawn cast long shadows across the sandy, mustard-colored earth. For the first time in daylight, David saw they were on a sloping hillside spotted with mesquite brush and small, egg-shaped, brown boulders.

A good hiding spot but nothing to eat for two nights running and a day of hiding. On the first night, they'd come across a stream and drank from it, but they had no way of carrying water with them. *Yuen warned me it'd be like this,* David reminded himself. *He still insisted on going due east, toward the Yellow River. It makes sense,* he admitted, annoyed by the reality. *The best way to get to the Nationalist lines near Xian is to float down the river…if we can get there.*

David had pointed out that the Yan River ran directly from Yenan to the Yellow, but the shallow, rock-strewn Yan was not navigable in late summer, and besides, Yuen was sure the Communists would be carefully searching the waterway. *Better to keep to the wilderness,* Yuen said. David pictured the course of the Yellow River in his mind and estimated the distance they'd have to travel once they reached it. *We'd head directly south and, depending on the current, might cover the hundred and fifty miles in a week or two.*

Anxious to move, David rose a little to see more of the land around them, but his mind spun. He slumped down against a rock and shaded his eyes against the flaring white disc of sunlight, not yet high in the cloudless turquoise sky but already fierce.

How hot today? As bad as yesterday?

Yuen stirred and slowly cranked himself to a seated position. Blinking, he glanced at David and yawned. Then Yuen took in the huge expanse of high desert, a forbidding landscape if there ever was one.

"We sure picked a good hiding spot," David said.

Yuen sniffed. "There's nothing here, and no reason for anyone to be here…unless of course they were looking for someone."

"Yuen, you're bleeding."

Yuen touched his face and there was blood on his fingers.

"It's your nose."

He clamped his nostrils shut while David tore off the left chest pocket of his shirt and handed the scrap to him.

Yuen stuffed the rolled fabric into his right nostril. "We have to find water," he said nasally.

"And food," David added.

"There's a town nearby, if I remember. I'll go now."

"Maybe we should move on that way together, save some time."

Yuen looked at him, eyes narrowed, fingers still compressing the nostril. "No. We are not very far from Yenan. There are plenty of loyal comrades looking for you. If anyone sees you...we both die."

Yuen walked four miles to the town of Yanchang. The town looked small from afar, a collection of low buildings scattered among a half-dozen parallel streets.

Yuen hesitated. *I'll stick out if it's a small place...the kind of place people might remember me.* Then he thought of David, and his own wretched hot throat and growling stomach forced him on.

The town was bustling with soldiers and military activity. A squad of men marched ahead of Yuen, going the same way, their drill instructor barking at them.

New recruits.

Yuen coughed from the dust kicked up by a passing truck, which was loaded with crates. The truck stopped ahead, in the center of the street, blocking both directions. A few soldiers jumped out of the cab.

He quickened his pace. Glancing between the short, wooden buildings, he saw an open field beyond the edge of town. Two platoons of men were assembled in a line. The crack of rifles. *Target practice.* Yuen climbed a few steps onto a raised boardwalk fronting a row of stores. Head down, he merged with other walkers whose clean clothes reminded him that his were soiled and blood-spattered. Directly ahead, a uniformed man walked toward him, and Yuen turned abruptly, mingling with a group of farmers heading for the other side of the street.

Presently, he found a water pipe and drank slowly, one handful at a time. He made sure not to fill himself up too much, as he knew that would bring on cramps. After drinking, he entered a bakery and asked for two balls of steamed rice wrapped in lotus leaves and two plain white buns.

"May I have that jar, please?" Yuen asked the storekeeper as he pointed to an empty jar on the floor behind the counter.

The clerk lowered his tarnished glasses and eyed him suspiciously. Yuen held out his few crumpled yuan. "This is all I have."

The old man assented but showed he was not pleased with the transaction. Then, begrudgingly, he stooped, got the jar, and set it down in front of Yuen.

"Thank you," Yuen said. He turned swiftly and left.

Moving again with small groups of people, he returned to the water pump and filled the jar. The stomp of feet made him look up. A band of refugees was coming into town from the east—men and women clothed in shabby rags with some of the men hunched, weighed down by heavy crates tied to their backs. There was a cart, laden with boxes and clothes piled high, pulled by a gaunt-looking ox. A woman shuffled beside it holding the hand of a child whose face was smeared with campfire ash.

"Welcome!" a Communist officer called to them, waving both arms above his head. "You are safe here. Our great Chairman Mao welcomes you and promises you food, water, and safety. Your young men will be helpful to our cause—would you like to join us and fight for China? Of course you would!"

The refugees, dispirited and worn, stared blankly at the well-dressed officer.

"Come with me—this way. We have food and water. Plenty for all."

The people went past like a legion of the dead. Yuen wrapped his arms around the food and the precious water jar. Keeping his head down, he left the town.

"Slow down." Yuen told David. "Moisten your mouth with two fingers before you drink."

David coughed and tried to do that. His eyes started to water as soon as the moisture tickled the back of his throat. Yuen handed him a small ball of rice and a white bun. David ate with small, mincing bites even though he wished to devour all the food in an instant.

The sun crept high and brilliant in the dry, blue sky.

Yuen watched David eat slowly, methodically.

He has known some hard living, Yuen thought. *But not living on the run. Not being hunted like an animal.*

It feels all too familiar to me.

David swallowed. He could feel the color rising in his cheeks, the heat from this vital nourishment sparking in his veins.

"How do you feel now?" Yuen asked.

David closed his eyes and lowered his head. The sun was hot on his neck. "Better," he said. "Thanks for getting the food. What was the town like?"

"There is a lot of military activity. A big mobilization beginning."

"Civil war?"

"Yes. More truly a continuation. Restarting what we left unfinished."

"Will you fight?"

Yuen scoured the low hills with his eyes.

"I will have no choice. Much as I would like to fade away, I will be called—that is, if I'm not shot as a traitor first."

"That's ridiculous. I think you're a hero."

Yuen scoffed. "If I am a hero then this country is blessed with a million of them. Perhaps we are all heroes. Either that or just men with guns."

"If you were an American, you'd have earned the Medal of Honor long ago, I'm sure of it."

"I'm no American."

David finished the rice ball and took a small drink of water. "Sometimes I'm not sure I'm one, either," he said. "I've lived more in China than anywhere else. Maybe I have no real nationality."

"You have a country, David. I have a Party. There is a difference. But I doubt the Party will ever trust me again—that's if they don't find it irresistible to kill me. Then again, with the new war, they may value old warriors like me. I can't fight for them if I'm dead, can I?"

"They imprisoned you, almost killed you, and you'd fight for them again?"

Yuen leaned back against a boulder and sighed. "What choice is there? That's where you Americans are so different. You have choices. We don't. We may live. We may die. As a prisoner, I was alive but felt I had died. Our only want is to survive. If there is food and water, that is enough. We accept our fate; there are no alternatives."

"What you're doing for me, saving my life—that was an alternative, Yuen."

Yuen shrugged, yawned, and stretched his arms. "You think too much. We should get some sleep. We'll move on after nightfall."

"You go first; I'm wide awake."

Yuen nodded and rolled to one side.

A minute later, David thought to say, "Yuen, thank you for rescuing me."

But Yuen was already asleep.

—

As the sun's bottom rim touched the western horizon, two Communist soldiers crouched behind a row of thorn bushes near the crest of a hill. They peered across the dusty slope, which fell away to the right, in the direction of the two small figures across the shallow valley.

The younger soldier, a thirty-year-old man named Jin Fu Ma, tapped his foot restlessly, still marveling at his good fortune. He'd caught a glimpse of Lin Yuen as Yuen had scurried a little too quickly across the street in town. Yuen had been around a long time, and he'd served with many men. Years ago, he'd been Jin's commander in the Eighth Route Army, back when the Communists' regular army was strong enough to more openly challenge the Japanese. He remembered Yuen was the perfect soldier: brave, loyal, and a killing machine. So he was shocked when his name came up as a wanted man, a possible accomplice to an American officer who'd murdered three comrades.

The orders were supposedly secret, passed verbally so that no record would exist. This was rare, a method reserved only for orders of the highest importance and sensitivity.

Perhaps they want to make sure the Americans don't learn of it, Jin thought. Secret orders or not, from the rumors of the last day and a half, Jin had no doubt that comrades everywhere were looking for the American.

After tailing Yuen in town, Jin had quietly recruited a soldier named Wang Shu to help him. Wang happened to be smoking on the step outside the bakery. He was in Jin's unit, but the former shoemaker was a raw recruit, one already earning a reputation for laziness and a dim mind. Wang was older, with a hawkish face and pale skin. He wasn't an ideal partner, but he was in the right place at the right time, and Jin had not wanted to take his eyes off Yuen.

"We'll move soon," Jin said.

Wang shifted uncomfortably beside him. His voice cracked as he said, "Are you sure you wouldn't like me to go get some backup?"

"Will you stop asking that?" Jin said, exasperated. "There's no time, and we can do this ourselves. I'll do everything. You just have to point a gun. Can you do that?"

Wang's eyes drifted down to his rifle: a Russian carbine, single shot, bolt-action.

Jin stared hard at the shoemaker but then said in a softer voice, "I know how to do this, but I'll need your help. We'll have surprise and we will succeed. Do not be anxious. I was right about following Yuen, wasn't I? He led us straight to the American."

Wang nodded. There was no doubt the tall white man must be the American. Jin imagined himself triumphantly marching the two prisoners back into town. There would be significant honor in capturing such important fugitives.

"What is your plan?" Wang asked.

Jin surveyed the topography one last time; he'd spent the last hour weighing the situation. "They look like they are not in a hurry to leave. We will circle down and go to the other side of their hill. Then we can take them from behind."

"But we'll lose sight of them—"

"So we better start moving," Jin snapped. "Before the sun goes down, too. Come on, follow me."

Jin felt foolish rushing Wang, but he didn't apologize. It was Jin who'd insisted on waiting over an hour to see what Yuen and the American might do. Now the sun was setting and there was no choice but to act.

Wang was right, it was a risk to go around the hill, but Yuen was a formidable foe, and complete surprise was the only way to apprehend him without a fight.

The two soldiers descended the back side of their hill and jogged to a point behind the American's hill. They cautiously climbed the gentle slope, the eastern side, which was dark and cast in shadow. Their steps sent gravel and loose rocks tumbling down the hillside.

Jin cringed. To him, the only sounds were Wang's loud footfalls. *Will you be quieter?* Jin screamed inside his head.

At the summit, Jin shielded his eyes from the sun and looked straight down on Yuen and the American. This side was much steeper. Scattered bushes dotted the slope, but there was little cover for their approach. Yuen and the American were talking, but Jin could not hear them. Both men were sitting; no weapons in sight.

He looked at Wang. "Point that somewhere else!" he hissed, shoving the bayonet of Wang's rifle away from him.

Wang clung to his weapon, white-knuckled. Jin whispered, "We'll rush down and take them prisoner."

The older man regarded Jin for a moment.

"Just follow me," Jin said.

He sprang up and started downhill. It took all of Jin's concentration to hop and jump and stay on his feet. Small avalanches of rocks followed him as he descended. A few times he stumbled. Once he fell to one knee but got up quickly and went on.

There was a loud thump, followed by a soft cry as Wang lost his balance on the loose scree, fell on his backside, and slid down past Jin. Jin cursed him and got well out of his way.

Yuen was up and moving, turning around.

Jin skidded to a halt ten feet above Yuen and David. He had the advantage and his rifle was ready for either man. However, much to his dismay, Yuen was standing with his pistol drawn and aimed at Jin's chest.

"Who are you?" Yuen demanded.

"You are both under arrest!" Jin shouted.

Yuen's brow furrowed, a hint of recognition.

"You..."

"Yuen, it's me, Jin Fu Ma."

"What are *you* doing here?"

"We have orders to bring you in."

Wang came stumbling over. Taking a position beside Jin, he covered David with his rifle.

"How did you find us?" Yuen said.

"We followed you from the town. Now, I want you to put your pistol down. We don't want to shoot you; we just want you to come with us."

Yuen glanced at David.

"Damn it, Yuen. Put it down!"

Calmly, Yuen said, "Listen to me, Fu Ma. You're a good man. Whatever they told you is false. This American's innocent; the Party has framed him."

"He killed three comrades."

"He didn't kill anyone." Yuen's eyes narrowed. "*I* did."

"What?"

"If you lay down your rifles, I'll explain."

Jin stole a glance at Wang, whose gun was visibly trembling, then he looked back at Yuen. "I know you're not a liar, but I'm not stupid. We're bringing you in. Now put—"

Yuen fired.

Jin cried out and fell backward, hit in the left shoulder.

Wang squeezed off a round.

David ducked. The shot went wide, the bullet ricocheting with a musical whine. A puff of deep blue muzzle smoke hung suspended in the dry air.

Wang stared at Yuen, who jabbed his pistol at him and moved closer. The old man took a shaky step back and dropped the rifle.

Yuen's pistol cracked again.

Wang dropped into a seated position. He looked down in disbelief at the dark red circle expanding on his shirt. He emitted a little bird-like cry and toppled over on his side.

The two soldiers lay side by side. Jin was howling and clutching his shoulder; Wang was in his death throes.

Yuen now looked to David, whose eyes were on the wounded men. David didn't move or speak.

Yuen walked to Jin and fired a round into his forehead. The bang reverberated, bouncing off the stony hills.

Yuen turned to Wang, who strained to raise one arm. Yuen touched the barrel of his gun to Wang's temple. Then he hesitated, and looked at David once more.

David set his jaw. His eyes drifted to the ground.

Without waiting another moment, Yuen cocked the pistol and pulled the trigger.

FORTY-SIX

The hills were darkened shapes that broke from the lighter, star-pierced black of the heavens. Yuen watched David cut the scrub brush that grew in the dry sand and place it over the shallow graves. *This should make it tougher to find the bodies*, Yuen thought.

The moon was full but somehow yellowed like old paper, and it cast an eerie glow across the high desert landscape. *Out there, somewhere, I know there are others—the ones ordered to come if Jin did not return right away. I can feel them out there. Somewhere.*

When the graves were covered, they moved off from the hillside. Soon the ground leveled out, and David lengthened his stride. Above his head, he recognized the belt of Orion and the twinkling coppery star that was the constellation's right shoulder.

Usually the familiar sight of Orion gave David comfort, but not this night. He couldn't shake the thoughts that had writhed in his brain since he'd dug the graves.

I could have stopped Yuen from killing those men. We could've knocked them out or tied them up.

He stared at Yuen's back as he followed him. Yuen walked confidently even though he still had a lopsided gait.

His conscience is always clear, David thought. *If we hadn't killed them, they would've told others about us. So maybe it was them or us...and maybe Yuen was right...but it still feels wrong.*

David felt himself breaking into a sweat, yet the frosty air made him shiver. His eyes darted from one tumbleweed to another. The night seemed full of low, dead-looking, bunched-up plants—the kind that thrive on no water. Peering into the shadows of these sullen shapes, David saw the crouching men—wool-uniformed, heavy-collared men.

Communists.

In his fevered mind, they leapt out of the shadows, red-star caps in moon glow, bayonets silvery, ready to slay the traitors: himself and Yuen.

David rattled his head to purge the hallucination. But the faces of the men Yuen executed took its place. The scene of their death replayed, spooling forward and back, over and again.

He shook his head once more, took deep gulps of air, and tried to calm himself. Above him, the stars glittered in diamond waves that seemed to cleanse his thoughts—if only for a few moments before the phantoms returned.

The gradual change in terrain was familiar to David now, as the dusty loess lands gave way to more verdant pastureland. Tall spruce and stunted cherry trees dotted the countryside. Wild yellow grass gained a hint of green, a sign that the river was close and the desert was behind them.

They'd agreed to keep moving, day and night. Now there were streams coming out of every fissure in the earth, and beside one, they ate their fill of wild cherries. Smaller berries grew in profusion all around the water, and David filled his pockets with the red and purple fruit.

When Yuen saw a bobcat in a skeletal tree, he drew his pistol and shot it. It was toward morning and the sun was already beginning to burnish the hills. To David's surprise, Yuen said they would make a daytime fire and roast the animal. He'd never eaten cat, but there were a lot of things he hadn't eaten before coming to Yenan.

Their march continued right after the meal, but not before the offal and cat bones, ash and coals, were buried deep and their tracks gone over with a spruce bough. Using the sun, David knew they were headed east, but he had no idea how many miles they walked—*was it ten or twenty miles a day?* He did not know.

Sometimes, at night, Yuen stopped for several minutes to gaze at the stars. On cloudy nights, he'd pause and listen for the wind, or so it seemed, and David squinted to make out distant peaks or other landmarks. Yuen relied on his instinctual sense. Occasionally, David thought Yuen was lost, but he always followed him without a word.

Five days out of Yenan, they stumbled out of a wood and onto a wide, rock-strewn plain, covered by water only a few inches deep.

"Is this it?" David asked.

Yuen gazed all around. No one in sight. "This is part of it. Normally all this would be underwater. It's been a dry season. Let's keep walking."

They sloshed in and out of the water. After the desert, David liked the feeling of water inside his shoes. The river deepened and merged with a larger tributary. Sandbars and large rocks littered the expanse, but the water came to their knees. *Enough to float on*, Yuen decided.

They spent the rest of the day gathering driftwood and cutting thin saplings. Using vines, they roped the wood together and built a narrow raft.

The next morning they were ready to launch.

"We're going to have to carry this thing a lot of the time," David observed, squinting across the river. Sunlight danced off ripples on the water.

"Just be thankful there is no one here to see us," Yuen said.

"Right. I bet we're the only idiots to ever try navigating this stretch."

The raft rode low in the water, and they made several stops to tighten the vines. After a few hours, they learned the best positions for balance and buoyancy, and at last, the craft floated steadily.

The monotony of the next three days comforted both of them. With greater skill at piloting the raft, and a lucky tailwind, they made speedy progress to the south, and the river grew in depth and width. David felt as if the worst was behind them now, and the river created the illusion that they were the only two men in the world.

On shore, Yuen shot two wild pheasants. He showed David how to clean and roast them. After the bitter taste of the cat meat, this was the most succulent thing David had ever eaten.

That night, the two men rested by the light of a crackling fire. David sat at the water's edge and drew his knees up to his chest. Nearby, a night bird, perhaps a bittern, glided low and disappeared into some tall cattails in the marsh.

Yuen whittled a toothpick out of a dry piece of wood and went to work on his teeth. When he finished, he washed out his mouth in the river. Face dripping, he asked David, "Will you marry that woman when you get back?"

"You mean Katherine?"

Yuen nodded.

"I hope so…if she's willing, that is."

"Then you will take her back to America?"

"I don't know. Haven't thought that far ahead."

"I'm surprised at that," Yuen said with a small chuckle. Then he asked, "Is America really such a wonderful place?"

David poked at the fire with a flame-blackened pine stick. "It can be…if you have money. The Depression was tough, but still, it wasn't a war. Not like here. Even then, there were plenty of houses with big yards, cars, and telephones. You should go there someday."

"I might like that."

"You can come visit my family in Philadelphia. I've got aunts and uncles there."

"Would they welcome me?"

"Of course! But I'll apologize in advance because they'll try to convert you."

"To what? Christianity?"

"That's right." David grinned.

He watched his friend gather more driftwood. After all their walking, Yuen still moved like he wasn't very tired.

"I still don't understand why you feel ashamed of your Christian god," Yuen said, dropping the wood in a pile next to the fire. "Is it only because you are upset with your father?"

How much did I tell him about that? David wondered.

"Maybe that's true," he admitted. "Maybe I've ignored God because of him, and maybe that's wrong…"

"But what did he do that made you dislike him so much?"

David looked away. *Have I ever told anyone before?*

Do I even remember?

"You really want to know?"

Yuen nodded.

The sound of water lapping the bank filled several seconds of silence. Yuen discovered an uneaten pheasant thigh, and he went to work on it—the meat was white and hot underneath the black-seared skin. For a long time, David remained quiet, sifting through memories. Finally, he drew a deep breath and stared into the flames as he spoke.

"After my mother died, I had nightmares all the time. I was just a child. My father acted like she'd never existed. He put away all pictures of her. We never talked about her. Maybe that was his way of coping, but I never forgave him for it, or for ignoring my pain all those years. Then, after I got past it, I just hated him. I saw arrogance and self-righteousness in everything he did. When we talked—which wasn't often—it was always an argument about school, my friends, politics. I don't know when it happened, but at some point I just wasn't afraid of him anymore."

David moved to one side and stretched out flat on his back. Staring past the densely packed branches of a river-bent hemlock, he saw the moon poking through the tight needles.

"I turned seventeen, and he told me he'd arranged for me to go to his old school, Yale. I'd never heard the idea before—he just came out with it one day. Honestly, I had nothing against going to school in America, but disappointing him was one way of hurting him. Running away was a way to make him even sorrier. So the week before I was supposed to leave for school, I took off on a freighter instead, and that was it."

"And you haven't seen him since?"

"No."

"I think you are angry at your God because you are angry with your father."

David shrugged. "There was a time when I doubted whether God existed. But this year, with you, I've seen death. I've taken life. And right now, I feel more certain than ever that God *does* exist, and maybe He's watching us, right now."

Yuen threw the pheasant bones into the fire, which began to eat them hungrily.

"Do you believe in some kind of god, Yuen?"

Yuen laughed. "Good communists don't believe in God, remember? And the Chinese don't think in such ways—not anymore, anyway. Your Christian god is so much a reflection of who you think you are. But I am glad that you believe in your god. I know I did not say so before, but I think this is a good thing."

"Can I ask you a question?"

"Is this not what we're doing?" Yuen said.

"What I'm wondering is…what did you do before you were a soldier?"

"I told you—I was a student."

"Is that all? The men always thought it might be more…interesting."

Yuen rubbed his chin and smiled thinly. "Oh, yes. It was most interesting…" He paused, then said, "I was a piano teacher."

"What?" David sat up.

"It's true. The island I come from is nicknamed the 'Piano Island.' The rich Westerners brought so many pianos that we had more than any other spot in Asia, I suppose. I was much better at piano than I was at schoolwork. When I was fourteen, I started earning a little money teaching it to other Chinese, and I taught private lessons while I was at the university too."

David beamed at his friend. "I don't think I'll ever be able to picture you in front of a piano. The men would have loved this!"

Feeling his rough, calloused hands, Yuen added, "I haven't played in over a decade, but I bet I still could."

All at once, a black duck came in for a heavy landing on the water, and a rippling, moony "V" spread out behind it. It bobbed and splashed for a bit, then paddled into shadow.

Both men stared at the river, and then Yuen looked at David. "Now I'd like to ask you a question."

"Go right ahead."

"Why did you not stop me from shooting those two men?"

David's smile fell.

He looked at the duck that had come around into the moonlight again and didn't say another word.

FORTY-SEVEN

David sat aft, wielding a wide piece of driftwood as a paddle and rudder. Yuen had a straighter pole, which he used to gauge the water's depth and push them clear of rocks and sandbars. Both sides of the river were densely forested, and as they floated, David couldn't help thinking of *The Adventures of Huckleberry Finn*.

I'm Jim and Yuen's Huck, he thought. *He's the only reason I'm still alive. Out here, I'm a helpless target...at least until I reach the Nationalists.*

He swatted at a buzzing sound near his ear, and the fly scattered to the wind. A few feet away, a fork-tailed swallow alighted on a half-submerged log, then, as soon as it touched the sun-exposed wood, it flew off.

Yuen, eye to the river, also watched the riverbank. "We will stop early and fish again tonight," he said.

David raised his forearm and wiped the sweat out of his eyes. "Sounds fine."

Near Hancheng, Yuen had swum ashore and crept to a small bamboo dock where he found lines, hooks, and pebble weights coiled on top of a barrel. Nearby, a sleeping fisherman dozed in the sun. David watched as Yuen selected a handful of tackle and slipped off the edge of the dock into the green water. A moment later, he was on the raft again.

That night Yuen caught six fish: four orange-gilled, gray-striped perch and two silver-sided catfish. Six days on the river, and they'd seen only a handful of people. One old fisherman waved to them from a flatboat across the river and Yuen waved back. The old man was far off—too far to worry about being recognized. There was also a group of women scrubbing clothes on rocks by the water's edge, but they toiled without looking up.

A strong, southerly current pulled them ever toward the sea. In his mind, David pictured the Yellow River's sharp turn to the east, east of Xian. *That's where we've got to go, and it can't be much farther.*

The prospect of fleeing undetected for hundreds of miles had once seemed impossible, but now he felt a strange sense of hopefulness. *The peaceful river is either a sanctuary or an illusion. They could be waiting for us around any bend—but any day now, we could be safe.*

The next morning David and Yuen awoke to streaming sunlight. Lying on his stomach over a patch of soft grass, David hid his eyes in the crook of his elbow and felt the bristly hairs of his beard scratch his sunburned chest.

Yuen rubbed his eyes. The raft was tied to a dogwood tree ten feet away.

"It's late," Yuen said. "We should leave now."

David lifted his head and spat the sour, rusty taste of sleep out of his mouth. They'd made a habit of striking out before dawn each morning, but this time, they'd slept well past sun up.

"Come on," Yuen prodded. "Get up."

David got to his feet. Barefoot, he began to untie the raft as Yuen gathered the pole and fishing tackle.

"Hello!" came a strange voice.

Startled, David jumped. When he turned to see who was there, he saw a teenage boy standing in the meadow grass. He wore a homespun, brown jacket tied at the waist with a rope belt. A bulging knapsack hung over his right shoulder.

"Good morning, how are you?" Yuen said amiably.

"Good." The boy smiled, and then he looked at David curiously.

"What is your name?" Yuen asked.

"Cheng Hao. Yours?"

"My name is Soong, and this is an American missionary who doesn't speak Chinese. We were just in Hancheng on a visit. Now I'm escorting him back to his church in Luoyang."

"Really? You better be careful if you plan to stay on the river. The Nationalists are gathering south of here. They say there could be fighting any day."

"You know something about military things?" Yuen asked.

The boy put down his knapsack. "I've already begun training with the Communists. I'm from a small village not far from here. My unit's in Yongji, but I got a five-day furlough. I'm heading back today."

"Good for you! It's important to serve your country."

The boy stared at David. "I've never seen a foreign devil," he said. "What side is he on?"

"He's neutral. A good man...he tries to help all Chinese."

The boy knelt down to open his bag and withdrew a bundle, wrapped in cloth. "Would either of you like to share some man tou I've brought here for my breakfast?"

He unwrapped the cloth and produced three small yellow rolls. "My mother insisted I bring too much. I left before dawn, but she still made these fresh for me."

"That is very kind of you," Yuen replied.

The boy passed out the yellow buns.

"Please, let us sit," Yuen said, gesturing to the large root of an oak tree.

The boy sat down. David and Yuen sat on the grass beside him. For a few minutes, the three watched the river and ate without speaking.

"It's an exciting time to join the Communists," the boy said to Yuen. "You should consider it. Now that the Japanese are kicked out, we can build a new China."

Yuen nodded. "I have given some thought to this. They have some good ideas, for sure."

"Our political officer said we could expect our unfortunate Nationalist brothers to lay down their arms and join our side once they understand us better."

"Wouldn't that be nice."

Finished eating, the boy stood up, and Yuen's hand moved to the hilt of the knife that hung from his belt. The hoarse call of a squirrel made Yuen snap his head in that direction.

The boy grinned and said, "You're nervous. I'm just going to take a piss. Help yourself to this jar of milk, if you like."

The boy moved out of earshot.

"What are you planning?" David whispered.

Yuen's jaw muscles quivered. His eyes were set hard on the bushes where the boy had disappeared.

"You know what must be done."

"No!" David hissed. "Why don't we tie him and gag him?"

Yuen scoffed. "Don't be a coward. Someone would find him, and then they'd *know* we are fugitives. We have to make sure he cannot tell anyone. Don't worry, I will do it."

"Don't hurt him," David said.

Yuen's eyes narrowed. "Will you never understand? Do you want to live?"

"Don't do it."

The boy came out of the bushes and saw Yuen untying the raft. He knelt down to cinch his knapsack shut. "How much longer will your journey take?" he asked.

Yuen said, "A week."

"You should be on the road, not the river. You don't want to get caught in any crossfire."

"Good advice, thanks."

The boy stood up. "Well, I have to be going. They expect me by noon."

"Thank you for sharing your food. We'll remember what you said about the road."

David stepped onto the raft, and Yuen used his pole to push off. The boy was soon out of sight.

"Thank you," David said.

Yuen sneered. "You are a fool. It was stupid to let him go."

"I'm sorry you feel that way."

"What I feel does not matter. That boy will go straight to his unit, find out who we are, and report us."

"You don't know that."

"But I do." Yuen spat into the river. "It *will* happen. You think you're some great, generous person because you spared his life? You're not the only one whose life is at stake. I thought I could help you without anyone knowing about it. Then Jin Fu Ma followed me to get to you. Me! That means they've linked me to you—"

"Well, that guy's dead. They don't *know* you're helping me—"

"Are you an idiot? You think it matters if they don't have evidence? If they suspect me they'll treat me as guilty. They may have already hurt my family—or worse."

"You don't know what they'll do. I still don't think they know you're with me."

Yuen turned his back on David.

David raised his voice angrily: "I'm sorry, all right? I'm sorry. I didn't ask you to come with me. If you feel it's a big mistake, and I'm an idiot, then leave."

Yuen made a raw, guttural sound deep in his throat. With sudden, violent movement, he cracked his wooden pole over his knee. "It's too late for that!" he shouted, red-faced. He looked at the two sticks clenched in his fists and threw them into the river.

Then he crossed his arms and sat down hard on the raft.

David spent the rest of that morning staring at Yuen's back. Yuen never turned, never said a word. Nor did either man see anything on the river except the flash of a bright blue kingfisher with a tiny minnow in its beak.

FORTY-EIGHT

The sound of water lapping the raft sent Yuen's mind back to the small dock on Gulangyu. His father would wield the long bamboo pole with deftness and precision. The hook was bigger than Yuen's hand. He was a boy who never seemed to quit moving, but for those hours with his father, he was still as a stone, content to watch the arcing casts, the float bouncing on the waves. His eyes never wandered, alert for the strike, and when his father would yell, "I got one! Yuen! Hurry! Come with the net!" Yuen would leap into action and hold out the net with both hands tight, shoulders arched back, ready for the weighty deposit. Then he would watch the strain on his father's face as he flung the rod up and back, then down and to the side. Most times, the expression would change to a smile, and if it was a particularly large fish—perhaps a snapper or tuna—his father would pat him on the head and say, "Mother will be happy with this one. We'll tell her how we fought it together." And for that moment, Yuen would be the happiest boy in the world.

To his right, the sun was dropping, suspended just over the treetops. Yuen flexed his fingers, forming a fist that he opened and closed repetitively. The tension from the earlier part of the day—the anger at David and the worry that the boy would give them away to the authorities—was slowly seeping out of him.

He wondered if he'd been wrong.

Maybe that boy did not tell anyone.

Maybe after all these days they've given up on finding us.

He looked back at David. The younger man was worn out. His head was down, his body was still, but his arms kept moving, paddling as if driven by some internal motor.

Yuen faced forward again. *No. They will find out and probably already have. They'll know we are on the river.*

He scanned the water: no sign of anyone or anything. *We would be safer on land.* But just then he felt a gust at his back, and the wind drove the raft forward with a fresh and faster pace. He looked down at the raft's front edge as it drove steadily through the water. *But we are moving quickly now.* He eyed the gleaming disc of blood orange that was the setting sun, and noticed the leaves of the trees just beginning to glow with the sun's color. *We'll stay on the water. After nightfall there is little chance of being found. We'll go all night if we can and leave the raft before morning.*

The raft bucked and Yuen looked back. David was sitting down, just steering now, the raft following the current's course. *We must be close,* Yuen told himself. *The Luo and Wei will converge with the Yellow. The river will become much larger.*

A bothersome thought reoccurred to him. *It will be thick with soldiers: theirs and ours. When we get there, both sides might shoot at us. And if we do reach the Nationalists? Even the stupidest Nationalist soldier would know not to shoot an American, but what about me? Would David be able to protect me? Would they just let me leave freely?*

Yuen felt a prickle on his arm and smacked it with his opposite hand. He frowned at the thin smear of blood on his skin and looked at the dead mosquito in his palm. *Been sucking our blood all day, haven't you?* He wiped the hand on his pant leg. *You're not the only one who wants us.*

He sat down and let his mind drift to Mei Fong, and he wondered what she might be doing at that moment. He didn't entertain the thought of not seeing her again.

There isn't any proof I've helped David.

And they have a traitor's body already…Lu Gao.

And then the image of Lu Gao's poor wife leapt to mind. She'd lost her son and husband. *They will wreck Lu Gao's name,* he thought sadly. *Or perhaps they will cover the whole thing up. Either way, the poor woman does not deserve it.* He dipped his fingers into the sliding water. *And me? They will punish me for certain. Maybe they will have evidence; maybe they will not. It does not matter. I'll spend weeks or months in confinement…or worse. But if I can survive it…I might get my family back.*

Yuen's eye picked up a flicker on the water, far ahead. *What's that?* He blinked, focusing. The sunset cast long shadows, right to left, across the dark and rippled water. He struggled to make out the shape, and then he thought he heard a noise and shushed David even though David hadn't spoken. The noise was low but growling. He peered hard, straight ahead. Then, he saw it.

Yuen spun around.

"David, to shore!" He pointed. "A boat!"

423

"Boat?"

"*Motor*-boat. Peasants don't have motorboats. Go!"

David angled the rudder and Yuen knelt down, reaching for the river bottom with a long, warped pole.

Too deep.

He raised the bamboo stick and began to paddle with his hands to turn the raft. A few seconds later, he looked at the raft, the water, and then out in the distance.

Maybe they can't see us; we're smaller.

But the noise suddenly rose in volume. The patient hum increased, and the dark shape sped up.

Yuen tossed the pole in the river. "Leave the raft. Swim for it!"

David obeyed without a word. Leaving their weapons, they dove into the dark, cold water and swam. The raft spun aimlessly behind them, following a whorl in the current.

A minute later, they crawled, dripping, onto the east riverbank. Water squirted from their shoes as their feet made imprints in the mud. Yuen's head was pounding. He wanted to knock the water out of his ears, but he didn't dare stop. The woods were filled with trees just inches apart—hemlocks, weeping willows, and birches with thin, peeling, papery bark. They ran away from the river, scraping their elbows and arms against the trees. Their feet tripped on roots in the darkness of the forest.

Several minutes later, Yuen stopped to listen. Along with their breathing, only the sound of a lonely warbler broke the stillness of the impenetrable river woods.

With a wave toward David, Yuen ran farther. The ground was bare save for a few leaves and scattered pine cones. They weaved through thin trees that would barely conceal a man standing sideways.

Yuen stopped. The army of trees hemmed them in and shut out the violet nightfall.

Then, a shout in the distance: clipped Mandarin, incomprehensible.

Yuen looked at David.

"Over there," David whispered, pointing into the darkness. Yuen looked but didn't see. He felt David grab his arm and pull him to the right. Closer now, Yuen saw the land dip and heard the sound of running water.

A stream.

There was thicker brush, tall ferns, and a declivity going down to a streambed. The ground was marshy and moist. David and Yuen flattened down on the shallow ridge, the stream singing behind them.

Yuen dug his feet into the mud. The side of his face was in the humus, one closed eye partially covered in black mud. The other eye rolled and saw shades of black—the sloping ground, the stream, the darkened trees, and the air between it all.

The sound of footsteps, close ones, approaching. Yuen held his breath. Someone came near—very near. A foot crunch. Then—

"Ahh!" a voice cried, surprised.

The man tumbled down the embankment not ten feet from Yuen. He cursed, and Yuen imagined him kneeling in the ferny mud. They heard him trudge across the stream, lunging as his feet sank in. Grunting, he stumbled into the forest beyond.

David and Yuen lay still for perhaps a half hour. For a long time, the only sound was the thin wind wailing softly in the trees.

Finally, David raised a mud face to Yuen and whispered, "Do you think they're gone?"

"Not sure."

"Would they come back this way to the river?"

"Don't know."

"Should we get going now?"

"Wait. It is better to stay hidden."

They waited.

One hour turned into two, and Yuen struggled to stay alert. *Don't fall asleep*, he told himself. He felt his heavy lids begin to drop, and so he shook his head and bit his tongue to stay awake. He heard David shift a little, and his breathing became deeper, more regular. *Did he doze off?*

Yuen heard the voices again. *Returning to their boat?* He could not make out the terse Mandarin, and the voices soon stopped. One pair of footsteps drew nearer, and Yuen's heart raced a little faster.

The man, close now, scrambled down the embankment on the opposite side of the stream. Yuen lay on his back, peering at the soldier's dark, upright shape. The man could be staring right at him, but only if he were looking in the right direction.

Yuen drew his knife, eyes glued to the man's movements and the long, narrow outline of his rifle. The soldier splashed into the stream, moving slowly, careful not to fall. Yuen's fingers tightened around the handle of the knife.

The man was ten feet away.

Five feet.

Yuen's eyes were now fully adjusted to the lack of light; he could see the soldier well. He sucked in a deep breath.

Closer…closer…

There was a shout off to Yuen's right.

"You see anything?" someone said.

"Shut up, will you?" the man by Yuen said.

His boot was close enough for Yuen to smell the seal oil on it.

The other soldier said, "I can't see a thing."

"Pretend you're an owl."

The other sighed and spat. "I'm eating mosquitoes," he complained. "Let's get out of here."

The soldier close to Yuen turned and walked to the right.

Yuen exhaled slowly.

Suddenly, David stirred and coughed.

Yuen pounced, clapping his hand over David's mouth.

"Hear that?" came the close voice.

"What?" asked his comrade.

"I heard something…right near here."

There was a long silence, and then, "Leave it. Might have been a bird. There are ravens nesting. Saw them and heard them when we came in."

David's pupils were wide saucers. Yuen released his hand, and together they remained frozen. They could hear the far-off thud of boots fading into the distant woods.

They waited a while longer. Yuen's leg fell asleep, and the needles of pain prompted him to shift it slowly.

"I think we should move now," he whispered.

"Only if you think they're gone," David murmured.

Yuen rolled onto his back. "The moon's coming through. Let's go."

They rose to their feet. David stopped to take a drink at the stream, and then Yuen heard a new sound.

"Dogs!" he hissed.

David listened.

Down by the river, the way they'd come, the barks and bays of dogs were echoing in the woods.

Yuen stole a look skyward then spun around, searching for the way south. Moonlight began to break through; the forest was infinite, homogenous, the trees forming maze-like walls of brown and green.

Yuen chose a direction and ran. The barking grew louder, the voices, too.

The light was enough to see the ground, and they moved faster than before. After twenty minutes of hard running, they crested a slight rise, and a fresh breeze touched their faces.

What's that ahead? Yuen stared hard. The sound of water, an open plain. He saw it now, the wide, dark band.

The river! Much bigger. It must be flowing east.

"That's it!" he said to David.

They ran on. Yuen began to zigzag, hoping to throw off the dogs. David went straight and pulled ahead. Ten minutes later, Yuen burst out of the woods to a panoramic view of the broad river. David was in front of him, standing hunched over with his hands on his knees, breathing hard and staring ahead. Yuen looked around: no soldiers, no pickets.

"Go," Yuen said, waving across the river. The water ran slowly right to left. The forest on the other side looked dark and quiet.

David turned his head.

"They will be over there, the Nationalists, I'm sure of it," Yuen said, coming up beside him.

"Come with me," David said. "I can protect you."

Yuen's chest rose and fell steadily. He managed a soft smile. "No, my friend." He put a hand on David's shoulder. "My place is here, where I belong."

"But they're right behind us!"

"So get going! I can still get away, if you'll just go—"

David didn't move.

"If I don't go back, they'll know I was involved. My family is sure to suffer—"

"You don't know that. We can try to get them out."

Yuen shook his head. "You don't understand. We don't want to get out. I *have* to return and do whatever it takes to survive and make sure my daughter can live."

Yuen stared at David. The younger man's face was torn, distressed.

So loyal, Yuen thought. *So naïve. He always has been.*

David pleaded, "Do you really think you can elude them now? They're right behind us! They'll be here any second!"

"I can make it. Now go!"

David hung his head for a second. Then he reached out and the two men embraced.

"Yuen, I'll find you. Somehow. We'll meet again."

Yuen nodded.

They separated. After one last gaze at his friend, David sprinted for the river.

Yuen watched him dive in and swim.

Always so optimistic, thought Yuen. *So American.* The splashing echoed loudly in the darkness. After a few minutes, he saw that David would make it across.

Then he sat down. He could hear the voices and dogs behind him.

He believed his chances for survival were good. He was a war hero with loyal friends in Yenan. It would be rough, certainly—many months and perhaps years of imprisonment, maybe even torture. But if he could endure it, the chance that he might live to see Mei Fong grow up would be worth the suffering.

Shouts behind him. "There he is!"

He turned. Flashes of lantern light between the trees. Two black dogs barking and gnarling, jumping at their leashes. Ten soldiers came out of the pine trees, rifles aimed at Yuen.

"Where is the American?" came a sharp voice.

The soldiers stared across the river. Yuen raised his hands slowly and took one last look behind him beyond the tracery of trees.

The river was empty.

The soldiers descended on him, knocking him to the ground, swinging their rifle butts. The hard toe of a boot smashed his ribs. Another kick broke his nose, and blood flowed freely. He gasped and blinked. In his vision, he saw lightning bolts and surprising colors that mixed with his view of the dirt and stomping boots. Then something smashed his spine, and a terrible pain shot up his tailbone.

"Enough!" a voice commanded. "Bring him!"

The soldiers stopped. Yuen heard their heavy breathing. They propped him up, but he couldn't stand. The voice cracked an order. Two soldiers grabbed Yuen under the arms and dragged him back the way they'd come.

They came to a clearing and dropped him on the ground. Yuen tilted his head and saw a new man emerge from the shadows into the clearing. He walked slowly. His uniform was neatly pressed, and he wore his green cap at a rakish angle.

One soldier saluted him and spoke in a hushed tone.

The political officer erupted. He threw down his hat and stomped on it. His face swelled, red with anger. Spittle spewed from his mouth as he screamed at the cowed soldiers.

Yuen knelt on the ground, steeling himself for the abuse that would surely come. He wanted to block out the shouting and tried to picture Mei Fong playing in the schoolyard, smiling, throwing a ball, running into his arms…

A new, more timid voice spoke and Yuen recognized it. He looked up. The political officer hovered over one soldier, a boy. The boy nodded and muttered something. Then he stole a glance at Yuen, and Yuen saw that it was Hao, the boy from the riverbank.

Yuen stared at the ground. He didn't care about what might have been. David was free, and he was glad for that. He was surprised that the political officer hadn't hit him or even shouted at him yet. Instead, the officer was haranguing his men and had walked around behind him.

The last sound Yuen heard before the bullet shattered his brainstem was the crickets chirping. They were so loud and resonant, and in that moment, it was if they were speaking directly to him. He did not see the officer's pistol pointed at the base of his skull. He did not hear the pistol hammer click. There was a whiteness—a flare—as the woods lit up brighter than the moonlight, and then Yuen saw and felt nothing.

The chastened soldiers jumped at the pistol's sharp report. As Yuen's body crumpled forward, his executioner's hand trembled. He was consumed by one worrisome thought—that with this failure, he too might soon meet with a similar fate.

EPILOGUE

Xian 1990

Gazing though the minibus window, the old man felt relieved to see the old city gate. The large stone tower was blackened, sooty, but still recognizable. He'd found little else familiar in the ancient, walled city. He peered skyward at the polluted gray haze that blotted out the sun, then down, at the road filled with hundreds of bicycles and many taxicabs, but no regular cars.

The bus inched along in the mass of cyclists. Its musty and metallic smell irritated his nose, and he tried to breathe through his mouth. Springs within the hard, high-backed bench poked at his sore tailbone. *I'm getting too old,* he thought moodily.

Outside, people looked at him and the others curiously, a novelty. He remembered that look. They wore masks to mitigate the fumes emitted all around them, and so he could only see their eyes. They wore the same drab cotton coats and trousers as they had in the old Yenan days. Yes, he could still make out the old China in these people, despite the drab, modern buildings and urban sprawl.

What had brought him back? A letter from the year before: a thin, blue aerogram that appeared to have been opened and then sloppily resealed. The letter, in neat block letters and blue ink, was addressed to him.

Pastor David Parker, 120 Elm Street, New Haven, Connecticut.

It came from a woman named Mei Fong, but David couldn't place her; he hadn't thought about China in so long. Unfolding the thin paper, he saw that the letter was short. In her first lines, written in English, she identified herself in objective terms, as a doctor might present a patient:

I am a fifty-three-year-old Chinese woman living in Xian. I work in a factory making umbrellas.

The next line took David's breath away.

You knew my father, Lin Yuen, during the war.

The words released a floodgate of feelings and then memories. *Yuen.* The man with whom he'd forged a bond of brotherhood in battle. The man he'd spent years trying to locate, to no avail. As the years passed, his efforts waned, and Yuen became a memory, a man that David put on a pedestal in his mind. Much later, Yuen became a kind of ghost that haunted him in his dreams. Sometimes David wondered if the man had ever really existed. But again, this was because he was in his seventies now, and perhaps his memory was beginning to fail, or even trick him.

David read on.

I write to you because I think you might like to know that I am here, in Xian, and that if you ever come back to China, I would be pleased to see you. I have a son and a baby grandson. We send you warm greetings and best wishes.

David had immediately called Katherine at home, and right away, she said she would start looking into a trip. They discovered the best way of traveling was with an organized tour group. After the Tiananmen Square Incident, the government was wary of outsiders, especially Americans. If David tried to go about the country independently, he might have trouble. And the fact that he was a pastor would make things worse; the Communists were wise to American Christians who called themselves tourists or English teachers, but who really planned to save souls—just as they had for a century and a half.

They signed up for the typical four-city tour. They'd walked the Bund in Shanghai, toured the Forbidden City in Beijing, and cruised the Li River near Guilin. Now they had one day in Xian to see the famous terra cotta warriors. They stayed in pleasant Western hotels and were permitted to shop in "Friendship Stores," whose shelves were filled with trinkets and dishware similar to goods one could find in any Chinatown back home. In every city they met a new guide, usually a young and earnest university student majoring in English.

The group consisted mostly of David's countrymen. There was one couple from Mexico and another from Spain, *but you can always pick out the Americans,* David had thought. *They're the ones who wear shorts, carry clunky camcorders, and sport atrocious pastel hip packs.* One adolescent boy from Texas irritated David to no end. He found it amusing to ask the guides how free they felt, whether censors read their mail, and how much money they made.

Today, Katherine and their grandsons, James and Winston, were going with the group to see the terra cotta statues. David planned to stay behind. He'd written Mei Fong and asked her to meet him at their hotel for lunch. He asked if Yuen would be there. She wrote back a short note that she would come, but there was no mention of Yuen. David found that odd, but he felt sure he would see his old friend again at last.

The tour group left and David hung back, telling the guide that he wasn't feeling well. The other tourists couldn't believe that he would miss the main attraction—the only reason anyone would come to visit Xian. David went back up to his room, waited for a while, and then went back downstairs to sit in the lobby.

As he waited, he felt himself becoming almost shaky with excitement. The prospect of seeing Yuen made his heart leap. He accessed memories that had not surfaced in decades—their farewell, the swim across the river, running into Nationalist pickets with his hands up, yelling for them not to shoot. He'd made it back to Chungking. It had been October—*or was it November?* He couldn't remember exactly. There was a joyous reunion with old friends—they'd not known his fate for several weeks. His best friends, Jack Service, John Davies, and Ray Ludden were no longer in Chungking, and David wrote to let them know he was alive. The Communists had offered no explanation for David's disappearance—or Major Enfield's—and had gone through the motions of a city-wide search. Poor Katherine had been beside herself, closing herself off from everyone and scarcely able to write a word for her newspaper.

When David reappeared in Chungking—back from the dead—he and Katherine vowed never to be apart again. But first, he reported his survival story to Ambassador Hurley and filed a long written report. No one questioned him; his tale was too unbelievable to be fiction. They asked about Major Enfield, whose body was never found, but David pleaded ignorance, deciding not to explain how he'd killed the major. His conscience was clear on this, and remarkably, the decision had never bothered him.

By that time, the August talks between Mao and Chiang had proved fruitless. The prospects for a negotiated settlement were slim, but there remained one last hope—General George C. Marshall was coming to try to broker a deal. Hurley assured David that General Marshall would get David's report and take it under advisement. David never knew how his ordeal influenced policy—or if it did at all. He was surprised to learn later that the Dixie Mission had stayed in Yenan until 1947, and he assumed that someone important decided his little fiasco was not enough reason to break off relations with the Communists prematurely.

Shortly after reuniting with Katherine in Chungking, they decided to go to England so he could meet her family. They married in Cardiff, then sailed to New Haven to visit David's father—the first time David had seen him since he'd run away at seventeen. For the next few years, David wrote scores of letters to friends and officials in China, trying to open a connection to Yuen. Most of his contacts never got a response, and to others, the Communists pleaded ignorance. Then, in 1949, the civil war entered its final phase, the Americans pulled out, and the curtain came down on relations between the two countries.

But here she was! Mei Fong approached, alone and stoop-shouldered. She was short and thin, with wrinkled skin and a weary but friendly smile.

They shook hands. Her hands were the rough, worn hands of a person who'd labored for many years.

David glanced around the lobby again, but there was no mistake, no Yuen. He suggested they move to the hotel restaurant, where they sat down a few minutes later.

"I'm so glad we are able to meet," David said in Mandarin.

"Do you like to speak in Mandarin?" Mei Fong asked.

"It makes no difference to me," he answered, smiling.

"Mandarin is good." Mei Fong stared at him in a curious way, just as he was staring at her, searching for Yuen's face. It was difficult; he could hardly remember Yuen's face at all, and Mei Fong's awoke no memory of it.

"Please tell me about yourself," Mei Fong said.

David told her of his family with Katherine: two sons, one married with the resulting two grandsons. He was the pastor of a church in Connecticut. Mei Fong explained that she'd lived in Xian for forty years following her move there right after the Communists rose to power.

The city had changed, she said. The tall, modern buildings were still a sight to see. She was happy. Her husband worked at the power plant on the river. She'd kept the same factory job for almost twenty years. Their only son had done well for himself and become a dentist. His little son, the light of Mei Fong's life, was only three years old.

And then David asked the question he'd wondered about for forty-five years.

"And where is your father?"

By Mei Fong's look of surprise, David knew something was wrong.

Mei Fong spoke slowly, quietly.

"Mr. Parker, my father was executed the day you swam across the river to the Nationalists."

David felt a shockwave of numbness wash over him. He felt light-headed. His eyes filled with tears. He tried to stop them, but they came anyway. In that silent moment, a thousand buried images ran through his mind. He saw the precise angle of the river and remembered the sharp cold as he entered it with Yuen. He saw the hemlocks and the birches growing so close together, and he heard the cough of ravens in the dead sticks of pines. He saw the moonlight as it filtered down through the place where he and Yuen had hidden by the little stream. It all came back, but in a brief and spasmodic interplay of imagery clicking too fast to calibrate.

And then he remembered where he was, and who Mei Fong was, and what she'd said.

"My God, my God," he mumbled, pressing his face with both hands and wiping away the tears.

"You didn't know," Mei Fong said.

"No, I did not."

She gave him a moment. The old man's tears touched her, as did the way he rocked his body back and forth between stifled sobs.

Finally, she said, "Although he died when I was very young, I loved him very much." Now she felt tears of her own. "I only know what happened because my father's friends found out. For years I'd been told he'd left on an emergency mission and gone missing. After the Party took over the country, he was declared dead and actually honored in a ceremony for all those lost in the war. They called him a hero."

Mei Fong sniffed and wiped her eyes with a napkin. "Then, when I was in my twenties, a dear friend of my father's told me the truth. He found out that my father helped you escape and was killed moments after you parted."

David gazed across the table through red, wet eyes. *Yes, I do see Yuen in her now.*

"Mei Fong, your father saved my life more than once. He was the greatest man I've ever known. We talked a lot, and I know that you were the light of his life. You were the only reason he never gave up. I think you were the reason he didn't come with me that day."

For two more hours, they shared more stories and tears. David told Mei Fong everything he remembered about her father. She so clearly craved every one of David's memories that he racked his brain to recall everything he could. She talked more about her family. Her mother had never remarried. Mei Fong sensed that there were secrets about her father that her mother would never tell, and she took them to her grave.

Mei Fong intimated that times had been hard in the 1950s during the failed Great Leap Forward, and then during the Cultural Revolution, but she mainly kept to the positive things— her own family and the happiness she felt at learning more about her father. At the end, they parted with a hug and a promise to write one another.

That night, David lay in bed for hours, unable to sleep. He asked God why he'd lived when Yuen had died. He owed Yuen everything—his life, the years of happiness. Even the lives of his children and their children were gifts from Yuen. David wished his friend had lived a long and gratifying life instead of him, and he knew he would gladly trade his life to make it so.

Fresh tears began to roll down David's cheeks.

But he choked them back. What would Yuen think if he were to see him now? He would not pity David nor understand why any man would waste time and tears on what might have been but could never be.

And for the first time in years, Yuen's face was clear in David's mind. Perhaps seeing Mei Fong had indeed unlocked the memory, for there he was—the same weather-beaten face, venerable, strong.

David blinked back tears and laughed with joy as he smiled at his friend.

But Yuen didn't smile back. He didn't laugh. He merely nodded.

And before he finally drifted off to sleep, David breathed a prayer of thanks he hoped that Yuen could somehow hear.

HISTORICAL NOTES

THE DIXIE MISSION—Officially named the U.S. Army Observer Group, the Dixie Mission resided in Yenan from July 1944 to March 1947. It remains a unique connection between the U.S. government and the Chinese Communists. Proponents of the mission assert that it represented a "lost chance" to develop constructive relations with the Communists. Ongoing dialogue with the future rulers of China might have prevented China from strongly allying with the Soviets. Diplomatic relations with the Chinese could have influenced the Korean War, the Vietnam War, and the Cold War. Instead, a twenty-five year silence ensued. Others doubt that any such relations could have substantially influenced Mao's totalitarian state.

The public perception of the Dixie Mission has shifted through the years. Following the Communist victory in 1949, Jack Service and other diplomats were blamed for the "loss" of China. In the McCarthy era, several of the participants' lives and careers suffered as a direct result of their participation in the mission. Later, when Nixon reopened relations with China in 1972, historians began to view at the Dixie Mission more sympathetically, and the "lost chance" theory gained in popularity.

Few of the men who participated in the mission are still alive. Some will always wonder how history might have changed had their reports been received differently. This will never be known. It is clear by all accounts that they served their country with honor and devotion in a difficult and foreign land. That their views and admonitions went against the prevailing opinion among American policymakers at the time does not detract from their service—it amplifies it.

For further reading on the Dixie Mission, consider: *Lost Chance in China*, by John S. Service (Random House 1974); *Dragon by the Tail*, by John Paton Davies (W.W. Norton 1972); and *Dixie Mission: The United States Army Observer Group in Yenan, 1944*, by David D. Barrett (University of California 1970).

JOHN "JACK" S. SERVICE (1909-1999)—Jack Service paid a high price for the favorable reports he wrote about the Chinese Communists. When he returned to Washington in 1945, he was arrested and charged with leaking secret U.S. documents to *Amerasia*, a periodical with supposedly favorable views of Communism. He was later cleared of all charges. In 1950, Joseph McCarthy accused Service of being a Communist sympathizer, and he was dismissed from the State Department in 1951. In 1956, the Supreme Court determined that Service had been wrongfully discharged. Finally reinstated in 1957, Service's career stagnated, and he retired in 1962. Later, he became a curator at Berkeley's Center for Chinese Studies. In 1971, Service was one of a small group of Americans invited to visit China in advance of President Nixon's trip.

DAVID D. BARRETT (1892-1977)—The first commanding officer of the Dixie Mission served in China for most of his thirty-five years in the U.S. Army. In 1945, General Patrick Hurley accused Barrett and members of the Foreign Service of undermining his negotiations between the Nationalists and Communists. Hurley subsequently blocked Barrett's promotion to brigadier general. After the Nationalists fled to Taiwan in 1949, Barrett served as a military attaché to Chiang Kai-shek's government.

In later years, he taught Chinese language and history at the University of Colorado. In 1970, Colonel Barrett published an account of the Dixie Mission. In it he wrote, "As I look back on my service with the Dixie Mission I am perfectly willing to admit that in some ways I was unduly impressed by the Communists in Yenan...In admitting I was oversold...I think it only fair to myself to point out, now that Red China is the bitterest enemy we have in the world today, that hindsight is always better than foresight, and in the summer of 1944 it was not easy to see how completely Mao and his followers would eventually turn against us."

JOHN PATON DAVIES (1908-1999)—Convinced that John Davies was actively trying to sabotage his attempts to unify the Nationalists and Communists, General Hurley arranged for Davies' transfer to Moscow in 1945. Davies also served in Germany and Peru after the war. Like Service, Davies was accused of being a Communist sympathizer by Joseph McCarthy and was driven out of the State Department in 1954. Davies and his wife subsequently moved to Peru, where he ran a furniture business. They later returned to the United States and fought to clear his name. Davies was reinstated by the State Department in 1969.

RAYMOND P. LUDDEN (1909-1979)—Ludden received a Bronze Star for the mission to Fuping, during which Dixie Mission member **HENRY C. WHITTLESEY** was killed. Their nine-hundred-mile journey with the Communists lasted four months in severe winter weather. (It was this expedition that first inspired the author to write about a friendship between an American soldier and a Chinese guerilla on patrol from Yenan.) Although Ludden was investigated by the McCarthy hearings, he was never accused of supporting Communism. He later served in Europe with the Foreign Service.

PATRICK J. HURLEY (1883-1963)—General Hurley succeeded Clarence Gauss as ambassador to China in November 1944. He blamed his failure to negotiate an agreement between the Nationalists and Communists on State Department men he felt were biased in favor of the Communists. After the war, Hurley was a Republican candidate for the U.S. Senate from New Mexico in 1946, 1948, and 1952, but he lost all three elections.

Hurley's war whoop greeting to the Communists upon his arrival in Yenan, and the crash landing of the first American flight to arrive, are two memorable events in the Dixie Mission's history.

CHIANG KAI-SHEK (1887-1975)—After the failure of the Marshall Mission (December 1945 to February 1947) to bring the Nationalists and Communists to terms, the Chinese Civil War began in earnest. Despite a considerable advantage in arms, mechanized transport, and other military supplies, the Nationalists suffered from weak leadership, poor morale, and corruption. First defeating the Nationalists in northeastern China, the Communists steadily outfought Chiang's armies as the war moved south. On December 10, 1949, as the Communists laid siege to the last Nationalist stronghold at Chengdu, Chiang left mainland China for the last time and escaped to Taiwan.

As president of the Republic of China on Taiwan, his government continued to claim to speak for all of China. Although Taiwan had a democratic constitution, in reality, Chiang's government was characterized by single-party control, imposing martial law and limiting civil and intellectual freedoms during his rule. In 1975, he died at the age of 87 from renal failure after being hospitalized for a heart attack.

MAO ZEDONG (1893-1976)—Mao led the People's Republic of China from its inception in 1949 until his death. Some have admired him for unifying and modernizing China. During his reign, he established universal housing, improved healthcare, and promoted equal rights for women. Others have called him a tyrannical despot. After taking power, he instituted widespread land reform and oversaw the persecution and murder of accused counter-revolutionaries, academics, professionals, and former Nationalists. His social programs, including the Great Leap Forward and the Cultural Revolution, did enduring harm to China's economy and society. It is estimated that civilian deaths due to his policies numbered in the tens of millions.

ZHOU ENLAI (1898-1976)—The consummate diplomat, Zhou was the first premier of the People's Republic of China from 1949 until his death. His political skill and care never to threaten Mao's leadership helped him to survive when other leaders were purged by Mao through the decades. He is credited with working to mitigate Mao's violent policies during the Cultural Revolution. He was instrumental in arranging President Richard Nixon's visit to China in 1972. Beloved by the people of China, there was widespread expression of grief upon his death in 1976.

PENG DEHUAI (1898-1974)—One of the Communists' best military commanders, Peng ably led Chinese armies in World War II, the Chinese Civil War, and the Korean War. He later served as Defense Minister from 1954 to 1959. Peng criticized Mao for aspects of the Great Leap Forward in 1959, and Mao responded by stripping him of his responsibilities and arresting him. He was later humiliated and tortured during the Cultural Revolution. In 1978, the Party posthumously reinvestigated Peng's case and reversed its prior judgments against him, clearing his name and affirming his contributions to the Chinese Revolution.

LIU SHAOQI (1898-1969)—After his service as political commissar of the New Fourth Army during World War II, Liu served as vice chairman of the Communist Party of China from 1956 to 1966. During the Cultural Revolution, he was accused of being a "capitalist roader" and traitor. He was expelled from the Party in 1968. His death has been attributed to medical neglect—Mao ordered all medicines to treat his diabetes and pneumonia withheld. His body was surreptitiously cremated and buried under an assumed name. The people of China were not told he had died for ten years. In 1980, the Party reinstated Liu and honored him with a state funeral.

ADDITIONAL NOTES

The Bao'an political prison described in this narrative is fictional; however, Colonel Barrett's memoir, *Dixie Mission: The United States Army Observer Group in Yenan, 1944*, indicates that there was a concentration camp for political prisoners near Yenan—one that the Americans were never allowed to see.

Although Communists guerillas are supplied with American weapons in this story, the Communists never actually received any arms from the United States.

ACKNOWLEDGEMENTS

Though writing is primarily a solitary exercise, no author can successfully produce a book without the assistance of others. This book would not exist without the help and generosity of several people whom I am blessed to call friends.

I am grateful to Scott Kim, one of my closest friends and a fellow physician-writer, for helping me conceptualize this book at the outset and for being my earliest and strongest supporter.

I am also indebted to my friend, Gerald Hausman, another kindred soul whose editorial skills and sagacious wisdom continually humble me.

Deep thanks to my agent, Alice Tasman, who never wavered in her conviction that this novel would find a wide and ready audience.

Patton Dodd, my editor at Bondfire Books, has my gratitude for his commitment to this story and for the innumerable things he did to bring this project to fruition. I'm also grateful to Bondfire's Rachel Mueller, for her dedication to sharing my novel with readers everywhere.

Special thanks to: Anita Shreve, for generously showing interest in a first-time novelist; Jonathan Spence, for his mentorship and for reviewing the manuscript; Chris Min Park, for her ever-present encouragement and helpful advice; Todd Skinner, for his editorial assistance; Jesse Morrow, for lending his design talents to the project; and Stephen Lu, for carefully critiquing early drafts.

Additional thanks to: David Agahigian, William Benson, Bernard & Alice Chang, Cynthia Chen, Brad Foster, Tara Hart, Lorry Hausman, Philip Lam, Wilfred & Esther Lam, Geoff Leung, Florence Lu, Ted & Michelle Steger, Daniel Tam, Isaac Tam, William Tasman, and Ray & Ann Wee.

And finally, my deepest thanks are reserved for my wife and best friend, Christina. Every day, I am the beneficiary of her wise counsel, keen insight, and unmatched dedication to family. Nothing would be possible without her love and support.

ABOUT THE AUTHOR

Andrew Lam was born in Philadelphia and raised in central Illinois. He graduated *summa cum laude* in history from Yale University, where he studied military history and U.S.-East Asian relations. He subsequently went to medical school at the University of Pennsylvania, followed by specialty training to become a retinal surgeon. His first book, *Saving Sight*, was released in 2013. He is currently an Assistant Professor of Ophthalmology at Tufts University School of Medicine and resides in western Massachusetts with his wife and four children.

Photograph by Todd Lajoie

ABOUT BONDFIRE BOOKS

Bondfire Books is an independent publisher based in Colorado and New York City. We publish fiction and nonfiction—both originals and backlist titles—by today's top writing talent, from established voices to up-and-comers. Learn more about Bondfire and our complete list of titles at www.bondfirebooks.com. Follow us on Twitter @bondfirebooks and find us on Facebook at facebook.com/bondfirebooks.

CPSIA information can be obtained at www.ICGtesting.com
Printed in the USA
LVOW08s0021120815

449787LV00005B/167/P